CHANGEMAKER

CHANGEMAKER

A data-driven guide to being an effective activist

LISA MUELLER

First published in the UK in 2024 by
Footnote Press

www.footnotepress.com

Footnote Press Limited
4th Floor, Victoria House, Bloomsbury Square, London WC1B 4DA

Distributed by Bonnier Books UK, a division of Bonnier Books
Sveavägen 56, Stockholm, Sweden

First printing
1 3 5 7 9 10 8 6 4 2

Copyright © 2024 Lisa Mueller

The right of Lisa Mueller to be identified as the author of this work has been asserted in accordance with the Copyright, Designs and Patents Act 1998.

All rights reserved. No part of this publication may be reproduced, stored in a retrieval system, or transmitted in any form or by any means without the written permission of the publisher, nor be otherwise circulated in any form of binding or cover other than that in which it is published and without a similar condition being imposed on the subsequent purchaser.

A CIP catalogue record for this book is available from the British Library.

ISBN (hardback): 978-1-804-44126-8
ISBN (ebook): 978-1-804-44127-5

Printed and bound in Great Britain
by Clays Ltd, Elcograf S.p.A.

CONTENTS

Introduction: Changemaker 1

1. "Hundreds of Flowers, Abloom":
   Mobilizing Protest Participation 21
2. The Truth About Slacktivism: Online Versus
   Offline Protesting 49
3. Give Peace a Chance: Violent and
   Nonviolent Resistance 77
4. "The People United Will Never Be Defeated!":
   The Secrets of Successful Coalitions 103
5. Money Talks: Fundraise Like a Pro . . .
   Without Losing Your Soul 137

Conclusion: Activists Are Not Robots 171
Acknowledgments 179
Reading Guide: Tips and Inspiration for Activists by Activists 181
Notes 183
Index 211

CHANGEMAKER

INTRODUCTION

A DATA-DRIVEN GUIDE TO BEING AN EFFECTIVE ACTIVIST

History has shown the power of protest to transform the world. The American and French Revolutions spurred experiments in popular rule that resonate to this day. Anti-colonial struggles helped to expel foreign occupiers from Latin America, Africa, and Asia. Union strikes secured fair wages and humane working conditions for generations of laborers. The US Civil Rights Movement culminated in landmark legislation enhancing the rights and freedoms of African Americans. The Arab Spring and "color revolutions" in ex-Soviet countries loosened dictators' grips on power. More recently, students from New York to Nairobi walked out of classrooms to draw attention to climate change, forcing their cause to the top of policy agendas.

While none of these uprisings completely eradicated any social ills, all were astonishing successes in light of the odds stacked against activists who were often armed with little more than the symbolic might of their bodies in the streets. It is impossible to count the number of times ordinary folks have fought for, and won, significant concessions from intransigent authorities. These are the uplifting stories that history books glorify and artists immortalize. Popular culture depicts protesters as selfless defenders of justice and inspirational writers of history. Nations erect statues to honor heroes who vanquished tyrants. Beloved Broadway musicals like *Hamilton* and *Les Misérables* romanticize revolutionary sacrifice and bravery. Protesters even reenact roles in real life from popular struggles of the past; in Nicaragua's 2018 revolt against President Daniel Ortega, participants recreated famous episodes from the 1979 Sandinista Revolution.[1] In the wake of the Arab Spring and Occupy Wall Street, *Time* magazine named "The Protester" its 2011 Person of the Year.

However, as I write this book, protests worldwide are failing at record rates.[2] One doesn't need to look far to find pessimistic counternarratives lamenting the inability of activists to make meaningful or lasting gains. French revolutionaries had barely tasted democracy before Napoleon declared himself emperor and dragged France into a long period of restored dictatorship. Jubilation surrounding the Arab Spring dissipated as new autocrats clamored to replace ousted ones. Occupy Wall Street, once hailed as a triumph of "the 99 percent," fizzled out before the "occupiers" could obtain much in the way of economic redistribution or other concrete reforms. The 1965 Voting Rights Act looked like a monumental victory for African Americans and their allies, but sobering research revealed how white communities in the American South responded to the ban on Jim Crow segregation laws by doubling down on incarcerating Black citizens.[3] The most cynical interpreters of history argue that dominant groups extend rights to the marginalized *only* when it is in their interest to do so, such that any apparent step forward for progressives is really no step at all.[4]

But cynicism has not gotten the better of activists, who soldier on. The turn of the twenty-first century ushered in an age of mass protests unlike any the world had seen before. From the Hong Kong democracy movement to Women's Marches to Black Lives Matter, global protest frequency rose by an annual average of 11.5 percent between 2009 and 2019.[5] This spike eclipsed previous waves of protest, including the turbulent 1960s. Many of the protests capturing headlines during this ongoing wave have involved thousands of participants, sometimes braving tear gas or worse to voice their grievances and lobby decision makers for concessions, ranging from pensions to free and fair elections.

When do such efforts work? Under what conditions do protesters get what they want as opposed to coming up empty-handed, or winding up even worse off? These questions are timeless, and not just among scholars or seasoned activists. Plenty of people have at least dabbled in activism, even if only by posting a few words on social media or displaying a bumper sticker on a car. Some individuals have invested dearly in the causes they care about, risking their livelihoods and even their lives at protests where arrest and physical repression were real dangers. Many more have followed protests from the sidelines, glued to news feeds about the latest outbreak of unrest in a faraway country or their own backyard. No matter how small or great your investment in activism, you might reasonably ask whether it was worth it.

Here I should pause to clarify what I mean by *activism*. While this book discusses highly visible forms of activism like marches and sit-ins, I follow geographers Susan Hanson, Deborah G. Martin, and Danielle Fontaine by opening the category of *activism* "to consider actions and activities that, because of their limited geographic reach, normally are considered too insignificant to count as activism" and yet have potential to catalyze change.[6] Quiet activism—behind the scenes and underground—figures prominently in this book. Not all activists shout into megaphones. Some, whom we will meet in later chapters, pursue change by supporting comrades on the frontlines, clandestinely subverting oppressors, or even by simply existing.

Our personal experiences and observations make it tempting to speculate about the causes of protest success or failure. If activists got what they wanted, you might infer that it was because they knew the right slogans to chant or had strong allies on their side. If activists came up empty-handed, you might blame low turnout at a rally or a spokesperson's overly aggressive statement to the press. However, what happened in the past is not necessarily the best guide for how to protest in the future. There are two problems with relying on intuition to decide which ways of resisting the status quo are more or less impactful.

First, we can't be sure that an experience from one protest applies to protests elsewhere or at other points in time. Perhaps a lawmaker changed her vote in response to a social media post today, but will the same post work next year, or on another lawmaker? Would a differently worded bumper sticker solicit the same number of supportive honks, and does it depend on the neighborhood you're driving through? Some protesters in sub-Saharan Africa borrowed mottoes from the Arab Spring,[7] but it's unclear whether echoing the cries of Egyptians and Tunisians had any influence on democracy in places like Senegal and Malawi, which differ in numerous ways from the North African countries where the Arab Spring unfolded. As the cliché goes, an anecdote is not a dataset. We cannot generalize about how to make protests work by studying one case, or even a handful, in isolation. As science historian Naomi Oreskes affirms, "Just because someone is close to an issue does not mean he or she understands it."[8]

There is a second reason to doubt our intuitions about the ingredients and qualities of successful protest: we can never wind back the clock to see how history would have played out had protesters employed different tactics. Consider the case of the US Civil Rights Movement. Some activists stood up for racial equality by exercising civil resistance—boycotts, sit-ins, and other peaceful gestures endorsed by Martin Luther King Jr. Others took more extreme, militant action in self-defense when confronted with police repression and violence, in the tradition of the Black Panthers. These two camps frequently butted heads over which basic approach—restraint or radicalism—was more promising. For decades, laypeople and experts alike could only guess who was right, because they could never observe the counterfactual of a more violent Martin Luther King or a more peaceful Black Panther Party and see how politicians and citizens would have reacted under those hypothetical scenarios. Simply comparing scoresheets across the two factions provided few hints, because wings of the Civil Rights Movement varied not just in terms of (non)violence, but also in terms of geographic origin, economic and religious profiles of members, and so on. This difficulty, of identifying the cause of an outcome, is what social scientists call the "Fundamental Problem of Causal Inference." It is why activists up until now have had little choice but to select strategies based on their gut instincts about what works, what feels right in the moment, and which actions conform with their "tactical identities" (for example, as radicals or pacifists).[9]

Activists should care about discerning cause and effect, because the potential rewards and losses of activism are enormous. Protests erupt when people are desperate to redress serious grievances, such as inequality and oppression, and manage to coordinate their actions. On the one hand, an activist victory could mean compelling decision makers—elected or appointed officials, business owners, religious leaders, and others—to enhance well-being for millions of people far into the future. To cite a key example, abolitionists convinced the British government to ban slavery in the nineteenth century, laying the groundwork for other global powers to do the same. The practice of owning human beings went from ubiquitous to unthinkable.

On the other hand, a defeat for activists could mean prolonged hardship, from both withheld concessions and any repression suffered in the act of resisting. The philosopher William MacAskill ponders a terrifying alternative history in which Quakers, freed(wo)men, and other activists did *not* persuade British rulers to incur the substantial political, economic, and military costs of enforcing a ban on slavery. Abolition was not a foregone conclusion, as some historians once argued; it was highly contingent, hinging on "moral weirdos" effectively standing up for what they believed at a time when slavery was considered normal, and even natural.[10] Without antislavery protesters (a) advocating for their beliefs and (b) succeeding, it is entirely possible that institutional slavery would still be widespread today. Given such high stakes of making protests work, activists need a better game plan than winging it. Fortunately, they no longer need to grope in the dark for effective tactics. Exciting scientific breakthroughs offer unprecedented possibilities for learning which strategies actually work better than others. This book is neither idealistic nor pessimistic. It is a realistic guide for how to choose tactics that win.

AN EVIDENCE REVOLUTION FOR REVOLUTIONARIES

The twentieth century saw brilliant achievements in the natural and physical sciences: a polio vaccine, humans walking on the moon, the spread of air travel and personal computers, the rise of the internet. In our current century, the *social* sciences are having their moment in the spotlight. Advances in statistics, economics, political science, and other fields have revolutionized countless aspects of life, large and small. Hit books proclaim that empirical analysis holds the secrets to success in sports (*Moneyball: The Art of Winning an Unfair Game* by Michael Lewis), government (*Moneyball for Government* by Jim Nussle and Peter Orszag), philanthropy (*Doing Good Better: How Effective Altruism Can Help You Make a Difference* by William MacAskill), and, ultimately, "everything" (*Freakonomics: A Rogue Economist Explores the Hidden Side of Everything* by Steven Levitt and Stephen Dubner).

The "Evidence Revolution"[11] left a conspicuous mark on politics and policymaking. Elections have become "victory labs" in which candidates exploit sophisticated polling, forecasting, and marketing analytics to get an edge on rivals.[12] Modern-day government officials update their beliefs, preferences, and behaviors in light of new evidence on effective policies.[13] Nobel Prize–winning economists Abhijit Banerjee, Esther Duflo, and Michael Kremer pioneered experimental methods for testing anti-poverty initiatives, so that development personnel could have "more than good intentions."[14]

The central tenet of the Evidence Revolution, also known as the "What Works Movement," is that empirical social science holds the key to gaining political influence and making genuine societal impact. Diverse fields have espoused this philosophy, notwithstanding concerns about devaluing community-based knowledge and condoning a "tyranny of experts"[15] or a "tyranny of metrics."[16] Whether one fully welcomes the change or not, a burgeoning number of academics have escaped the "cult of the irrelevant"[17] to produce research for solving real-world problems. In this book, I will try to reassure you that big data, randomized controlled trials, and other empirical methods are "weapons of math destruction"[18] only when put to ill use. In the hands of progressive activists, they can be means of liberation.

Curiously, the Evidence Revolution has not taken root in actual revolutions. A wealth of rigorous political science has studied effective protest tactics, yet there are few hints that activists are deploying it on the ground. In the 1950s through the 1970s, protest scholars routinely emerged from the front lines of the civil rights, anti-war, and women's rights struggles. Linking theory and praxis came naturally to these scholar-activists. But over ensuing decades, research on protest and social movements grew more technical and more opaque to nonacademics, even as rising academic standards of data transparency and causal inference made it more credible. Such "disciplining" of activism[19] generated confusion and suspicion between scholars and activists, in the rare event that they crossed paths at all.

This schism matters, because activists might be missing out on information that could enhance their odds of success. For instance, some protests start out peaceful but turn violent when the crowd's temperature rises or protesters feel they have no choice but to answer violent repression with more violence. However, there is a strong scholarly consensus that peaceful resistance is more effective than violent resistance under most circumstances.[20] If activists knew and embraced such evidence, they could adapt their tactics accordingly, and perhaps alter the course of history: political scientist Omar Wasow statistically simulated the 1968 US presidential election ten thousand times while assuming that no violent protests had occurred in April 1968 following Martin

Luther King Jr.'s assassination. The results suggested that had civil rights protests been more peaceful, the election outcome would have been reversed, with Hubert Humphrey beating Richard Nixon in three-quarters of the simulated races.[21] We cannot observe the counterfactual election directly, but this simulation gives us reason to seriously contemplate the potential impacts of our protest tactics. While popular movements achieve stunning victories from time to time, sheer enthusiasm isn't the most effective plan long term. Political science lends more promising tools than ever for making activism work, and we need to make these tools accessible for the people who could *put them to work* promoting social justice, responsive government, environmental awareness, and other goals.

There are, of course, already guides for activists, many written by activists themselves (see the reading guide at the end of this book). Yet a majority of them are meant to inspire, not to communicate scientific facts. Activist, author, and "radical doula" adrienne maree brown writes in *Emergent Strategy*, "I'm sure there are science people who could write a contrarian book to anything in here. If that's you, then yay! I bet you're hella smart—help us all get free!" I love this quote because it highlights how a book like mine, centered on empirical data, can be in conversation with books like brown's, which offer insights about powerful activism from nature and personal wisdom. Veteran activists might possess valuable firsthand knowledge about how to change the status quo, but social science exists to test even our most deeply held intuitions about which approaches work better than others. And sometimes, science reveals our intuitions to be misleading. The biologist Edward O. Wilson put it bluntly: "Such is the paradox of the social sciences. Familiarity bestows comfort, and comfort breeds carelessness and error. Most people believe they know . . . how institutions evolve. But they are wrong."[22] A person whose car keeps breaking down has experiential knowledge of what it feels like to sit on the side of the road waiting for a tow truck. But the average driver still needs professional mechanics and engineers to make sense of the car's problem, prescribe fixes, and develop new and better cars that don't break down in the first place. Social scientists are to activists what mechanics and engineers are to motorists.

The 2017 Women's March on Washington became an infamous example. Organizers and many participants instinctively thought that assembling an inclusive, intersectional coalition of feminists, environmentalists, and other left-leaning constituents was the best way to strengthen their opposition to Donald Trump and the Republicans. However, my experimental and statistical analyses of eleven countries, including the United States, show that protesters are more likely to sway incumbents and the electorate if they articulate clear, cohesive demands rather than a hodgepodge of claims.[23] This could explain why the Women's March struggled to win any tangible concessions, while the conservative pro-life movement achieved major victories such as sympathetic Supreme Court appointments and state limits on abortion access. Each year since 1974, pro-life activists have gathered at their own rally in Washington, the March for Life, with a sharp and singular message about overturning *Roe v. Wade*—a goal they finally achieved in 2022. The 2017 Women's March was a cacophony in comparison. Could feminists have prevented the Supreme Court from rolling back abortion rights with a better protest strategy? There is no way to know for sure, but the evidence suggests they could have.

I did not write this book to tell activists they are wrong, but rather to arm them with information that might currently be hidden or confusing. As the activist and author Cynthia Peters said, "If activists were more visionary, more seriously oriented toward winning profound change, perhaps we would look to social movement theory for guidance in critiquing and analyzing what we need to win.... We need to look for the evidence of what works and why—not as an exercise in understanding, but because we want it to inform our work, improve our skills, make us better at what we do so that we can win."[24]

This book is the first to translate and synthesize cutting-edge scholarship on protest and social movements into a neat package.

Drawing on my own research and work by my colleagues in political science and sociology, I illuminate lessons from familiar cases as well as international cases that many Western activists know little about. The evidence in this book may embolden would-be activists to take the plunge into activism with greater confidence that they can make a difference.

Years ago, I went to a political protest in Minneapolis. A few hours in, my voice was hoarse from chanting, my feet weary from marching, and my arms sore from waving a poster in the air. I was exhausted, yet energized by the communal atmosphere—a strange mix of indignation and hope. As the sea of humanity charged away from downtown to go occupy the freeway, I felt a tap on my shoulder. It was one of my students. "Professor Mueller!" he yelled above the commotion, as hoarse as I was. "Are you here to study us?" I understood his query as serious; he knew me primarily as a protest scholar, not an activist. "No," I replied. "I'm here because I'm pissed off!" For days afterward, as the euphoria of that night faded and reality set back in, I grappled with whether I had accomplished anything at all by protesting. That tension drove me to recommit to my research and reconsider how I could make my findings available to the public.

Think about the last time you attended a demonstration. I imagine you may have felt the same confusion, ambivalence, and hunger for clarity about the power of protest. I empathize, and have written this book both for you and for myself. My journey as an amateur protester and a professional social scientist has led me to believe that activists should avail themselves more of the empirical research on protest and social movements published in the twenty-first century: a new science of social change.

"TRUST SCIENCE"

One of the innumerable characteristics that made Donald Trump an outlandish president was his disdain for science. His attacks on the scientific community went beyond refusing to wear a mask during the COVID-19 pandemic, touting homeopathic remedies like injecting disinfectants, or insisting that environmentally friendly light bulbs cause cancer. He waged a wholesale populist culture war against scientists and intellectuals, portraying them as self-serving elites and avatars of the mythical "deep state." Scholars charted a steep rise in anti-science rhetoric in the United States during the Trump administration and documented how anti-science extremism globalized to other countries, fueled by Russian propaganda.[25]

Scientists fired back by organizing the inaugural March for Science in 2017. The marquee rally in Washington, DC, spun off into more than six hundred satellite marches across the country and around the world. A frequent chant at these protests was "Trust science!" The COVID-19 outbreak was still three years away. Little did the demonstrators know just how urgent their refrain would become in the midst of anti-vaccine conspiracy theories, mass misinformation about viral transmission, and death threats against medical officials like Dr. Anthony Fauci. The United States would go on to suffer one of the worst COVID death tolls of any country, including poorer nations that were far less equipped to respond to the emergency.[26] Many factors probably led to this tragedy, but mistrust in science was at least partly to blame. The historian Naomi Oreskes grieved, "COVID-19 has shown us in the starkest terms—life and death—what happens when we don't trust science and defy the advice of experts."[27]

The 2017 March for Science did not erase science skepticism. On the contrary, surveys of Americans taken before and after the march show that it had mixed success at best. Leading up to the march, liberals and conservatives were polarized in their attitudes toward scientists and experts, with liberals generally feeling more favorable toward the scientific community than conservatives. Survey respondents were even *more* polarized after the march, indicating that the protesters had failed to mobilize a consensus around respecting scientists. Moreover, conservatives became no less likely to agree with the statements, "Research is politically motivated" and "You simply can't trust scientific research."[28] Knowing now how deadly science denial would become in the COVID era, it is hard not to wonder how many lives could have been spared if the March for Science had been more successful at making people "trust science." Sociologist Robert J. Brulle remarked that the marchers' tactics were doomed from the start because scientists were the wrong spokespeople for the movement.[29] By seizing the megaphone, scientists inadvertently emphasized the divide between experts and nonexperts. They never paused to ask whether their communication strategy would be effective.

I bring up this example not to disparage lab coat–clad demonstrators for falling short of their mission, but to point out that not even scientists instinctively turn to science when organizing a protest *about trusting science*. If you forgot to read a stack of academic papers before attending your last protest, you are entirely normal. The human brain evolved to help us survive and propagate the species (to seek food, dodge predators, and find mates), not to sit around thinking about the intricate mechanisms driving political processes.[30]

Protesting often feels visceral and spontaneous rather than methodical. Engaging in activism, whether in the form of a one-off demonstration or a sustained movement, can be a dizzying emotional ordeal. One classic political science text described protests as "moments of madness."[31] Scholars note that people protest not only for instrumental reasons like raising the minimum wage, but also for more intrinsic reasons such as releasing emotions, asserting identity, or feeling part of a community.[32] Activists tend to think with their hearts as much as their heads. The archetypal protester is driven by (com)passion, righteous outrage, or a variety of other laudable emotions, urges, moods, and commitments.[33]

There is nothing inherently bad about emotionally protesting. Some feelings (such as shame, paranoia, and exhaustion) can work against protest success, but others (like joy, hope, and love) can work toward it. In any case, scholars have by and large discredited the idea that emotions derail rationality; people are perfectly capable of thinking and feeling at the same time.[34] The savviest, most strategic protester can experience anger, fear, or pride while taking to the streets. Activists are not wrong to follow their hearts.

Nevertheless, some critics worry that feelings and identity have gained undue primacy in protests and social movements at the expense of results.[35] They contend that we should walk away from a protest not just feeling warm, fuzzy, and righteous, but also having built something. Without denying the positive motivational role that emotions and identities play in activism, I propose that activists can make a greater impact by anticipating the effects of their methods. This advice may sound obvious, but research shows that when reacting to a problem, humans do not automatically foresee the downstream consequences. Instead, we are susceptible to all sorts of cognitive biases: We gravitate toward causes that are the most visible, but not necessarily the most urgent or tractable. We help people nearby who are like us, rather than distant strangers with the most need. We default to solutions that expend the least energy, yet might be fruitless. And we sometimes perform altruism to boost our own social status, versus prioritizing the well-being of the people we are ostensibly trying to aid.[36] None of this is our fault. We cannot flip a switch in our brains to reverse biases that evolved over many generations; the most recent known example of human evolutionary change happened about three thousand years ago.[37] However, our animal instincts can hamstring our efforts to help others, and we can choose to temper them if not suppress them outright.

Psychologists have found that some intense feelings, especially severe anxiety and guilt, distract us from the mission at hand and short-circuit our problem-solving capacity.[38] In the context of activism, the problems in need of solutions could be logistic (publicizing a rally, transporting protesters, raising bail money) or conceptual (designing a logo, composing a speech, drafting a petition). Problem-solving entails thinking through various contingencies, weighing trade-offs, and calculating risks. All of these processes are difficult to undertake when reacting from the gut, as we are inclined to do after a triggering event such as a contentious election, an unpopular court ruling, or a hate crime. Surgeons, astronauts, and marines know that humans are not born with an innate ability to execute complicated tasks under stress. Cultivating this ability requires intention, practice in calming emotions, and a willingness to adjust one's behaviors in light of new information. When even a subset of activists commits itself to such deliberate and systematic problem-solving, protests become more than cathartic; they are potent catalysts for social and environmental change.

But what information should guide activists? Which sources can they trust, and which should they treat with suspicion? That's where social science comes in.

Although this book is first and foremost about *empirical* science (relating to the way things are), it raises important *normative* questions (relating to the way things should be). These include: What is protest for? How should we cope with uncertainty? Should "optimizing" strategies and winning concessions be the ultimate objectives? Can protest also be about catharsis, camaraderie, and simply being heard? Am I selfish if I protest mainly to feel better about stressful situations? Is it wrong to have fun at a protest about a serious issue? Is it arrogant to think I can transfigure the world? What does responsible allyship look like? When is protest merely performative? I will confront such philosophical dilemmas head-on.

A SCIENTIFIC *AND* RADICAL AGENDA

One morning, a bewildered parent wearing a name tag stopped me outside the building where I teach. She was visiting Macalester College with her teenage daughter, a common sight during application season. The mother glanced up at the engraving above the doorway, which says Carnegie Science Hall. She then looked back at me and sheepishly asked, "Excuse me, but can you please tell us where the ... um ... *real* science building is?" Apparently, she had entered Carnegie searching for a physics or chemistry classroom, only to discover that it housed political science, economics, anthropology, and other social sciences. Disguising my mild offense, I politely directed her toward the other end of campus.

What *is* scientific about social science? And what's the difference between social science and "real" or "hard" science? I pose these questions to cohorts of incredulous undergraduates at the start of each semester. Students often enroll in political science courses expressly to *avoid* the kinds of learning that they associate with science—rigid note-taking, dispassionate inquiries into the mechanics of the natural world, math of any kind. Especially at Macalester, a school with a radical, left-leaning reputation, many political science majors regard the classroom as a space for consciousness raising and community organizing, and as a refuge from hypothesis testing and data analysis. A student taking my required Empirical Research Methods class once declared, "It is dehumanizing to reduce human suffering to numbers in a spreadsheet!"

I relish the challenge of convincing students that social science can be both scientific *and* radical (and even humanizing!). It is scientific because it aims to uncover truths about how the world works, by testing our intuitions from lived experience against empirical facts. But unlike the natural and physical sciences, social science takes as its subject matter human behaviors and human-made institutions. Yes, this makes it "messier" (less precise) than biology or astronomy, and raises particular ethical concerns when researching human subjects. Most political science studies take place not in a controlled laboratory, but in the pandemonium of elections, legislatures, wars, and revolutions. However, the socialness of social science also lays bare how scientific findings relate to our lives, more so, perhaps, than studies of arcane chemical reactions and pathways of celestial objects. Social science can reveal why our activism achieves desired results or not. And it can suggest why people choose to participate in protests or not, pulling back the curtain on our own behaviors and the proclivities of individuals we hope to mobilize. What's more radical than science that helps protesters win?

Some of my students remain unconvinced, claiming that thinking like a scientist is the opposite of thinking like an activist. Scientists are known to be patient, objective, open to being wrong, and, I am willing to admit, somewhat boring. Many activists, in contrast, are quick to react, fervent, resolute, and thrill seeking. "How can we sit in this classroom staring at datasets when there's a struggle in the streets *right now*?" students plead. It can be tough to argue with them, especially at flash points like the murder of George Floyd in 2020, which occurred just a few miles from campus. I sympathize with their pain and anger and admire their drive to take action. But I also contend that slow intellectual projects are necessary for ensuring that whatever happens in the streets, now or in the future, is not futile or, worse, harmful. My students have a point that there is not always time to retreat to the classroom or the lab following a triggering event. That's why I wrote this book—as a quick-reference guide that activists can pick up to complement their bravery, sacrifice, and good intentions.

While the notion of radical social science strikes my young students as novel, my older colleagues are keen to remind me that politically engaged research on protest is nothing new. Indeed, social movements helped populate sociology and political science departments in the 1960s and 1970s, when it was commonplace for professors to maintain ties to activist networks. A consensus came out of the 1968 American Sociological Association meetings "that if your research was focused on the relatively powerless and disadvantaged, you had a moral obligation to enable them to use the results; that the study of social movements ought to provide movement activists with intellectual resources they might not readily obtain otherwise."[39] Civil rights, anti-war, free speech, and feminist activists found comfortable homes in universities through roughly the late 1990s.

The trouble was that some of these early social movement scholars got *too* comfortable in the ivory tower, losing touch with their activist roots and downplaying relevance in their work. They became more eager to impress journal editors than empower people still fighting for justice in the trenches. Twenty-first-century research on contentious politics is more quantitative, jargon laden, and incomprehensible to nonspecialists than research from preceding decades. After the tumultuous 1960s and 1970s, university departments sought to hire technicians rather than activists. Meanwhile, estranged protesters chanted, "People power, not ivory tower!"

There is no shortage of commentary bemoaning this shift from engaged to disengaged research. Backlash was inevitable. A vocal contingent of academics is now calling to demote peer-reviewed publications as the gold standard for professors' tenure and promotion. They want to resurrect "publicly engaged academic work" that "encompasses different forms of making knowledge about, for, and with diverse publics and communities."[40] The subtext is that universities must correct their mistake of divorcing scholarship from activism.

These critiques overlook the fact that social scientists' bookish deviation in the late 1990s and early 2000s had many benefits. By stepping back from the front lines of protests, scholars carved out space for themselves to hone their analytic skills, interrogate their intuitions, and produce increasingly sophisticated research. Here, "sophisticated" refers to research that is verifiable, transparent, robust, and relatively free from once-common pitfalls such as overgeneralizing from a small number of cases, inferring from unrepresentative samples, ignoring alternative explanations, and conflating correlation with causality. To a large extent, albeit imperfectly, referees at academic journals did their jobs. Empirical research on protest and social movements published after the Evidence Revolution is arguably more credible than work published before. Even if scientific findings will never be 100 percent certain, the burden of proof has risen for claiming that a given protest tactic works. The Evidence Revolution introduced the principle that political interventions—encompassing activism, economic development, and public policy—should be subject to the same clinical vetting and peer review as medical interventions have for a long time. Individual *scientists* are not infallible; history is littered with their foibles and some egregious cases of malpractice (Nazi experiments, the invention of nuclear bombs, etc.). But *science* is self-correcting, constantly updating, and, at its best, resistant to prejudice and conflicts of interest. Good scientists pledge themselves to truth, not to profit or ideology, so we can trust their empirical claims more than those of nonscientists. The catch is that a lot of potentially useful scientific evidence remains impenetrable to people without a PhD.

I wrote this book because I believe that public engagement and scientific rigor can and ought to coexist, and that I am responsible for communicating my research to people who are in the best position to apply it. Social scientists do not need to choose between generating relevant knowledge and knowledge that passes peer review. The reason why these two forms of knowledge sometimes *seem* mutually exclusive is that cutting-edge social science tends to be highly technical. However, scientists in far more technical fields than political science have already demonstrated that it is possible to translate even the most esoteric ideas for the general public. If astronomers like Carl Sagan and Neil deGrasse Tyson could demystify the cosmos for lay audiences, then social scientists should have less trouble communicating research on protests and social movements to current and prospective activists. The following chapters are my attempt to do just that, and to make social science radical once more.

A TACTICAL ARMS RACE

Why is this book important right now? Current events and evolving technologies create a pressing need for a new science of social change. Democratically minded protesters are under pressure to keep up with authoritarian leaders, who are quickly learning how to manipulate computer science and data analytics to get the upper hand on anyone who would oppose them. Political scientist Erica Chenoweth worries that we are entering an "age of smart repression" in which savvy dictators will harvest public data and manipulate social media to efficiently target and entrap their opponents.[41] Chenoweth recounts how Sudanese strongman Omar al-Bashir tasked state agents with posting fake Facebook events to lure people to the streets for a supposed Arab Spring protest, only to round up thousands of unsuspecting youths. Reporter Roderick Kefferpütz warns that China is exporting its brand of "digital dictatorship" to countries like Uganda, shipping spy cameras and drones and hosting seminars on advanced censorship and surveillance.[42] Big-data processing, facial recognition software, automated text analysis, and artificial intelligence have supercharged autocrats' ability to monitor and subdue citizens. For instance, Chinese authorities have used cell phone and genetic data to identify "dissidents" and incriminate the minority-Uighur population.[43] Traditionally, activism is a skill learned through years of informal experience, but time is a luxury that citizens in repressive regimes no longer have. To protect themselves and future generations, the defenders of democracy and human rights need a crash course in promising strategies, along with a framework for evaluating their risks. This book can help, in a small way, to level the playing field between the enemies and guardians of freedom.

WHAT'S AHEAD

Each of the next five chapters addresses a different theme in the new science of social change: protest turnout, online versus real-world protesting, violent versus peaceful tactics, coalition building, and fundraising. I organized the book around these themes in an attempt to make an extremely broad and deep literature easier to digest. I also included numerous endnotes, both to support my empirical claims and to provide further reading for anyone who wants to delve deeper into the evidence. However, you can still get all the benefits of this book even if you ignore the endnotes.

One way of looking at the chapters is as ingredients in a recipe for success. In scholarly literature, *success* often means activists winning concessions in line with their nominal demands. The specific concessions in question vary from protest to protest or movement to movement. They might include raising the minimum wage, capping carbon emissions, or legalizing gay marriage. However, *success* is a blanket concept covering additional outcomes such as public sympathy toward protesters, awareness of various causes, and the longevity of groups organizing protests. Each of these phenomena requires its own set of explanations, and I endeavor to stay clear about the outcome of interest as I walk readers through diverse studies.

The coronavirus pandemic, climate change, and other titanic concerns have a tendency to overwhelm and paralyze us. In democracies and autocracies alike, actions like voting and writing letters to government officials can appear useless in the face of gridlock, polarization, and inequality. Activism offers an alternative. Thanks to progress in social science, the potential for activism to really work has never been higher. People just need reliable information to unlock that potential.

1. "HUNDREDS OF FLOWERS, ABLOOM"
Mobilizing Protest Participation

As a girl in China in the early 1900s, my great-grandmother endured the excruciating ritual of adults binding her feet with gauze and squeezing them into tiny "lotus shoes."[1] Foot-binding, which often required breaking the toes, was a Chinese custom dating back to the tenth century. Unnaturally dainty feet epitomized femininity and distinguished the leisure class from farmers who needed their full mobility to work the fields. A woman who could barely walk remained housebound and subservient to her husband. By the nineteenth century, almost all upper-class Han Chinese women had bound feet to signal their elite status and secure their marriage prospects.[2]

Given such cultural pressures, my great-grandmother's mother was bold to untie her daughter's feet in 1909. She took a political risk by relieving her child's suffering: would flouting society's expectations doom the girl to become an outcast and a spinster? Instead, this act of resistance emboldened my great-grandmother to pursue independence throughout her life. As she grew up, her feet and her mind ran free. She dreamed of studying medicine, made the unconventional choice to marry for love rather than money, and then escaped to America when Japan invaded China during World War II. The expression "I have big shoes to fill" carries a special connotation for women in my family. We celebrate the fact that foot-binding has gone virtually extinct. The last factory manufacturing lotus shoes shuttered in 1999.[3]

This story of one woman's protest against a repressive custom, while inspiring, obscures the fact that ending foot-binding once and for all was a *collective* effort. A coalition of actors, not all of whom saw eye-to-eye, struggled for decades to make foot-binding socially unacceptable and eventually illegal. Anti-foot-binding associations proliferated around the turn of the twentieth century, founded by Christian missionaries fighting "barbaric" local practices, Chinese nationalists aspiring to raise China's standing in the eyes of foreigners, and grassroots feminists hoping to liberate their sisters from oppression.[4] One such feminist, Qiu Jin, unbound her own feet, dressed as a man, and attended college in Japan where she learned archery and fencing in physical education classes. She wrote home to her brother, "I am tough and healthy. I take part in gymnastics every day to keep me fit."[5] Upon returning to China, she devoted herself to the anti-foot-binding movement and wrote in a poem:

> Unbinding my feet to pour out a millennium's poisons,
> I arouse the spirit of women, hundreds of flowers, abloom.[6]

Oral poems helped to spread the message of *fangzu* ("letting feet out") to illiterate communities. Women untied their feet en masse at rallies. The ladies of the Letting Feet Out Society published a pamphlet instructing older women on how to loosen their bindings and care for corns and calluses.[7] My great-great-grandmother spared her daughter from pain and disfigurement, but she could not singlehandedly upend an entire nation's norms and laws. Systemic reform would entail mobilizing, in Qiu Jin's words, "the spirit of women, hundreds of flowers."

This chapter is about the importance of collective action—people working together toward shared goals. It can feel empowering to protest alone, but rarely does one person effect momentous change. Even high-profile "solo" protests tend to involve concerted effort behind the scenes.

African American icon Rosa Parks famously refused to give up her bus seat to a white passenger in segregated Montgomery, Alabama, in 1955. The usual telling of this story in public schools suggests that Parks was weary one day after work, impulsively defied segregation, and inspired the Montgomery Bus Boycott. However, progressive educator Herbert Kohl notes that this account "misrepresents an organized and carefully planned movement for social change as a spontaneous outburst based upon frustration and anger."[8] As Kohl documents, Parks was not the only Black person to disobey segregation laws. Civil rights leaders were already devising a bus boycott and contemplating which protester would make an ideal face of the movement. They strategically chose Parks because they knew her to be a hardened activist who could withstand severe public backlash, including death threats. Kohl stresses that revising the history of Rosa Parks does not diminish Parks's heroism. On the contrary, "this story of collective decision-making, willed risk, and coordinated action is more dramatic than the story of an angry individual who sparked a demonstration; it is one that has more to teach children who themselves may one day have to organize and act collectively against oppressive forces."[9] Parks may have been a hero, but it is a myth that she was acting alone.

Depicting protests as smaller than they really are is not always an innocent oversight. Political elites are known to deliberately mischaracterize protesters as uncoordinated anomalies in order to downplay activists' strength, numbers, and strength *in* numbers.[10] A year after the January 6 riot at the US Capitol, investigators were still debating how many people descended on Washington that chaotic day. The Secret Service publicly estimated attendance at around 20,000 rioters, but leaked documents suggested that the true turnout could have been as high as 120,000. The reporter who published the classified numbers surmised that Trump's detractors deflated the estimates because they did not want to publicize that 120,000 people believed Biden stole the election.[11]

Another reason why people sometimes underestimate the size of movements is that activists may hide their numbers to avoid detection.[12] Verónica Cruz runs the nonprofit *Las Libres* ("The Free Ones"), which successfully pressured the Mexican Supreme Court to decriminalize abortion in 2021. Following that victory in her own country, she formed an "abortion underground" to help American women skirt new laws restricting abortion access after the US Supreme Court overturned *Roe v. Wade* in 2022. The underground works like this: American retirees living in Mexico, affectionately called the "Old Hippies," purchase hundreds of abortion pills legally over the counter, smuggle them across the Texas border in toiletry bags and earring boxes, and mail them to accomplices who distribute the medication to women wishing to end their pregnancies. Cruz underscored that her impact would be minimal without a clandestine network of allies risking imprisonment to defend reproductive rights. Reflecting on her journey as an activist, she described herself as part of an ant colony—"one of the countless workers toiling beneath an unbroken surface, carving intricate paths toward their goal."[13]

If you are reading this book, you are probably an activist or thinking of becoming one. Through an activist's eyes, collective action can seem inevitable in the face of injustice. You might be wondering, *How could someone* not *stand up against foot-binding, racial segregation, and laws that deny women their bodily autonomy?*

Yet, many social scientists have a quite different reaction to protests and social movements: they are more surprised when people *do* rise up than when they do not. Nationally representative surveys show that activists make up a minority of the human population. The truth is that most people, even those who are deeply upset with the way things are, never take to the streets or orchestrate covert movements. Resistance is the exception, not the rule.

Figure 1 summarizes the percentage of people in a diverse mix of countries who said they have participated in a peaceful

FIGURE 1: Protest Participation Around the World

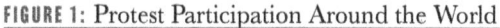

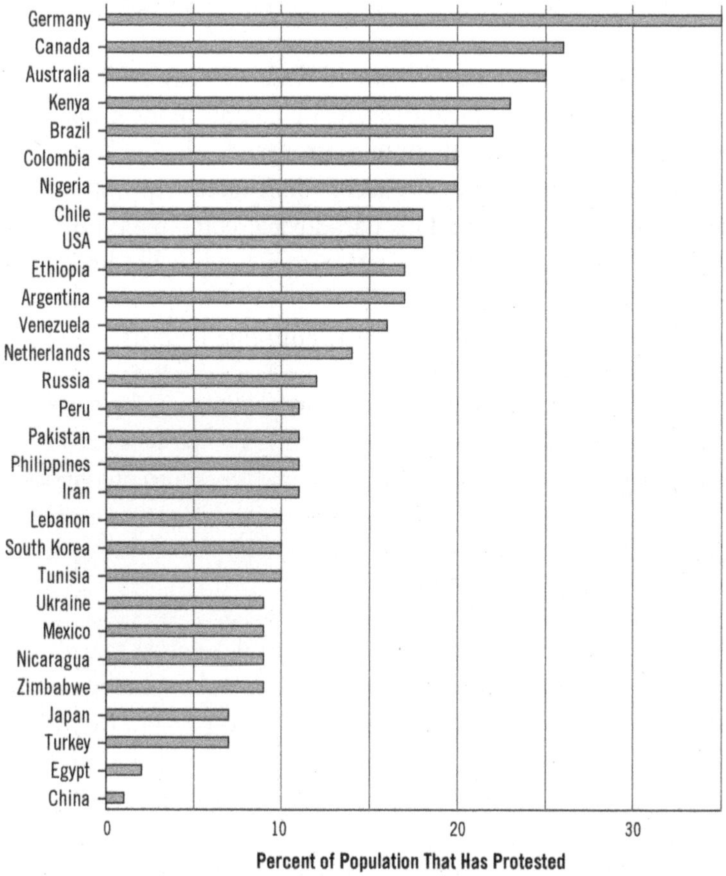

demonstration at some point in their lives.[14] The rates vary, but they are lower than one might expect in light of abundant anxiety-inducing problems in the world, from climate change to economic inequality. In a 2022 poll by the American Psychological Association, 87 percent of respondents said the rise in prices of everyday goods, such as gas and groceries, was a "significant source of stress" in their lives.[15] Nearly three-quarters felt "overwhelmed by the number of crises facing the world right now," including

COVID-19 and the war in Ukraine. The vast majority feared nuclear war (69 percent) and had trouble coping with "global uncertainty" (81 percent).

Despite Americans' widespread dissatisfaction with the status quo and concerns for the future, we can see in the graph that less than 20 percent of them have protested, whether to reduce inflation, expand healthcare access, halt nuclear proliferation, or for any other reason. This paradoxical combination of pervasive grievances and low protest participation is not limited to the United States. A 2021 UNICEF survey of more than twenty-two thousand respondents from twenty-one countries showed

> **EXERCISE:** To make these figures more relatable, write a quick list of all the issues that worry you lately. Then, put a star next to each issue that you've protested about. Protesting could mean taking to the streets, signing a petition, donating to a cause, et cetera. Chances are, you drew very few stars.

Feeling concerned is practically universal, whereas *voicing* concerns is exceedingly rare, even during an age when the frequency of protest events is at an all-time high.[17] Anti-foot-binding advocates, civil rights activists, and the Old Hippies of the abortion underground are unusual. Most people who yearn for change sit on the sidelines of social movements.

Why do so many aggrieved people remain politically quiescent? Does this matter? And if so, what can be done about their inaction? That's what we'll explore in the coming pages. This chapter covers the science of collective action. It explains why there is (often) power in numbers, illuminates the barriers to mobilizing protest participation, and recommends proven ways to overcome those barriers. It also addresses why acting alone can still be a good idea, even if mass movements are more likely to make history.

BIGGER CROWDS ARE BETTER... OR ARE THEY?

According to crowd-counting experts, the largest wave of protest in United States history unfolded after a Minneapolis police officer killed George Floyd in the summer of 2020. Floyd's slaying was one of at least 135 deaths of unarmed Black Americans at the hands of law enforcement since 2015.[18] It ignited rallies near the murder site, which then spread like wildfire. An estimated twenty-six million people protested nationwide.[19] The Black Lives Matter movement spun off demonstrations around the world from Jamaica to Japan. "There is a George Floyd in every country," said a journalist in South Africa.[20] Activists demanded concessions that ranged from convicting the officers directly involved in Floyd's death, to launching investigations of broader ties between white supremacists and law enforcement, to the complete defunding of police departments.

Did the unprecedented size of the Black Lives Matter movement make any of these concessions more likely to materialize? To pose the question more generally: Does higher protest turnout improve the odds that protesters will win?

The intuitive answer is yes. For one thing, large uprisings are physically more onerous for authorities to deflect than small disturbances. In 1989, throngs of East Germans flooded the streets of Leipzig on thirteen consecutive Mondays, demanding democratic elections, the ability to travel to other countries, and German unification. Enormous crowds became self-fulfilling: the more people who took to the streets, the more obvious it was to bystanders that the regime was unpopular, encouraging even more people to rise up. This "informational cascade" helped to coordinate the opposition, resulting in a wave of unrest unlike any the socialist leaders of East Germany had witnessed before.[21] When Communist Party chief Erich Honecker ordered his deputies to crack down on the protesters, his security chief snapped back, "Erich, we can't beat up hundreds of thousands of people."[22] On October 9, senior politburo official Egon Krenz rushed in on an emergency flight to thwart Honecker's plans to open fire on peaceful demonstrators, fearing the harm that public carnage would do to his party's domestic and global image. Honecker backed down and resigned ten days later. Within a month, the Berlin Wall fell, marking the end of the East German regime. The sheer size of protesting crowds seemed to avert a bloodbath and change the course of the Cold War.

Even if authorities manage to shut down huge demonstrations, it can be costly. East German leaders anticipated the political fallout of repressing activists, and recent evidence from other countries suggests that they had good reason to be cautious. An experiment in Uganda showed that excessive police violence tends to trigger a backlash, decreasing citizens' support for security forces and increasing their willingness to dissent.[23] Scholars studying Chile have observed similar patterns.[24] Repression only works when the oppressor can credibly threaten retribution, which is more difficult against immense crowds. When threats are not credible, repression has the opposite-from-intended effect of emboldening the opposition.[25] This is why Saudi crackdowns have failed to silence online objectors. Researchers found that imprisoning Saudi activists deterred only the prisoners themselves from speaking out against the regime. The prisoners' Twitter followers, realizing that authorities could not capture them all, *escalated* their online criticism of the ruling family and calls for revolution. If anything, the arrests drew more attention to the regime's illegitimacy.[26]

The costs of repressing large protests can be economic as well as political. After residents of Hong Kong rose up against the mainland Chinese government in 2019, authorities added a new line item to their budget: "safeguarding national security," with a price tag of $1 billion. This was on top of a 25 percent increase in the policing budget, amounting to another $3.3 billion.[27] Economic costs can also take the form of international sanctions. The European Union expanded its sanctions on Iran in 2022 after 336 Iranian demonstrators were killed and 15,100 detained in uprisings following to the death of Masha Amini, who had been jailed by morality police for violating Muslim dress codes.[28] Even the most brutal dictators rationally hesitate to stifle protests if the costs are too high, and those costs inflate with crowd size.

Giant demonstrations trap power holders in a double bind: repression is expensive, but so is letting protests run their course. In 2022, big-rig drivers parked their trucks at multiple points along Canada's southern border to protest the Canadian government's COVID-19 vaccine mandates for cross-border truckers. During two days in February, police estimated that five thousand people protested in Ottawa and one thousand vehicles clogged the streets.[29] On the internet, countless more anti-vaccine activists raised funds to send supplies to their comrades on the ground. When all was said and done, Canada's transportation bureau calculated that the "freedom convoy" cost the country up to $2.9 billion in trade activity.[30] While the blockade was deeply unpopular among mainstream Canadians, it succeeded in rallying the far right, seized the attention of national leaders, spurred a revolt against the Conservative Party leader, and galvanized similar movements in the United States and France.[31]

In one of the most influential studies on protest turnout, political scientists Erica Chenoweth and Maria Stephan argued that even a slight uptick in the number of active participants can make a campaign over 10 percent more likely to achieve its goal.[32] In a TED talk, Chenoweth popularized the so-called "3.5 percent rule"—the idea that no government can withstand a challenge from 3.5 percent or more of its population without conceding or crumbling. That works out to about 11.5 million Americans, or less than half the number of people who participated in the George Floyd protests. Numerous studies point to a link between higher protest participation and a higher likelihood of protesters getting what they want.[33] The implication for organizers seems clear: mobilize as many bodies as you can.

However, the best strategy is not always so simple. Social scientists, including Chenoweth, have recently updated their assumptions about the causal relationship between crowd size and protest outcomes.

One of the biggest puzzles vexing protest scholars is whether large crowds actually cause success, or whether turnout and success simply correlate. If protesters join crowds when they expect to win concessions, then favorable odds of success might cause high turnout and not the other way around. It's a classic chicken-or-the-egg problem.

Scholars deal with this problem by finding natural experiments. For ethical and practical reasons, social scientists cannot conduct randomized controlled trials on protesters, like medical scientists randomize patients into treatment and control groups in drug trials. But if some factor outside of researchers' control *naturally* makes protest size vary at random, then researchers can infer whether turnout, and not another variable, caused protests to succeed or fail.

Rainfall creates just such a natural experiment. Whether it rains on any given day is effectively random. Moreover, rainfall tends to suppress protest participation (apparently, many activists are willing to fight for change, but not if it means getting wet). A team of economists found that bad weather reduced the size of Tea Party Tax Day rallies by 58 percent.[34] They then showed that high rally attendance on fair-weather days predicted higher Republican vote share in the 2010 midterm elections, as well as more conservative voting behavior by lawmakers: a 1-percentage-point increase in the share of Tea Partiers protesting raised the share of Americans voting for the Republican Party by 12 percentage points, and having a rally on a clear day equated to approximately one additional vote for conservative legislation in Congress. For the Tea Party, larger rallies generated sizable political gains.

The Tea Party study implies that activists should work to maximize protest turnout, so long as their goal is to win at the ballot box and on the floor of Congress. However, activists might have other goals, especially in autocratic regimes where the whims of dictators have more bearing on citizens' daily lives than votes and legislatures do. Under dictatorship, activists are often less worried about election results than about securing free elections in the first place.

When scholars study a wider range of protest outcomes in authoritarian countries, it is not so clear that crowd size has the same advantages that it does in American party politics. Instead of measuring protest success by party vote shares or lawmaker behavior, social scientists Charles Butcher and Jonathan Pinckney measured success by whether the ruling regime offered concessions in response to a specific protest event.[35] They focused on Muslim-majority countries, which provide another convenient natural experiment: Friday is a day of prayer when many Muslims have fewer work responsibilities and gather at the mosque for religious services. Fridays therefore serve as a focal point for collective action. In some countries, up to 80 percent of Muslims report attending Friday prayers on a regular basis. It's practical to protest when the community is already gathered in one place; it's no coincidence that mosques were critical organizing hubs during the Arab Spring. And because mosques are considered sacred spaces, they are less vulnerable to repression even in countries with rules against public gathering. Studying the outcomes of Friday protests in Muslim countries solves the chicken-or-the-egg problem: if people protest on Friday, we can assume it's because they find it easier to coordinate on that day, not because they are jumping on the bandwagon of protests that they already expect to succeed.

Surprisingly, Butcher and Pinckney's findings were the *opposite* of those of the Tea Party study: in predominantly Muslim countries, larger crowds *reduced* the likelihood that protests would receive concessions. The authors interpreted this unexpected result by remarking that Friday protests convey little new information to powerholders, precisely because they take place like clockwork. Authorities know that organizing demonstrations on Friday is easy. Therefore, Friday protests send a weaker signal of the opposition's power than protests on other days of the week. Butcher and Pinckney concluded that large crowds yield concessions only if they catch incumbents by surprise. Effective protests must reveal shifts in the balance of power between the regime and the opposition. Getting bodies into the street is not always enough to win.

Science is a humbling profession. It demands that scientists self-correct when fresh evidence overturns their prior conclusions. Erica Chenoweth, of "the 3.5 percent rule" fame, acknowledged Butcher and Pinckney's discovery by writing in a paper, "Data suggest that campaign size is a more unreliable predictor of success than previously understood, particularly in contemporary mass movements. Many campaigns fail despite achieving large-scale participation during peak events."[36] Examples of giant protests that failed include Bahrain's anti-monarchy uprising of 2011 (mobilizing 7 percent of the population) and Iraq's protests against Saddam Hussein in 1991 (mobilizing over 8 percent of the population). Conversely, some smaller protests have succeeded, such as Mongolia's 1989–1990 pro-democracy movement in which less than 1 percent of the population participated. Such exceptions to the 3.5 percent rule have led some activists to declare the rule "broken."[37] Answering these concerns, Chenoweth's revised message is that mass participation alone is not enough to win concessions; it also matters *whom* organizers mobilize. Getting new people, especially the regime's own supporters, to join the resistance is more powerful than just mobilizing hardcore opponents that rulers expect to raise a ruckus anyway.

With this latest insight in mind, we can update our reading of historic protests that seemed to win merely by virtue of being large. Recall the Monday demonstrations in East Germany. A careful inspection of history uncovers just how close the situation came to a bloodbath. Authorities planned to implement a "Chinese solution" to crowd control, referring to the state massacre of hundreds to thousands of demonstrators at Tiananmen Square earlier that year. East German authorities were poised to pull the trigger: they distributed extra helmets, shields, batons, and respirators to police and instructed hospitals to brace themselves for an inundation of gunshot wounds. By the time Egon Krenz arrived in Leipzig to intervene in Erich Honecker's violent plot, special combat units, cops, and police dogs were already stationed around the city. Krenz probably would have been too late to prevent the slaughter. However, rank-and-file security forces shocked everyone—not least the participants in that day's Peace Mass—by refusing to carry out the massacre at the last minute. Their passive defection became known as the "Miracle of Leipzig."[38] In reality, it was not just the sea of humanity flooding the streets that broke the East German regime, but also the conscientious resistance of particular individuals—the regime's own troops—whose rebellion Honecker least expected.

THE ADVANTAGE OF DISADVANTAGE

Muslims who protest on days other than Friday and defectors from a ruling coalition have something in common: they make costly, and therefore credible, displays of their dissatisfaction with the status quo. The effectiveness of costly protest implies a radical and exciting hypothesis: the *most* oppressed populations may, ironically, have the advantage over more privileged folks when it comes to getting powerholders to grant concessions.

Political scientist LaGina Gause explains this logic in her book *The Advantage of Disadvantage*. She points out that the costs of protesting are not equal for everyone. For instance, someone who earns minimum wage at an hourly job suffers more economic hardship from taking a few hours off from work to protest than someone with a lucrative salaried job. Likewise, protesters from marginalized racial or ethnic groups may experience more physical harm or legal and emotional repercussions from protesting than less marginalized protesters.

The January 6 riot on Capitol Hill was one of the most flagrant displays of a racist double standard in contemporary social movements. Despite the overt crimes that rioters committed—illegal entry, assault, disorderly conduct, weapons offenses, theft, conspiracy—Capitol police arrested barely a few dozen people. In comparison, Black Lives Matter protesters suffered more than fourteen thousand arrests, as well as harassment and rubber bullet wounds, in the months leading up to January 6, despite being overwhelmingly peaceful. The conspicuous difference seemed to be that the Capitol insurrectionists were mostly white, whereas the Black Lives Matter protesters were mostly Black people and their allies. The Black Lives Matter Global Network Foundation condemned the double standard: "When Black people protest for our lives, we are all too often met by National Guard troops or police equipped with assault rifles, shields, tear gas, and battle helmets. When white people attempt a coup, they are met by an underwhelming number of law enforcement personnel who act powerless to intervene, going so far as to pose for selfies with terrorists."[39]

Although this unfair treatment is distressing, the story does not end there. The odds are not as bleak as they appear for organizations of marginalized people like Black Lives Matter, thanks to the advantage of disadvantage. This theory refers to how the uneven costs of protesting affect the way powerholders react to protests by advantaged and disadvantaged groups. Politicians look for the most credible signals of public opinion, so that they can respond to popular demands and thereby enhance their odds of reelection. When privileged people—who may able to take time off work or pay for childcare—attend a protest, politicians tend to dismiss protesters' demands as cheap talk. But when marginalized folks rise up, they're risking much more; they may sacrifice their wages, jobs, and personal safety. As a result, politicians know there must be a deep grievance at stake. Gause, the political scientist, found that legislative support for protesters' demands increased by 39 percentage points following protests by low-income people, but by only 7 percentage points after protests by high-income people. Similarly, lawmakers were more than twice as likely to support non-white protesters as white protesters.[40]

The moral of the story is that costly protest can be more effective than easy protest. Gause's research reframes the costs of protesting as *investments* in likely success. Marginalized activists make considerable sacrifices in their struggles for justice in terms of time, money, safety, and mental health. The good news is that their sacrifices need not go to waste. According to empirical evidence, the power of protest depends on *who* participates, not just how many. Counterintuitively, a crowd of disadvantaged demonstrators has more clout than a crowd of demonstrators who are already powerful in other ways.

HOW TO START A MOVEMENT

Let's say you want to start a movement. You realize you can't go it alone, but you're aware that the people you need most might be the *least* willing to join you: Perhaps they have yet to join your side of an issue. Or they are socioeconomically disadvantaged and feel like they can't afford to take the risk. Or maybe they are just too busy living their lives. What can you do to mobilize your fellow citizens?

A first step is to understand the behavioral psychology of collective action. There are two main categories of problems that hinder collective action: *coordination problems* and *cooperation problems*. This section of the chapter will help you surmount both.

Coordination problems happen when a group of people all want to do the same thing—say, meet for dinner, hold a meeting, or attend a protest—but they lack the necessary information: the dinner host forgets to forward the restaurant reservation to all guests; the office manager never emails the date and time of the meeting; nobody advertises where and when a protest is happening. Coordination problems are easy to fix with modern communication technologies like email, text messaging, and social media. Organizers have repeatedly used Twitter to assemble mass demonstrations in a matter of hours.

For example, pro-democracy activists in Hong Kong managed to stage massive protests against the Chinese government with hardly any centralized leadership at all, relying only on social media. An eyewitness recounted an astonishing feat of coordination over four days in 2019:

> On August 19, someone posted to the LIHKG forum [a Reddit-like platform]. . . . Very soon thereafter organizing groups appeared on Telegram [a messaging app]. They came up with a map and logistics for how many people would need to be where. Soon, Telegram groups had formed for each segment of the route, which would shadow the MTR subway system. The day of the protests, volunteers updated real-time maps and polls showing where people were heading, and which MTR stations needed more attendees. Volunteers at the subway exits helped with staging, ensuring that when the protest started at 8 PM, everyone was already in position and there were no gaps. A Telegram group organized the final action of the night, having each protester cover their eye and chant "give back the eye" at 9 PM [a reference to a protester who had been blinded in one eye by a police bean bag round].[41]

Three years later, even China's Great Firewall was no match for the deluge of social media posts coordinating protests against harsh COVID-19 lockdowns. Chinese activists skirted censors by recording videos from odd angles and taking videos of videos, which confuses surveillance algorithms. One censor, speaking on the condition of anonymity, told the *New York Times* that platforms such as WeChat would need to hire ten times more staff to silence protesters.[42]

Coordinating protests was arduous back in the era when messages traveled by horses and smoke signals, but these days it is difficult to imagine a protest fizzling because communication broke down. In a lecture called "Don't Sleep Through the Revolution," Martin Luther King Jr. warned Americans not to be like Rip Van Winkle, who dozed off before the American Revolution began and awoke after George Washington was already president. In the contemporary telling of this fable, Rip would be roused by a notification on his phone and rush into battle with the other soldiers. Modern technology has largely relegated coordination problems to the past, except in the remotest rural areas where low population density still inhibits mass movements.[43]

Today, the more daunting task when initiating movements is getting people to *cooperate*. Unlike with coordination problems, when everyone already wants to participate in the collective action, cooperation problems involve getting people to participate when they don't want to make the individual effort. The masses you hope to mobilize may very well share your anger about the status quo and, in principle, fully support your cause. However, protesting carries costs and risks. Plenty of aggrieved people are reluctant to give up their time, money, and potentially their safety by attending activist meetings or taking to the streets—especially, as we learned from the Tea Party rallies, if it's raining.

Another barrier to mass mobilization arises when people can enjoy the outcome of a movement even if they do not contribute to obtaining it—this is called "free riding." For example, if a labor union wins a higher minimum wage, a worker can benefit from the new policy whether or not that worker marched on the picket line. Likewise, a successful democratic revolution achieves democracy for every citizen, including those who were too scared or lazy to confront the dictatorship when it mattered most. Economists have a term for goals like a high minimum wage and democracy: these are "non-excludable goods," that almost anyone can consume at will. When the outcome of a movement is non-excludable, people are tempted to free ride on the participation of others. Free riding is easy to forgive when protesting is very dangerous, like in a repressive regime. However, free riding can deter collective action even when protesting costs nothing more than an hour of one's time. The concept of free riding helps to explain how widespread grievances can coexist with low protest participation: being pissed off is a necessary but insufficient condition for the masses to rise up, because many dissatisfied people prefer to let others win concessions for them.

Despite these discouraging cooperation problems, plenty of movements have successfully gotten off the ground. Social science reveals how. Namely, organizers have two main tools at their disposal for getting people to stop free riding: *selective incentives* and *coercion*, colloquially known as the carrot and the stick.

Selective incentives can be material, psychological, or social. They fix the free-rider problem because they are *excludable* goods, accruing only to people who participate in a collective action.

Material incentives for protest participation are effective. An experiment in Hong Kong showed that offering students forty-five dollars to attend an antiauthoritarian demonstration and report back on turnout rates increased attendance by 10 percentage points compared with offering no incentive.[44] This finding would not shock most social scientists; the entire field of economics rests on the principle that people respond to incentives.

But from an activist's standpoint, the practical implications of the Hong Kong experiment may be ethically uncomfortable. Material incentives for protesting are often scandalous. Donald Trump habitually accused progressive activists of paying protesters to attend events such as the controversial Senate confirmation of Supreme Court Justice Brett Kavanaugh. He tweeted, "The very rude elevator screamers are paid professionals only looking to make Senators look bad. Don't fall for it! Also, look at all of the professionally made identical signs. Paid for by Soros and others. These are not signs made in the basement from love! #Troublemakers." Trump was not alone in suspecting grassroots movements of astroturfing: Google searches for "paid protesters" surged around the time of the 2018 Kavanaugh confirmation hearings, the 2017 Women's March, and the 2017 "Unite the Right" rally in Charlottesville, Virginia.[45] Trump's own campaign reportedly paid actors fifty dollars apiece to pad the crowd at his presidential campaign announcement.[46]

While fact-checkers have debunked some of Trump's protest-hiring accusations,[47] paid protesting does in fact happen. A town hall meeting in Camarillo, California, heated up when a man took the floor for nearly three minutes, grilling municipal leaders on a proposed construction project. "I'm just a concerned citizen coming up here speaking to you," he professed. This "citizen" later outed himself as Prince Jordan Tyson, a struggling actor from Beverly Hills. He confessed that he had received one hundred dollars and a script of talking points from Crowds on Demand, a publicity firm that discreetly supplies professional protesters for publicity events and political campaigns.[48] "Whether your organization is lobbying to move forward a healthcare, financial, energy or other social initiative, we can organize rallies and get media attention for your causes and candidates," the Crowds on Demand website promises. "We also assist individuals, companies and political organizations with protests and picketing campaigns. We've protested governments, corporations and everything in between." Not surprisingly, Crowds on Demand has drawn criticism for deceiving the public and civil servants with political theater. The firm battled a lawsuit over allegedly running an extortion campaign against a Czech investor.[49]

Aside from moral and legal gray areas, using material incentives to induce protest participation can backfire on activists by fueling cynicism that casts doubt on *all* demonstrations, including those where nobody has been paid to show up. Organizers may therefore prefer using *non*-material incentives to mobilize the masses. These can be psychological, like the chance to vent one's frustration with the status quo. Laboratory experiments confirm that feeling angry about social injustice makes people more willing to protest as an emotional release.[50] And in a groundbreaking series of oral histories in El Salvador, political scientist Elisabeth Wood found that peasants who took up arms against an oppressive government reported reaping no material gain from putting their lives on the line. Instead, they fought for the insurgency because it gave them "pleasure in agency"—an intangible sense of making history.[51] Salvadoran insurgent leaders, many of whom emerged from local Catholic organizations, spread the message of liberation theology. This framed high-risk collective action as a chance for emotional fulfillment.

The opportunity to have fun, even at a protest about a serious issue, serves as another selective incentive to participate in collective action. Research suggests that people are more eager to join large demonstrations that have an upbeat atmosphere, and that such demonstrations are more common on the ideological left than on the ideological right. For instance, a study of protests in Germany showed that right-leaning rallies focused entirely on speeches by extremist politicians, with no music or entertainment to lighten the mood.[52] In contrast, the Berlin nightclub community put on a raucous counterprotest called "Blow Away the AfD" (referring to the anti-immigrant and anti–European Union Alternative for Germany party) featuring a free concert studded with pop stars. Because you could only enjoy the concert if you attended the protest, this selective incentive worked to overcome the free-rider problem and helped to draw approximately twenty-five thousand people compared with just five thousand at a concurrent AfD march. Right-wing organizers who want to boost turnout at their rallies would be wise to increase the fun and dial back the sermonizing.

Social esteem is a further incentive for joining a protest. Anyone who has posted a selfie at a protest and watched the "likes" roll in knows the warm feeling of social approval. Humans evolved to seek social status because acceptance in a group was important for surviving in paleolithic times. Groups shared food, hunted together, provided mates, and helped each other raise offspring.[53] Uncooperative tribe members risked ostracism and starvation. Although likability is no longer a matter of life and death for most of us, our brains still instinctively crave the approval of our tribe.

Understanding this general human craving for social esteem can help activists mobilize mass movements. To prove the point, political scientist Gwyneth McClendon collaborated with an LGBTQ+ organization that was hosting a pride rally in New Jersey to demonstrate support for marriage equality.[54] At the time, same-sex marriage was still illegal in the state and the governor was outspokenly against legalization. The organization agreed to let McClendon randomize the wording of emails that went out to 3,651 prospective rally goers. One version of the email only included basic information about the purpose, time, and place of the event. A second version added text that was crafted to instill social esteem: "We have the greatest admiration for anyone who takes the time to support LGBT causes, so we will be listing the names of people who attend in our monthly newsletter, to be shared with and celebrated by all of our supporters." A third version invited participants to post photos on an event Facebook page "so that friends can show their support for attendees by 'liking' the posts." McClendon measured actual attendance by asking people to present a code from their email as a raffle ticket at the door of the event. Both the newsletter and the Facebook treatments significantly increased turnout, by 71 to 76 percent, compared to the information-only treatment.

Building on McClendon's experiment, newer research shows that historically marginalized communities award higher social esteem for participating in social movements than historically dominant communities. This may be because lacking voting rights forced those groups to place extra social weight on non-electoral forms of participation such as protest. Strong activist norms developed as a result. Political scientist Allison Anoll found that Black and Latinx Americans view new neighbors as more likable and respectable when they hear that the neighbors attend annual political rallies. White Americans do not evince the same preferences for activist neighbors, suggesting that people of color offer more social rewards for activism than white people.[55] Anoll also found that people of color place even more value on activism when they live in more racially segregated neighborhoods where in-group members can easily observe and enforce one another's participation in movements. The comparative ease of mobilizing the masses in marginalized communities is another dimension of "the advantage of disadvantage" that we examined earlier.

Just as social approval can stimulate protest participation, social *dis*approval can deter people from free riding on the activism of others. Put differently, coercion (the stick) complements selective incentives (carrots). In extreme cases, coercion can be physical. This is how some armed rebel movements forcibly recruit child soldiers.[56] However, coercion can also be effective and safe in nonviolent movements, in the form of gentle shaming.

A peculiar story from Switzerland illustrates the value of social pressure for mobilizing collective action. Swiss leaders introduced a national vote-by-mail option in the late 1990s, hoping to boost voter turnout by saving citizens a trip to the polls. They expected this to be especially successful in remote rural areas where travel was inconvenient. And yet, turnout failed to increase even with the lower cost of voting; in some places, it even *decreased*. Economist Patricia Funk argued that this was because voting by mail removed a key impetus to vote: social criticism for abstaining.[57] It was no coincidence, she noted, that turnout dropped the most in small villages where everybody knew everybody and gossip about abstainers spread fast. If the farmer down the road doesn't see you at the polling station, you might get nasty looks from everyone at the market later that week. But if voting by mail is an option, then you have plausible deniability. Your abstention is no longer public, so you don't feel as much pressure to cast your ballot.

Voting is not identical to protesting, but we can apply the logic of social pressure to other forms of collective action like attending a protest. On Election Day in the United States, it can feel awkward to be the only person in a room not wearing an "I voted" sticker. That's because judgmental comments or sideways glances from sticker wearers activate abstainers' innate dislike of social sanctioning. Different from guilt, which is an *internal* sanction, *social* sanctions include the disapproval, ostracism, shame, and pressure to conform that we receive from other people. More painful than knowing you didn't vote is knowing that *other people* know you didn't vote. In one poll, 41 percent of regular voters admitted that their reason for voting was "My friends and relatives almost always vote and I'd feel uncomfortable telling them

I hadn't voted."[58] Unless you go through the trouble of buying or stealing your own "I voted" sticker, your lack of a sticker will unmask you as an abstainer.

Fear of social sanctioning may explain why married people tend to vote more reliably than single people. It's difficult to hide the fact that you didn't vote from the person you live with. Spouses have ample opportunities to pressure each other to vote and fewer inhibitions on sounding impolite by calling each other out for uncooperative behavior. Researchers measured survey respondents' willingness to enforce voting by asking whether, upon learning that someone did not vote in the election, "I would disapprove, and let him or her know," "I would disapprove, and keep it to myself," or "It wouldn't matter to me at all." Married people who agreed with the first statement (the strong enforcement option) were most likely to say their spouse had voted.[59]

By extension, handing out "I protested" stickers or encouraging your spouse to protest could prod reluctant activists into action. If you give someone a hard time for not attending a protest that you asked them to attend, the sting of your disapproval might motivate them to show up to the next protest. Like in-person voting in Switzerland, any technology that allows organizers to monitor individual participation in a collective effort can enhance turnout at a group event. This could be as simple as asking people to wear branded buttons or shirts after a demonstration, register their attendance at the entrance to a rally venue, or post about their participation on social media. Research on collective action also suggests that it takes less effort to mobilize people within your own social circle, whom you can easily contact and nudge into participating. In Uganda, people who are in the same tribe[60] contribute more to collective goods for their co-ethnics (like chipping in money at school fundraisers) than people who are in different tribes.[61] Like married couples and residents of racially segregated neighborhoods, tribal members have built trust from shared culture and can track one another's participation.

IF COLLECTIVE ACTION IS SO IMPORTANT, DOES MY INDIVIDUAL ACTIVISM STILL MATTER?

So far, this chapter has focused on the importance of *collective* action and how to mobilize it, which might lead you to an unsettling conclusion: "My *solo* activism doesn't matter." In this final section, I want to reassure you that your personal actions—including protest participation, social media posts, letters to lawmakers, donations to charitable causes, and signatures on petitions—can still make a difference, but maybe not in the way you once thought.

There are two questions to ask yourself when deciding whether the individual action you are planning is worthwhile: First, what is its *expected value*? Second, how much influence will my action have on the behavior of others?

Below are two common arguments in response to the question "Does my individual activism matter?"

1. **Your individual activism doesn't matter at all, because the probability of you alone deciding the outcome of a movement is extremely small.** The premise of this claim is plausible: one more body in a crowd, one more dollar donated, or one more signature on a petition is, in most cases, just a drop in the bucket. Especially in movements that are already large, one more participant probably won't be the factor that decides victory or defeat. The problem with this argument is that it is incredibly demoralizing. If everyone thought this way, then movements would never take off, let alone succeed.
2. **Your activism matters, but only if you derive benefits from it that don't depend on the overall outcome.** In other words, it's still rational to protest even if your participation doesn't make victory any likelier. Perhaps you enjoy intrinsic benefits from participating, like camaraderie or the ability to vent your anger, whether or not your side ultimately wins. This argument is only reassuring if you don't care about the outcome of protests. However, if you are reading this book, it's safe to assume you *do* care about outcomes.

A third, rather less intuitive, argument comes from economics, statistics, and applied ethics:

3. **Your activism matters if your expected value from participating makes it worthwhile for you.** To calculate expected value, simply multiply the value you assign to an outcome by the estimated probability of getting that outcome.

To understand how this works, we can adapt an example from philosopher William MacAskill's manifesto on effective altruism, *Doing Good Better*.[62] First, ask yourself, "How much is it worth to me if my social movement wins?" Let's say you value a victory at $1,000, maybe because you are fighting for a higher minimum wage that would put an extra $1,000 in your bank account next year. You then estimate, conservatively, that the probability of your individual participation deciding the policy outcome is one in sixty million. This puts your expected value of participating in the movement at 0.0016 cents (1,000 x 1/60,000,000). Objectively, that is not very much, so you may decide not to participate.

However, many activists protest to benefit others, not just themselves. Suppose that winning a higher minimum wage is worth $314 billion to you, because you anticipate that a victory will benefit millions of people. In that case, even assuming no change in the probability of you singlehandedly deciding the outcome, your expected value leaps to $5,200 (314 billion x 1/60,000,000). Most reasonable people would be willing to protest for that much money.

The upshot of the expected value framework is that it can be worthwhile to invest your energy in very low-probability outcomes so long as the value of those outcomes is sufficiently high. You can run these kinds of calculations the next time you are deciding whether to join a protest or a social movement.

If you are not content to bank on unlikely outcomes, you can magnify the probability of your individual efforts making a difference by letting your actions inspire others to act as well. These days, "influencers" often have a negative reputation as narcissistic social media personalities who hawk cosmetics and dubious vitamin supplements. Although such people are unlikely to catalyze the next progressive revolution, they illustrate a tenet that altruistic activists can adopt for virtuous ends: the bigger your following, the more people's behavior you can influence with your own actions.

Seasoned civil rights activist Gary Chambers Jr. knew exactly what to do after he called out a member of the Baton Rouge, Louisiana, school board for online shopping during a public hearing on renaming a high school named for Confederate General Robert E. Lee. He shared a video of the confrontation with his 26,000 Instagram followers on Juneteenth. In the clip, Chambers does not mince words at the podium: "I had intended to get up here and talk about how racist Robert E. Lee was, but I'm going to talk about you, Connie. Sitting over there shopping while we're talking about Robert E. Lee. . . . You should walk out of here and resign and never come back because you are the example of racism in this community. You are horrible." The video quickly racked up 1.8 million views and Chambers's follower count jumped to 200,000.[63] On its own, the speech would have been easy for intransigent bureaucrats to dismiss as the rant of an eccentric local troublemaker. However, by publicizing his discourse, Chambers catapulted the issue of Confederate monuments to national prominence and incited an outpouring of public sympathy that the city council could not ignore. After a four-year struggle to rename Lee High School, a committee finally renamed the school Liberty Magnet High School. Chambers made a calculated decision to be more than an activist; he became an influencer.

So, here's what we know:

- Most successful social movements have historically been collective actions, not individual actions.
- Protests that appear small often involve many people working behind the scenes.
- Protest participation is rare, even for folks who care about the issues. A fun concert at a rally or a judgmental glance

for not attending a protest can motivate fence sitters to
stand up.
- Larger crowds are often, but not always, more effective
  than smaller crowds.
- Crowds are most powerful when they involve defectors
  from the ruling coalition and disadvantaged groups for
  whom protest is costly.
- Individual activism is can still make a difference under
  two conditions: 1) it produces a high expected value; or
  2) it influences other people to rise up, transforming a
  solo act into a movement.

2. THE TRUTH ABOUT SLACKTIVISM
Online Versus Offline Protesting

In 2004, the *Oxford English Dictionary* started picking a Word of the Year: "a word or expression reflecting the ethos, mood, or preoccupations of the past twelve months, one that has potential as a term of lasting cultural significance." *Oxford* inaugurated this tradition around the time that Mark Zuckerberg launched Facebook, so it is not surprising that many winning words over the years have related to digital communication: "podcast" (2005), "unfriend" (2009), "GIF" (2012), "selfie" (2013). In 2015, the Word of the Year was not a word at all, but rather the "face with tears of joy" emoji: 😂. "Vape" took the top prize in 2014, but it barely edged out "slacktivist," a portmanteau of "slacker" and "activist" meaning "one who engages in digital activism on the Web which is regarded as requiring little time or involvement."[1] Sharing, "liking," commenting, and changing one's profile picture are common forms of slacktivism.

Slacktivist might have landed on *Oxford*'s shortlist thanks to a social media frenzy that prompted many people to question the legitimacy of online protest. On the night of April 14, 2014, militants from the Islamist terrorist organization Boko Haram masqueraded as soldiers from the Nigerian Armed Forces and snuck into the Government Girls Secondary School in northeast

Nigeria. Local families knew it was risky to send their daughters to school; *Boko Haram* is usually translated as "Western education is forbidden." The school in question had been closed for months due to security concerns. However, classes had briefly reopened to allow students to take their final exams in physics. Seizing their opportunity, the militants kidnapped approximately 276 girls and torched the schoolhouse. Fifty-seven girls managed to escape, but the rest endured atrocities such as child marriage, sexual slavery, forced religious conversion, and human trafficking. The public outcry reverberated beyond Nigeria. Twitter and Facebook accelerated a global movement to #BringBackOurGirls. The hashtag was used more than a million times within three weeks.[2] Michelle Obama, Malala Yousafzai, and other celebrities threw themselves into the cause, broadcasting digital thoughts and prayers.

It did not take long for people to notice that the rhetorical outrage on social media seemed to be outpacing any substantial efforts to actually bring the girls back. Amnesty International estimated that at least two thousand *more* girls were abducted by Boko Haram the following year.[3] Nigerian American commentator Jumoke Balogun fumed in *The Guardian*, "Dear world, your hashtags won't #BringBackOurGirls."[4] Even if Western governments did take stronger action against Boko Haram, Balogun argued that this would only serve to abet a "military expansionist agenda." She implied that people outside Nigeria who tweeted solidarity, however well-meaning, were worse than slacktivists; they were complicit in violent neocolonialism. Foreigners were not the only offenders. Nigeria's then president, Goodluck Jonathan, came under fire for being slow to rescue the girls and for appropriating the crisis by using #BringBackGoodluck2015 in his reelection campaign.

There's no mystery to why people engage in slacktivism: It's a low-cost way to take a stand, and it can earn you praise from friends. As we learned in the last chapter, humans have a deep-seated hunger for social approval. However, skepticism—or even revulsion—lurks beneath superficial "likes" and retweets. The Pew Research Center reports that over three-quarters of Americans agree with the statement "Social media make people think they are making a difference when they really aren't." A similar proportion thinks that "social media distract people from issues that are truly important." This is more than the share of Americans who believe that social media "highlight important issues that may not get a lot of attention" (65 percent), "help give a voice to underrepresented groups" (64 percent), or "make it easier to hold powerful people accountable for their actions" (50 percent).[5] In the context of activism, techno-pessimists outnumber techno-optimists.

The #BringBackOurGirls episode is no exception. It is rare nowadays for any movement to *not* have a hashtag that people can cheaply publicize.[6] Prominent examples include #MeToo, #BlackLivesMatter, #Fightfor15, #RhodesMustFall, and #JeSuis Charlie. The proliferation of virtual activism raises several questions: Why do slacktivists tend to irritate us, even if we engage in slacktivism ourselves? Does slacktivism really hurt a movement, or can it help despite the negative reactions it provokes? Assuming that online protest is here to stay, how can activists make sure it's effective and not just symbolic? In particular, how can online activists withstand evolving attempts by autocrats to sabotage them? This chapter outlines evidence-grounded and sometimes counterintuitive answers to all of those questions. It also spotlights a problem that few activists are talking about: the way the internet fractures our attention and impedes what I call "deep activism." But don't worry; that problem is surmountable. This chapter concludes with multiple ways to make the internet work for, not against, social movements.

WHY DO SLACKTIVISTS SEEM ICKY, AND WHY SHOULD WE CARE?

It is imperative to understand why so many people find slacktivism off-putting, because backlash to online activism risks setting back a cause entirely. Many worry that audiences might dismiss a hashtag like #BringBackOurGirls as a joke, as most internet memes are made for entertainment and not for resolving human rights violations.[7] Hashtags can draw the wrong kind of attention to serious issues. Slacktivism creates branding problems for matters that deserve mindful solutions, not short-lived hype.[8]

No one knows this better than branding professionals. In 2020, amid the turmoil of COVID-19 and George Floyd's murder, the advertising trade magazine *Adweek* released an article cautioning companies against the trend of posting hashtags and images to support social justice. The headline read, "Want to Be Taken Seriously? Don't Be Fake. Be Consistent."[9] The piece cited evidence that activist messages can offend consumers if companies don't back them up with concrete action. For example, Nike aired a 2020 commercial swapping its famous slogan "Just Do It" with "Don't Do It" (as in, "Don't turn your back on racism" and "Don't pretend there's not a problem in America"). The advertising analytics firm Ace Metrix found that people gave the ad a high "empowerment score" but also a high "exploit score." Meanwhile, Ben & Jerry's faces little backlash for endorsing progressive causes, presumably because the ice cream company has a long track record of corporate social responsibility, dating back to its 1988 "Peace Pop" campaign to redirect 1 percent of the national defense budget to peace-promoting projects. In contrast, Nike has a reputation for aggressive profit seeking and a spotty record on labor rights and environmentalism.[10] Its abrupt swing toward "woke" language smacked of opportunism and hypocrisy, and consumers took notice.

To explain popular aversion to slacktivism, it helps to think about its opposite: popular ardor for heroes.

Wesley Autrey was waiting for the New York subway on an ordinary Tuesday afternoon in 2007, his two daughters standing by his side. The fifty-year-old Navy veteran was going to drop off his kids at home before starting his shift as a construction worker. Without warning, a man standing on the platform nearby started having a seizure and fell onto the rails. Autrey didn't have time to think before he saw train lights hurtling toward the station. He leapt onto the tracks and held the stranger down while five cars rolled over them, close enough to smudge grease on his cap. Both men survived with minimal injuries, but this didn't make Autrey's intervention any less impressive to bystanders, whose applause and sighs of relief rang through the station. Over the next months, Autrey, now dubbed the "Subway Superman," received an outpouring of gratitude: talk show appearances, a seat at the State of the Union address, a trip to Disney World, a five-thousand-dollar Gap gift card, backstage passes to a Beyoncé concert, and, of course, a new hat. Mayor Michael Bloomberg honored him with the city's highest award for citizenship, saying, "Wesley's astonishing bravery . . . is an inspiration not just to New Yorkers, but the entire world. His courageous rescue of a complete stranger is a reminder of how we are surrounded by everyday heroes in New York City."[11] Autrey demurred at the acclaim, telling the *New York Times*, "I don't feel like I did something spectacular; I just saw someone who needed help. I did what I felt was right."[12]

Autrey's actions won him a level of esteem that is hard to imagine anybody matching by nonchalantly posting a hashtag. Indeed, the Pew surveys I mentioned earlier indicate that a sizable share of Americans judge online activism *negatively*. Far from heroic, tweeting #MeatlessMondays or #TrustWomen can come across as insincere or self-righteous. At first glance, it is obvious why people don't win awards for tweeting. *Of course we react differently to the Subway Superman*, you might think. *When did a tweet ever save someone's life?*

However, the psychology behind our disparate responses to Autrey and slacktivists gets murkier when we consider the admiration that society bestows upon graduates of elite universities. Sure, a single tweet probably never saved someone's life, but neither did a Harvard diploma, at least not directly. Evidence shows that elite schools provide no better education than their less prestigious counterparts. Researchers sent faculty to observe six hundred classrooms at nine colleges and universities—three with "high prestige," two with "medium prestige," and four with "low prestige"—and had them rate the quality of instruction using a standard rubric. Elite institutions scored no better than non-elite institutions overall, and even *underperformed* along some dimensions, like supporting changes in students' views.[13] While this study had limitations, including a small sample size, it suggests that the educational value of a top-tier school is questionable. Even in the extreme case of winding up in the emergency room, having a doctor who attended Harvard no more guarantees living to tell the tale than having one who trained in a "lesser" program: An audit of nearly a million hospital patients treated by more than thirty thousand physicians showed no difference between alumni of higher- and lower-ranked medical schools in the mortality of their patients within a thirty-day time span.[14]

Despite its dubious utility, an elite degree confers social advantages. One experiment showed that job seekers with Harvard, Stanford, or Duke on their résumés were significantly more likely to get callbacks from employers than otherwise similar applicants who graduated from the University of Massachusetts–Amherst, University of California–Riverside, or University of North Carolina–Greensboro.[15] A first-class diploma helps on the marriage market, too. "The League," informally known as "the Harvard of online dating," is a dating app that screens prospective members' college pedigrees and verifies their credentials on LinkedIn. Once accepted to the League (there is a long waitlist), users can filter matches by education, ranging from "selective" to "highly selective" schools; community college grads need not apply. Even some actual Harvard students find the app too pretentious for their taste. An undergraduate reporter writing for the *Harvard Crimson* test-drove the League and described the vetting process as "kind of gross."[16]

The outsized respect that society pays to elite college graduates challenges the theory that we look down on slacktivists because they add little value to the world. Accumulating tens of thousands of dollars in debt to attend a selective university does not guarantee that someone will cure cancer or negotiate world peace, any more than tweeting #BringBackOurGirls guarantees a solution to terrorism in Nigeria. And yet, many people worship fancy degrees[17] while pooh-poohing hashtag activism. Popular disdain for slacktivists requires a different, less utilitarian explanation.

That explanation comes from evolutionary biology, and specifically *signaling theory*. Peacocks with magnificent feathers (the animal kingdom's equivalent of Harvard graduates) once puzzled zoologists because they seemed to violate the principle of natural selection. Ornamentation helped peacocks attract mates. But wouldn't being so flamboyant also attract predators? The answer to this puzzle is that only the fittest peacocks—those with the ability to fight off predators and produce healthy offspring—can afford to display elaborate tails; others die trying. Thus, natural selection made peahens prefer them.[18] A risky signal is credible; a weak bird that flaunts handsome plumage quickly becomes a carnivore's lunch. And because the stakes of finding the right mate are high—only the fittest offspring survive in the wild—animals (including us) developed a profound repulsion to deceit to match their preference for bold honesty.

Experiments confirm that people do not judge one another based on the immediate benefits they provide, but rather on the costs they are willing to incur to signal their quality as long-term partners.[19] Human courtship often involves exchanging gifts that are expensive but impractical (diamonds, roses, champagne, love poems).[20] Such symbols help us screen out frauds on the dating scene. They are useful signals even if they are unpleasant for one or both parties. There's a traditional Japanese play in which a suitor must appear for 100 evenings at the door of the woman he loves, to at last be admitted on the 101st night. We can assume that neither lover relished the wait, but at least the lady could be confident in her suitor's commitment to her.[21] It is useful to think about social signaling in the context of intimate relationships because it reminds us that our practice of sending costly signals to each other is rooted in our deepest animal instincts to mate with the highest quality partners—those who will care for us and not just themselves. In this light, it makes sense that people came out so hard against Nike's anti-racist video; although Nike spent some money on the ad, it was plain that the corporate giant mostly stood to profit from increased sales. Similarly, slacktivists aren't even leaving home to support the causes they claim to care about. Nike and slacktivists send cheap signals revealing their shallow concern for others, which is why they make us cringe.

Putting down slacktivists is also a way of coping psychologically with our moral imperfections. It's easy to disparage conspicuous hypocrites, like corporations that use sweatshops while preaching social justice or the Minneapolis mayor who tried to join a George Floyd protest after rejecting calls to defund the police (demonstrators duly booed him out of the march).[22] However, many of us regularly fail to live up to our signaled virtues: ardent environmentalists sometimes don't recycle; proud vegetarians succumb to bacon cravings; anti-poverty warriors treat themselves to gourmet dinners instead of donating more money to the poor. We emotionally berate ourselves for falling short even while intellectually accepting that we can't be morally pure. Psychologists note that people who transgress social standards feel guilty and ashamed, even if they haven't wronged anyone in particular, because they've internalized the standards of some "generalized other."[23] Aware of our own ethical inconsistency, we try to protect our egos by projecting our shortcomings onto other people. This is a normal, often subconscious, defense mechanism that goes into overdrive during stressful times.[24] Slacktivists raise red flags in our minds because they are like mirrors reflecting our blemishes back at us.

We now have the biological and psychological understanding to explain why someone with a Stanford diploma seems more impressive than someone who puts a rainbow filter on their profile photo in support of gay rights. An elite degree is like a peacock's feathers: While it carries little intrinsic worth, it is the surest way (and a financially costly one) to convince others that you are the type of person who could get into a selective school. The social media user with the rainbow filter *might* be a devoted gay rights activist, but as far as you know, also might be a slacktivist willing to make only trivial investments in a cause. Evolution explains why we take offense when people lie their way into elite schools, catfish on dating apps, or engage in slacktivism: natural selection made us prize truthfulness and abhor phoniness, all the more because we know deep down that we are occasionally phonies ourselves.

Wesley Autrey stole people's hearts because it is impossible to fake rescuing a man on the subway tracks. His courage won him high praise not just for producing immediate value (saving someone's life), but also for tapping into people's instinctive attraction to risky shows of strength. The human psyche responds similarly to Nelson Mandela, Malala Yousafzai, and less well-known activists who underwent captivity or injury in the name of justice. All of those individuals paid dearly for standing up to oppression. Their selfless courage was never in doubt. Conversely, cheap talk like Nike's "Don't Do It" ad activates our innate distaste for duplicity, making slacktivism seem icky and fueling cynicism toward the worthy causes that slacktivists unintentionally cheapen, from protecting children against terrorism in Nigeria (#BringBackOur Girls), to racial equity in the United States (#BlackLivesMatter), to women's rights everywhere (#MeToo).

And yet, as we will see in the next section, slacktivism is not all bad. Its net effects might even be more beneficial than harmful, notwithstanding the negative side effect of trivializing urgent issues. This raises a bigger point that I wish to stress in this book and that I hope you will find comforting: No protest strategy is perfect, and that's okay. Any social movement that "succeeded" by common measures (spurred policy reforms, won material concessions, or changed public opinion) hit bumps along the road to victory. Being a savvy activist does not mean banishing problematic tactics from your playbook; it only means weighing the pros and cons of each decision, minimizing damages to the extent possible, and keeping your eye on the prize. We'll walk through this process together at the end of the chapter. But first, let's finish our scientific tour of online and offline activism, with a few philosophical detours.

DOES SLACKTIVISM REALLY HURT A MOVEMENT?

If slacktivists are *merely* irritating, then they are like flies; just swat them away and go about your more serious activist business. However, some techno-pessimists warn that slacktivists are more like mosquitoes—disease-harboring parasites that infect would-be effective social movements with a false sense of achievement. The reasoning goes: If people believe they are making a difference by sharing a hashtag, they will become less likely to take meaningful action in the "real world." Social media junkies will opine on everything and act on nothing. The locus of protest will migrate from streets to tweets. Over time, the prevailing sentiment becomes "To save everything, click here."[25] Old-school tactics such as street protests, lobbying, and writing letters to lawmakers have worked in the past.[26] If lightweight digital activism crowds out tried-and-true approaches, then activists might have more trouble moving the needle on ambitious goals. Economic justice advocate Astra Taylor insists that movements need "real organizing," not "viral outrage." She maintains, "The goal of any would-be world-changer should be to be part of something so organized, so formidable, and so shrewd that the powerful don't scoff: they quake."[27]

Public intellectual Evgeny Morozov is one of the most outspoken naysayers of online activism. In his provocative book *The Net Delusion: The Dark Side of Internet Freedom,* he set out to deflate widespread faith in the "ridiculously easy group forming" powers of the internet[28] (see chapter 1 on how the internet helps to solve coordination problems). Morozov thinks that slacktivism not only displaces the costlier work that genuine changemaking requires ("Someone still has to go to prison," he writes); it *corrupts the human soul* by turning us into "clowns cracking jokes about the guillotine." Slacktivists are ineffectual, he says, but worse, they are inauthentic. In a net-deluded society, tweeting #BringBackOur Girls is tantamount to trying to impress your Instagram followers with filtered snapshots of your interior décor. Morozov calls into question the very existence of virtual politics. From his outlook, only analog activism will do.

Morozov's anti-slacktivist treatise can sound like an old man yelling "Get off my lawn!" A devil's advocate might reply that every aging generation has lamented the newfangled technology of younger generations. How can we know whether Morozov is paranoid or prophetic? Online activism has been around a long time, allowing researchers to take stock of its effects to date. Spoiler alert: slacktivists are more like flies than mosquitoes.

One way of testing the behavioral effects of online activism is to see how tweets correlate with subsequent in-person demonstrations. A team of scholars collected almost fourteen million tweets geolocated in countries that were part of the Arab Spring, and then measured how much Twitter users coordinated around hashtags.[29] They found a clear relationship between yesterday's amount of online coordination and today's number of protests on the ground. In a complementary study looking at individual behavior in Chile, heavy social media users were seven times more likely than light users to voice demands to authorities and three times more likely to attend political forums.[30] Evidently, online protest does not substitute for offline protest, but rather facilitates it.

Of course, correlation is not causation. To know whether slacktivism actually *causes* people to protest offline, the gold standard of evidence is a randomized controlled trial. Before getting to their experimental results, communication scholars Yu-Hao Lee and Gary Hsieh pointed out in an article that the theoretical literature is agnostic on whether slacktivism reduces offline activism.[31] There are two conflicting lines of thought:

1. Slacktivism discourages other civic actions because people who post online feel like they have already satisfied their duty to society. Known in psychology as *moral balancing*, this is similar to the *self-licensing effect* in health studies: "If I ate a salad for lunch, I can enjoy a whole pizza for dinner, guilt-free!" Analogously: "If I tweeted #BlackLivesMatter, I don't need to attend the BLM

protest this weekend." Therefore, slacktivism should *reduce* offline activism as Morozov feared.
2. The behavior that we find icky in others is no less icky when we detect it in ourselves. People know when they are being slacktivists, and it makes them uncomfortable. To avoid the discomfort of *cognitive dissonance* (essentially, feeling like a hypocrite), online activists subsequently join civic actions offline: They attend physical protests, donate money, and so forth. Following this theory, slacktivism should *increase* offline activism, ultimately making people slacktivists no more.

To see which theory is correct, Lee and Hsieh asked research subjects to register at *We the People*, a now-defunct government website founded by the Obama administration in 2011. Visitors to the site could sign petitions on a variety of issues, and if a petition reached 100,000 signatures within thirty days, the White House would issue an official response. Lee and Hsieh instructed a random group of subjects to sign a petition on gun control (either for or against, depending on their personal views), while a control group was not instructed to do so. Signing a petition represented slacktivism, because it is very easy to do. They then asked if subjects wanted to make a costlier statement by donating any of their participation incentive payment to either the National Rifle Association or the Brady Campaign (a nonprofit combatting gun violence). Lee and Hsieh found that slacktivists (subjects who performed the low-cost activism of signing a petition) were no less likely to donate to charity than subjects that did not sign a petition. There were even cases where slacktivism *increased* offline activism: signing the petition made donors more generous when the charity was congruent with their gun control views.

The authors cautioned that slacktivism might not increase *all* forms of offline protest. They asked subjects about their plans to engage in different types of activism in the future. Signing the petition increased intentions to sign more petitions and to write letters to the government, but it had negligible effects on intentions to participate in protests and eight other civic actions. No single study can defeat or vindicate the theory that slacktivism hurts social movements. However, a meta-analysis of the broader literature uncovered little evidence for the hypothesis that slacktivism discourages real-world activism.[32]

Another argument for slacktivism is that low-cost online engagement serves as a double coordination mechanism: it not only helps activists coordinate logistically, as I discussed in the previous chapter; it also creates common knowledge about social norms.[33] If seemingly everyone in your network is tweeting #BlackLives Matter—to the point that it starts to look trite when more people jump on the bandwagon—it suggests that sympathy toward Black Lives Matter has reached a critical threshold where practically everyone within a relevant community (e.g., American liberals) knows that everyone else supports the movement. Common knowledge eliminates plausible deniability; if you don't show at least minimal support for Black lives, you can't say you didn't know any better.[34] Saying nothing opens you to social sanctioning; "silence is compliance," the cliché goes. Such convergence of attitudes on social media can trickle up to the halls of power. Elected leaders wanting to keep their jobs are more willing to endorse policies—like investigating bad cops and requiring antibias training of the police force—that vast swaths of their constituency take for granted as good ideas. Many once-fringe progressive causes (universal health care, environmentalism, gay marriage) found their way into major party platforms after public opinion unambiguously fell in favor of addressing them. Slacktivism *makes* public preferences unambiguous. Precisely because it is so mundane, it helps to shift activist goals from obscurity into the mainstream.

The COVID-19 pandemic provides a handy analogy to elucidate yet another benefit of slacktivism. Viruses can't spread on their own; they require hosts within whom they can insert their genetic material and co-opt proteins to reproduce. Uninfected (and unvaccinated) organisms are efficient at spreading viruses because they don't yet have protective antibodies to fend off invaders—hence, why it was dangerous during the pandemic to invite never-infected, unvaccinated guests to a dinner party. Social movements, like viruses, need "fresh blood" in order to spread; organizers can't recruit people who are already members. This makes folks on the periphery of a movement extremely valuable. They represent opportunities to "infect" new activists with the movement's message and to incorporate them into the struggle. Peripheral people often are slacktivists who express some sympathy toward the cause but aren't yet deeply involved. A study of the Arab Spring showed that Twitter users who were central to a social network—those whose follower counts were at or above the 95th percentile of all users in their country—had no impact on protest frequency, whereas those on the periphery—users with relatively few followers—bore almost all of the responsibility for rising protest rates.[35] An effective way to recruit peripheral people into a movement is to organize short, multi-site protests, such as marches, as opposed to extended, single-site protests, such as sit-ins or encampments. Short, multi-site events can physically reach new audiences without demanding too much of their time.[36]

Although slacktivists have a bad name, seasoned organizers know the vital role they play in making a message go viral. Abdel Rahman Mansour cocreated the Facebook page "We Are All Khaled Said" after Said, a twenty-eight-year-old Egyptian man, was beaten to death by police. Early followers of the page hailed from activist circles, but this core group soon became the minority. Mansour reflected, "Of course, some of [those who joined the page] were part of university movements, some of them were part of political parties, some of them were part of the 6 April movement, but the majority were middle class members who weren't involved in politics."[37] The page eventually grew so popular that people started sending *him* invitations to follow it, not realizing he was the administrator. ABC News reported that Khaled Said was "the face that launched a revolution."[38] Mansour's small friend group could not have launched a revolution by themselves. It took legions of strangers, some only dabbling in activism, to change history.

Recall from chapter 1 that individuals prefer joining fun activities that reward them with social approval, while shying away from unpleasant activities where they experience social disapproval. Mary Joyce, founder of the Meta-Activism Project (a digital activism think tank), warns that using the derogatory term *slacktivist* could discourage first-time activists by raising the bar for participation too high and making rookies feel like failures from the get-go.[39] Like all difficult human undertakings, activism has a learning curve. Every veteran was a newbie at some point. Gatekeeping—expecting too much from novices and branding them slacktivists—can stunt social movements by making activism more intimidating than it needs to be. Joyce proposes that movements would be better off if people excised the word *slacktivist* from their lexicon altogether.

We have now reviewed ample scientific evidence validating what social movement leaders have long intuited: Digital and analog activism are not mutually exclusive. A hybrid approach is not just possible, but optimal. Online and offline tactics enhance each other by broadening participation to diverse demographics and, as we are about to see, by spreading risk in the face of counterrevolution. The renowned social movements scholar Zeynep Tufekci tries to put the whole slacktivism controversy to rest with a succinct rejoinder that is ready-made for you to throw back at someone who chastises you for being a slacktivist:

> The concept of slacktivism is not just naïve and condescending, it is misinformed and misleading. What is commonly called slacktivism is not at all about "slacking activists"; rather it is about non-activists taking symbolic action—often in spheres traditionally engaged only by activists or professionals (governments, NGOs, international institutions). Since these so-called "slacktivists" were never activists to begin with, they

are not in dereliction of their activist duties. On the contrary, they are acting, symbolically and in a small way, in a sphere that has traditionally been closed off to "the masses" in any meaningful fashion.[40]

MAKING SLACKTIVISM WORK

To say that slacktivism doesn't hurt movements is not to say that slacktivism always works. How can activists put slacktivism to the best use? We've covered one way: by incorporating "uninfected" people into an expanding activist network. But new research also suggests that organizers hoping to effect real-world change should target recruits who exhibit specific characteristics. Some slacktivists limit their involvement to casual online activism or disengage completely, whereas others take on increasingly demanding roles both online and offline. What makes the difference between those two groups?

As it turns out, our personalities have a lot to do with whether we make the jump from online to offline protest. And there is such a thing as an activist personality. Political scientists Jan Matti Dollbaum and Graeme Robertson borrowed a common psychology instrument for measuring personality traits across cultures, known as the Five Factor Model or the Big Five.[41] This questionnaire asks how much you agree with statements such as "I am the life of the party" and "I get chores done right away." You can find many online versions. It took me just a few minutes to take the test.[42] Perhaps unsurprisingly for a professor, I scored above average on extroversion (the inclination to seek attention, friendship, power, status, and excitement) and below average on agreeableness (the tendency to put others' needs ahead of one's own and to cooperate rather than compete with others). Dollbaum and Robertson argued that these two traits, in particular, influence whether and how people participate in activism: Extroverts are more prone to protesting, which requires being assertive, expending energy, and shouldering risk. And while disagreeable people make terrible party guests, they make good activists because they have a high tolerance for conflict.

The researchers found support for this theory in a large dataset of Russian opposition supporters. They observed that disagreeableness distinguishes Russians who merely endorse opposition politicians on social media from those who take the extra step of partaking in offline campaign activity. If you are trying to convince the slacktivists in your life to shift toward offline activism, don't count out the disagreeable ones; they may be the very allies you need to stir the right kind of trouble and lock horns with antagonists.

It's unrealistic for social movement organizers to ask every potential recruit to take a personality test, but they can infer personality traits from the sentiments in people's social media messages.[43] That attention-seeking friend who constantly posts about her vacations and picks fights with her uncle on Twitter? She might drive you crazy, but science suggests she is a prime candidate to mobilize into a movement.

As much as we might try to target the right personality types, people's personalities are beyond our control. We *can*, however, control how we craft online recruitment materials. Building on the research we examined in chapter 1 about the mobilizing power of emotions, political scientists Andreu Casas and Nora Webb Williams designed an experiment to see whether including images in social media posts affects activist mobilization.[44] By randomizing tweets about Black Lives Matter, some with images and some without, they estimated that a tweet with an image generated three more retweets than a tweet without an image. They also varied the emotions that images conveyed. For example, a picture of armed security officers evoked fear, a photo of a lively march evoked enthusiasm, and a portrait memorializing a Black youth killed by police evoked sadness. The experiment showed that enthusiasm had a greater mobilizing effect than fear, and that sadness was demobilizing. This study has practical implications for activists: To mobilize the most people online, include images in your posts and choose those that are exciting rather than scary or sad.

> **EXERCISE:** Imagine you are designing a social media post to advertise an upcoming protest for a cause that you care about. Can you think of what image you would include in it?

HOW AUTOCRATS BEAT ONLINE ACTIVISTS AT THEIR OWN GAME... AND HOW ACTIVISTS CAN FIGHT BACK

Making online activism work requires more than mobilizing sympathizers. Increasingly, it also necessitates warding off attacks from aggressors who want to see a movement fail. Repression of activists was once a concern mainly in the nastiest dictatorships, but internet crackdowns are creeping into more and more corners of the world. Democracy almost everywhere is "under siege," according to Freedom House, a nonprofit advocacy group. In 2021, nearly three-quarters of the world's population lived in a country where liberties such as free speech and the right to assemble were deteriorating.[45] In a recent report, Freedom House sounded alarm bells about government censorship and arrests of protesters in places like Algeria and Hong Kong. Even the United States, once a beacon of democracy, slipped from a freedom score of 94 out of 100 in 2010 to 83 in 2022. That ranks the US less free than Mongolia (84), Croatia (85), and Chile (94). Global internet freedom declined for the twelfth year in a row in 2022, and setbacks were not limited to the usual suspects like Russia and China. Internet users faced legal repercussions in at least fifty-three countries; forty-seven governments cut residents off from foreign content, and twenty-two governments proposed or passed laws restricting the transfer of personal data.[46] Censorship and surveillance capabilities are getting more sophisticated. The Chinese firm Semptian boasts that its Aegis surveillance system monitors over two hundred million individuals (a quarter of China's internet users).[47] Authorities from other countries can easily purchase products like Aegis at tech trade shows. Activists and autocrats are in an arms race to master the most advanced online networking tools. Autocrats often have the advantage, but activists can still win. Here's how.

One way that online activists can fight back is by adapting to restraints on technology use. Activists are not helpless victims of censorship; they tend to be highly resourceful at finding new ways to circumvent censors. Political scientists William Hobbs and Margaret Roberts noticed a strange pattern in the academic literature: evidence kept showing a *positive* correlation between censorship and anti-government opposition.[48] To decipher this perplexing relationship, they theorized that internet clampdowns have an ironic *gateway effect* on activism: when authorities block access to a popular social media platform, they unwittingly incentivize opposition members to seek alternative "gateways" to regulated zones of the internet.

The gateway effect took over as soon as the Chinese government shut down Instagram. Users who normally wouldn't be curious about virtual private networks (VPNs) suddenly had a reason to learn how to use them. VPNs restored access not only to Instagram, but also to numerous other websites where activists could engage in opposition politics. Internet traffic data from before and after the ban revealed an uptick in activism among previously apathetic social media users.

Another way to weather online repression is by mixing public-facing activism with clandestine organizing. Authorities can readily quash protesting that occurs out in the open, such as rallies and social media campaigns. Political scientist Christopher M. Sullivan points out that social movements can hold off government attacks on the front lines provided that they have reinforcements behind the scenes—steady leadership, secret cells, dispersed informants, safehouses, secure bank accounts, and so on.[49] In those cases, government crackdowns are like running a lawnmower over weeds: the weeds can strike back with a vengeance as long as the roots remain growing beneath the surface, and pulling weeds over and over again eventually wears down authorities. Sullivan illustrates his argument with archival documents from the Guatemalan National Police. Statistical analyses of police records showed that arrests and assassinations decreased challenges to the state only when they disrupted underground opposition activities such as holding meetings, training dissidents, and raising funds. Dispersing overt protests *increased* dissent. The takeaway: online activism can succeed, but maintaining an offline (and discreet) wing of your movement is a sound insurance policy against mounting digital assaults.

A big problem with online organizing is that the very tools that allow activists to coordinate protests also advertise those protests to authorities. Therefore, it is wise to use online platforms for coordinating multiple protests in different neighborhoods or cities, rather than just one centrally located protest. Even though this reduces the size of any individual crowd, parallel protests help a movement survive by spreading crowd control thin.[50]

THE PROBLEM THAT NOBODY'S TALKING ABOUT

The digital arms race between activists and autocrats looks straight out of *1984*, George Orwell's classic sci-fi cautionary tale about a dictator named Big Brother who uses the Ministry of Truth to rule through surveillance and propaganda. Although contemporary life can seem eerily reminiscent of Orwell's dystopia, it arguably bears more resemblance to Aldous Huxley's *Brave New World*, a novel set in a future where the instrument of social control is "soma," a drug that keeps citizens happy and docile. The cultural critic Neil Postman explained why Huxley's dystopia is closer to our reality than Orwell's:

> What Orwell feared were those who would ban books. What Huxley feared was that there would be no reason to ban a book, for there would be no one who wanted to read one. Orwell feared those who would deprive us of information. Huxley feared those who would give us so much that we would be reduced to passivity and egoism. Orwell feared that the truth would be concealed from us. Huxley feared the truth would be drowned in a sea of irrelevance.[51]

Remarkably, Postman was writing in the 1980s, before the rise of the internet. He was concerned about television's hold on people's attention; little did he know how smartphones, Instagram, YouTube, and TikTok would hijack our brains by delivering addictive hits of dopamine.[52] The internet, far more than TV, became our drug of choice—our soma.

While there is no shortage of hand-wringing over the "attention economy" and the internet's corrosive effects on our focus, almost nobody is talking about how digital distractions make us worse activists.[53] Zeynep Tufekci, the scholar who reassured us that slacktivists make important contributions to social movements, also emphasized that "Attention is a key resource for social movements."[54] However, she located value in the attention of activists' *targets*, that is, how activists capture the attention of recruits, allies, powerholders, and the wider public. I wish to underline the value of activists' *own* attention. How does what we pay attention to (or not) affect our capacity to advocate for others?

Our addictions to TikTok and cat videos (or whatever fads arise by the time you read this book) do not just steal the time we could spend writing letters to lawmakers, filing a legal case against a polluting company, or raising money to fly people to a protest. Worse, science shows that the algorithmically curated dopamine fixes we get from our smartphones alter our neurochemistry; repeated "hits" short-circuit the brain's reward centers and deplete our patience for anything *but* slacktivism.[55] Scientists also link unhealthy internet habits to mental illness, which can lead to burnout.[56] Winning the battle against climate change, racism, or any other major crisis will not happen overnight. But it may *never* happen if the internet continues to atrophy our concentration muscles.

There is good news. When scientists are not presaging doom about our hijacked limbic systems, they are churning out guidance on how we can reclaim our attention and put it to work for humanity and the environment. For instance, psychologist Gloria Mark recommends mono-tasking. Each time we shift our attention from one task to another (say, from writing a letter to a lawmaker to checking our social media feeds), it takes around twenty-five minutes to return our focus to the first task.[57] This "attention residue" is not only inefficient, making our performance suffer; it is also draining and stressful.[58] Techno-critic and computer scientist Cal Newport has written a series of books translating this psychology research into actionable advice. One of his tips is to block out time on your schedule for "deep work," which he defines as high-value activities performed in a state of distraction-free concentration that push your cognitive abilities to their limit.[59] While Newport devised the concept of deep work to apply in professional settings, I contend that working deeply is just as important for activists, who are producing social if not economic value.

Practicing *deep activism* does not require forswearing the internet. It simply involves making the internet work for, and not against, your activist endeavors. Use social media when necessary for coordinating logistics, but carve out time for more cognitively demanding tasks like studying social movement theory, composing strategic plans, preparing grant proposals, and meditating on where you want to direct your activist energy. You can try this right away by scheduling quiet periods to read the rest of this book. As the prolific writer, philosopher, and activist Susan Sontag reminded us, "To be a moral human being is to pay, be obliged to pay, certain kinds of attention. . . . The nature of moral judgments depends on our capacity for paying attention—a capacity that, inevitably, has its limits, but whose limits can be stretched."

IN DEFENSE OF "PERFORMATIVE" PROTESTING

This chapter, like this book as a whole, focuses on how science can make us more effective activists. However, anyone who has typed a tearful social media post about an injustice, felt the sting of a rubber bullet, or been fired from a job for demanding fair pay knows that it's impossible to capture the full human experience of activism in a dataset or statistical model. Protesting is not always a calculated decision; it can be more expressive than instrumental.

This distinguishes activism from other areas of life—electoral races, medical treatments, batting averages—where people have applied scientific evidence to gain an edge. There's an intangible quality of activism that transcends scientists' ability to fully explain it, at least with existing data and methods. Maybe this is why we have protest songs and poems—to take over when reason is inadequate to make sense of the moment. Activism is both an art and a science.

Recognizing this, scholars in the humanities have supplemented *empirical* studies of online activism with *aesthetic* defenses of slacktivism and "virtue signaling." Science is for ascertaining cause and effect: What incentives make people participate in demonstrations? Does tweeting deter offline protest? Art, by contrast, communicates feelings "directly from mind to mind" with no intent to explain causality.[60] From the perspective of actors, directors, musicians, and dancers, being "performative" is not problematic; performance is the entire point. In *The Net Delusion*, Morozov dismissed virtual politics as a feeble simulacrum of actually doing something. But for critical theorist James McMaster, "to signal virtue *is* to do something—by performance studies standards at least."[61]

As a work of art, a hashtag or a viral image is not just a device for moving people into action; it is a means for stopping people in their tracks. Like we saw in chapter 1, mobilizing the masses is a key ingredient of movement success. Wholesale quiescence won't solve anything. However, one could argue that there is also value in passively bearing witness to social problems. Political theorist Adom Getachew chronicles how "aesthetic practices—especially a visual politics of spectacle, pomp, and performance—were central" to the founding of an empowered Black subject in the interwar period of the early twentieth century.[62] Black-led parades, marches, and rallies forced white spectators to pause their everyday lives and acknowledge the humanity of Black people in their communities. Most of those spectators did not become instant allies, but they became witnesses. Likewise, someone who watches the disturbing footage of George Floyd's murder on social media might not automatically take to the streets, but neither can they go about their normal routine. While the clip is not a performance, it is a spectacle; witnessing it changes how viewers relate to an event they can no longer dismiss. Different from *voyeurism* (enjoyment from watching the pain of others, like at a public lynching), *bearing witness* involves emotional discomfort on the part of the viewer (hence, to "bear" witness).[63] It initiates a state of emergency in the viewer's mind that carries the potential for an emotional response to eventually morph into concrete solidarity. The pause precedes the action.

Extraordinary visual representations of the world, as the celebrated novelist James Joyce said, induce "aesthetic arrest."[64] Joyce was referring to beautiful art, but ugly sights that we stumble across while "doom scrolling"—a video of an innocent man's murder, images of emaciated polar bears in the warming arctic, insurrectionists storming the US Capitol—can be just as "stunning." If you've ever felt paralyzed in the midst of watching a crisis unfold, you know the feeling. This book prioritizes action, but thoughtless action can be worse than no action at all when it incites backlash or inadvertently offends the people you want to help. Forms of protest that do little more than make us think—a hashtag, a video, a song, spoken-word poetry, graffiti—invite us to step outside ourselves and connect with the plights of others. Such empathy is the precursor to effective activism. We are spectators before we are players. As mindfulness practitioners quip, "Don't just do something, sit there!"[65]

Acknowledging the aesthetic value of activism casts performative protesting in a new light. Performativity is not necessarily lazy; it can be thoughtful. An example from more than a century ago illustrates this point. Although slacktivism is usually associated with the internet, it has pre-digital antecedents. Critics have accused activists of empty symbolism from time immemorial. Marcus Garvey was a target of such accusations. The Jamaican pan-Africanist founded the Universal Negro Improvement

Association (UNIA) in 1914 with the goal to promote the interests of Black people worldwide. In 1920, he staged a grand spectacle to open the UNIA convention in New York. Getachew, the political theorist, describes the scene:

> A parade on August 2 started at the UNIA headquarters at W. 135th and wound its way through Harlem. Representatives of the Black Star Line and the Negro Factories Corporation, the organization's two commercial enterprises, led the parade. Following in automobiles were Garvey, Davis, William Ferris, Reverend Eason, and other "high officials of the association . . . wearing their [academic] regalia." Behind them, the procession included the Black Star Line Choir, divisional marching bands, the women's Black Cross Nurses, and the African Legion. Over 20,000 were present at Madison Square Garden where the parade culminated.[66]

While some observers responded to this pageantry with admiration (especially women and Irish people, who were fighting their own liberation struggles), others responded with horror. Getachew notes that even W. E. B. Du Bois, himself a Black civil rights leader, was suspicious of Garvey's flashy production. Du Bois advocated for *"reasonable* race pride" that would stimulate sympathy among white viewers. He worried that the UNIA parade was gratuitously theatrical, namely in the way that it glamorized Garvey as a messiah. Garvey "appealed to the crowd" with all the "arts of the demagogue," Du Bois wrote. An article in *Opportunity: A Journal of Negro Life* alleged that Garvey psychologically exploited bystanders who were seduced by the "love of symbols, craving of power . . . [and] showy parades."[67]

However, the UNIA parade, like many displays of activist art, was not primarily a strategy for winning allies or obtaining concrete concessions. Rather, it showed that the Black activists were already powerful by virtue of evoking such strong reactions from their audience.[68] Garvey and his followers had accomplished something significant, if only by striking a nerve. Spectators lining the streets of New York that day in 1920, like doom-scrolling social media users of our age, could not unsee what they had seen. The parade lent them a new framework for thinking about themselves and Black people, whether or not they were galvanized to dismantle racism. Getachew credits aesthetic practices with founding an empowered race that Garveyites called the "Universal Negro."[69]

You, too, can incorporate aesthetics into your activist repertoire. If you have an existing artistic practice, you can build on what you already enjoy doing. You might compose a protest song and distribute it online, make buttons, or produce a "shockumentary" spotlighting a cause you care about. Peggy Orenstein, author of the book *Unraveling*, remarks that knitters' needles have "been a sharp political tool, wielded to fight injustice, to express both patriotism and protest, especially when other outlets were forbidden. No matter how you ended up feeling about those pink pussyhats, it was no accident that the women's first collective act of dissent after the election of President Donald Trump was to knit."[70] You may opt for performance art such as slam poetry or "guerrilla theater." *El Teatro Campesino* (The Peasants' Theater) started in 1965 while Cesar Chavez was leading the Delano Grape Strike in California. The United Farm Workers union deployed actors who performed political skits on flatbed trucks to spread the word about Chicano and labor rights. El Teatro Campesino still operates today, "committed to generating social change through the arts."[71]

Artist-activists find camaraderie in hubs such as the Artful Activist and the Center for Artistic Activism in New York. In 2016, the radical art cooperative Indecline installed larger-than-life sculptures of a naked, pot-bellied Donald Trump in a handful of US cities. This stunt transpired in the physical world, but the anonymous creators cleverly tailored it for a digital age. Images of the grotesque statues circulated on social media and inspired a profusion of hashtags including #makeamericaweirdagain and #ithadnoballs. On other occasions, Indecline went viral for transforming a suite of Manhattan's Trump International Hotel and Tower into a rat-infested prison cell and for repurposing commercial billboards into tents for unhoused people in Oakland, California.[72]

Artistic expression does not substitute for more direct tactics. Organizers of the Delano Grape Strike could not rely on guerrilla theater alone to win historic contracts with employers that finally secured higher wages, unemployment insurance, paid vacation days, and the legal right to unionize. They took a multipronged approach consisting of picket lines, boycotts, negotiations, and coalition building (which included convincing longshoremen to refrain from loading shipments of grapes onto boats at the Port of Oakland, resulting in spoiled product and huge financial losses for big growers). Subversive art did not replace, but rather complemented hard strategies. Suburbanites could easily forget to boycott grapes at the supermarket, but when a truck screeched to a halt in the middle of a California road and a troupe leapt out to dramatize the plight of farmworkers, passersby were hard-pressed to keep on walking. Many stopped in their tracks and confronted, some for the first time, the struggles of people less privileged than themselves. Audience members don't buy tickets to guerrilla theater; they get swept up into the show. Agency rests with the performers. Even if scientists cannot estimate the true "treatment effects" of such encounters on policy outcomes or worker welfare, the actors of El Teatro Campesino were no slacktivists. They were powerful by the mere fact of being seen on their own terms.

There is more to slacktivism than meets the eye. Low-cost online activism is not inherently bad; it matters how you use it and how you combine it with deeper engagement both online and offline.

Here are some key action items for slacktivists and organization leaders alike:

- Although slacktivism can create branding problems for social movements, it also aids success by mobilizing new activists and by coordinating people's actions and norms.
- Short, multi-site protests are better for recruiting "fresh blood" into a movement than long, single-site protests.

- Organizers can make slacktivism better serve movements by recruiting slacktivists with the ideal personality types (extroverted and disagreeable) and by including exciting images in their recruitment posts.
- Stay up to date on emergent social networking technologies. The *gateway effect* means that movements can withstand, and even flourish under, repression if activists stay one step ahead of censors.
- Back up your online activism with clandestine organizing offline. If antagonists shut down your demonstration or your social media account, your underground movement can stay intact and bounce back stronger.
- If you are organizing in a repressive environment, hold parallel protests spread across neighborhoods or cities rather than one centrally located protest.
- Practice deep activism. Use the internet to accomplish mission-critical tasks, but block off time in your schedule for working on activist projects free from online distractions.
- Performative protest is great for making people stop and pay attention to your cause. Aesthetic forms of activism lay the foundation for thoughtful action.

3. GIVE PEACE A CHANCE

Violent and Nonviolent Resistance

Omar Wasow is a rare person who became famous twice, for very different reasons. He first made his mark as a tech entrepreneur in the 1990s, just as the internet was taking off. He launched New York Online, a virtual community for New York residents, and went on to build websites for major companies like the *New Yorker*, Samsung, and Pfizer. He then cofounded BlackPlanet, a social networking site for African Americans that he sold in 2008 for $38 million.[1] *Newsweek* listed him among the "fifty most influential people to watch in cyberspace" and *People* named him the "sexiest internet executive." He caught the notice of Oprah Winfrey, who invited him on her talk show for some "intense computer training," as she introduced the segment on air. His tutorial covered how to use a mouse ("I thought it was a coaster," said Oprah of the mousepad), click on links (Oprah called them "hook-em-ups"), check email, and run web searches. Wasow returned to the show in 2010 to teach Oprah how to use an iPad. For most people, receiving a standing invitation from the "Queen of All Media"[2] would certify a flourishing career.

And yet, Wasow felt restless. "I was on TV and making good money in the center of the most important technological transformation to happen to society in decades, but at a certain point

I realized it wasn't enough," he said in an interview.[3] Wasow was born into an activist family. His father joined the Freedom Summer Project in the 1960s, risking his life to register Black voters in Mississippi. Citing the racialized violence that he witnessed while growing up in New York during the late 1980s, Wasow still itched to understand the social problems that plagued his hometown. The best way to do that, he decided, was to start a new career as an academic. He enrolled at Harvard University, where he earned a PhD in African American studies and master's degrees in government and statistics. He poured himself into a multi-year project to estimate the effects of violent and nonviolent civil rights protests on election outcomes. His article based on that research landed in the *American Political Science Review*, one of the top-ranked political science journals.[4] This was great news for the budding academic, who by then was an assistant professor at Princeton. With a top publication on his résumé, Wasow could relax into his second professional act, out of the spotlight.

However, a twist of fate dashed any chance of Professor Wasow living a quiet life of the mind. On May 25, 2020, four days after he published his paper, police murdered George Floyd and reinvigorated the Black Lives Matter movement. Although nearly 95 percent of the ensuing protests were peaceful,[5] media fixated on isolated instances of looting and destruction, like a man who set fire to the Minneapolis Third Precinct police headquarters near the site of Floyd's death.[6] This was the kind of negative media coverage of Black protesters that Wasow's study showed can hurt left-leaning candidates in elections. Wasow's article broke records at the *American Political Science Review* for online shares. As of March 23, 2023, it had been tweeted 5,374 times; 81 percent of those tweets were not by scientists, but by members of the public. One tweet in particular would hurtle Wasow back into the limelight.

On May 28, 2020, a white political consultant, David Shor, tweeted a link to Wasow's article with a summary of the findings: "Post-MLK-assassination race riots reduced Democratic vote share in surrounding counties by 2%, which was enough to tip the

1968 election to Nixon. Non-violent protests *increase* Dem vote, mainly by encouraging warm elite discourse and media coverage." Activist Twitter instantly took umbrage. A Black organizer wrote in a representative reply, "Yo. Minimizing black grief and rage to 'bad campaign tactic for the Democrats' is bullshit most days, but this week is absolutely cruel. This take is tone deaf . . . and reeks of anti-blackness." Benjamin Dixon, a Black political commentator, dared Wasow, "Tell you what, go to Minneapolis and fill the protesters in about your findings. Be sure to video it for our viewing pleasure." (As I write this, Dixon's Twitter profile displays a GIF of someone punching a Nazi with the caption, "self-defense is a human right.") While it's unclear how many activists read Wasow's entire article, many interpreted its conclusions as blaming victims of racialized oppression who choose to defend themselves with righteous violence. One critic conceded that Wasow's study was "true empirically" but insisted that it was nevertheless "bad research . . . because what it does is single out the political effect of riots in a way that allows people to blame 'inner-city rioters' and ignore other causes."[7] Another agreed that it was "not helpful . . . to think about the rise of backlash as the fault or responsibility of people who spoke out on behalf of justice."[8]

Shor apologized for his offending tweet: "While I strongly admire @owasow's work, it's clear that I have not been, due to both my background and words, an effective messenger of his findings about the power of non-violent protest. I regret starting this conversation and will be much more careful moving forward." This mea culpa did not satisfy Shor's employer, Civis Analytics. Shor was promptly fired and forbidden from commenting any further about the episode. Wasow himself, startled to be back in the public eye, struck a conciliatory tone: "The rage has almost this funereal quality, and so I'm sympathetic to those who are saying, 'Don't talk to us about selling the home of our father when we're still at the funeral.' . . . But I'm also deeply sympathetic to David [Shor] because I mostly live in this analytical, 'let's really talk about the numbers' kind of world."[9] Wasow could have also referenced the closing line of his article, which acknowledged that "An 'eye for an eye' in response to violent repression may be moral, but this research suggests it may not be strategic."

The Wasow affair epitomizes a recurring tension between activists and the scholars who study them. I wrote this book, and this chapter most of all, to smooth over that tension—to help activists become more analytical *and* to help scholars become more sensitive. I am optimistic that these two communities can learn from each other.

In the following pages, we'll explore the empirical consequences of violent and nonviolent activism, paying special attention to how the science on this touchy subject interacts with activists' socially embedded beliefs about the "right" ways to protest. First, I'll challenge the assumption that there are violent and peaceful types of protesters at all—a myth that is more defamatory than analytically useful. Violence characterizes tactics, not people. We will see how iconic proponents of nonviolence such as Martin Luther King Jr. embraced armed struggle more than history books recognize, whereas activists who were branded as vicious troublemakers often considered themselves anything but.

Next, I'll zoom out on the voluminous scholarly literature about armed and unarmed resistance, summarizing key evidence on when violence works (or not) and why. Wasow's study wasn't by any means the first to show that peaceful protest is better than violence for achieving certain aims. Its notoriety stemmed less from its technical details than from the timing of its publication. The controversy reminded scholars that *how* they disseminate their work, or how other people disseminate it for them, can matter as much as doing the work in the first place. As I will demonstrate with an original analysis of 464,047 tweets, scholars and activists have different vocabularies for talking about science and evidence. Consider me your translator as we tour the scholarly landscape. By the end of the chapter, you will have information to help you discern for yourself whether an "eye for an eye" is occasionally necessary, or whether you prefer to heed John Lennon's anti-war anthem and "give peace a chance."

DO VIOLENT PROTESTERS EXIST?

I'll confess that academics can be out of touch with reality, spouting gobbledygook that few normal folks can understand, let alone use in their daily lives. That's why I wrote this book in the first place—to narrow the rift between scholars and everyday activists. I've tried to pick out only the most practical bits of knowledge from the scientific literature while stripping away the jargon. However, I stumbled upon an arcane academic concept that is too mind-blowing not to share. And it just might change how you think about protesters, including yourself. It's the idea that fish don't exist.

Journalist Lulu Miller lays out this bizarre notion in her enchanting book *Why Fish Don't Exist*. While researching the turn-of-the-twentieth-century ichthyologist (fish scientist) David Starr Jordan, Miller learned that contemporary biologists no longer regard "fish" as a relevant taxonomical category. The "death of the fish" began with the cladistics revolution in the mid-twentieth century.[10] Named for the ancient Greek word *kládos* ("branch"), cladistics is a method for classifying organisms by common ancestry rather than superficial traits. Just because two creatures look alike doesn't mean they are similar from an evolutionary standpoint. For example, a lungfish is more like a cow than a salmon because beneath its fins and scales lie a distinctly bovine heart and windpipe. Mushrooms mingle with grasses and flowers on the forest floor, yet they are more closely related to animals than plants (that's why a grilled portobello tastes "meaty"). Whales share a family with deer (ungulates), and bats are only a few evolutionary branches away from camels.

The old-fashioned practice of classifying organisms by sight lacked scientific rigor and was prone to human bias. Miller dares us to wonder: If we've erroneously grouped all scaly creatures with fins into the category of "fish," why stop there? Why not also create categories for animals with spots or men who wear plaid? As counterintuitive as cladistics might seem to the layperson (maybe you ate "fish" for dinner last night!), it carries a powerful message for anyone who has been unfairly categorized. We could easily replace "fish" with "violent protesters" in Miller's concluding thought: "The category 'fish' hides . . . nuance. Discounts intelligence. It gerrymanders close cousins away from us, creating a false sense of separation to preserve our spot at the top of an imaginary ladder." Society is quick to tag activists who act violently as menaces, like an ichthyologist unthinkingly threading a label through the fin of a specimen. But if you fancy yourself a "pacifist," keep in mind that under the right conditions—observing a grave injustice, getting swept up in the collective effervescence[11] of a rioting crowd—you might discover that you are not so different from an "extremist" after all.

Following their misguided intuitions about how evolution works, early taxonomists ordered fish into "higher" and "lower" categories (think the charismatic blue marlin versus bottom-feeding catfish). They proceeded to order human beings into hierarchies, spawning the eugenics movement. Eugenicists endorsed the sterilization and, ultimately, the extermination of "unfit" people, including the disabled, the poor, and the dark skinned. Taxonomy might be scientifically meaningless,[12] but it was politically expedient for maintaining power structures with white, rich, able-bodied men at the top. Taxonomy is also, less nefariously, how our brains tend to make sense of a complex world: labels are convenient shorthands for simplifying a (sometimes literal) sea of diversity.[13]

This brings us back to the widespread assumption that there are violent and nonviolent activists. History books paint a picture of two archetypes: Martin Luther King Jr. and Malcolm X. People celebrate King as a steadfast peacemaker. In 1962, when the Baptist minister and civil rights hero was addressing the Southern Christian Leadership Conference in Birmingham, Alabama, a two-hundred-pound American Nazi leapt onto the stage and started mercilessly punching him. King dropped his hands "like a newborn baby" as the blows rained down on him.[14] He later sat down with his attacker backstage and calmly reassured him that he would not press charges. This show of restraint cemented King's reputation as a pacifist. His saintly comportment in the face of cruelty backed up his aphorisms such as, "Nonviolence is a powerful and just weapon, which cuts without wounding and ennobles the man who wields it. It is a sword that heals." King won the Nobel Peace Prize for his apparently staunch commitment to advancing racial justice without the use of force.

In contrast to King, Malcolm X is remembered for such sayings as, "We declare our right . . . to be given the rights of a human being in this society, on this earth, in this day, which we intend to bring into existence by any means necessary." He led the Nation of Islam, which had violent showdowns with police in the 1960s. Malcolm X knew that people saw him as King's foil, writing in his autobiography, "It is anybody's guess which of the 'extremes' in approach to the black man's problems might personally meet a fatal catastrophe first—'non-violent' Dr. King, or so-called 'violent' me."[15] The scare quotes betrayed his skepticism toward facile comparisons between prominent civil rights leaders.

Vindicating Malcolm X, scientists have gradually questioned the taxonomy of violent and nonviolent activists, much like biologists overturning the taxonomy of fish. In 1985, political scientist James Q. Wilson and behavioral biologist Richard J. Herrnstein published *Crime and Human Nature*, in which they linked violent crime to "bad genes." This premise echoed stereotypes of the "negro brute" that proliferated during the Radical Reconstruction period after the US Civil War, an idea rooted in racism. More recently, geneticists have shown that genes account for only about 5 to 10 percent of extremely violent behavior; the rest likely results from environmental factors such as stress, poverty, family disfunction, and failing schools.[16] And it must be emphasized that any genetic predisposition to violence is *not* unique to any racial group. Indeed, there is more genetic variation within racial groups than among them.[17] Over-focusing on genes incorrectly shifts blame onto individuals and away from structural causes of behaviors. As neurobiologist Robert Sapolsky clarifies, biological factors don't so much *cause* behaviors as modulate them by changing thresholds for responding to environmental stimuli.[18] Genetics evidently plays some role in violent crime, but certainly not enough to justify classifying any people as inherently vicious.

Increasingly, scholars refer not to types of activists, but rather to "repertoires of contention"—"what people know they can do when they want to oppose a public decision they consider unjust or threatening."[19] Studying Palestinian resistance to Israeli checkpoints in the West Bank, political scientist Emily Kalah Gade notes that while individuals and movements "are rarely (if ever?) exclusively violent, specific acts are."[20] To study civilian attacks against the Israeli state in 2015, she created a typology of resistance *acts*, not people. On any given day, the same person might decide to launch rockets, go on strike, join a march, or practice *sumud* ("existence as resistance") by disobeying state agents. Gade's interviews showed that if a checkpoint prevents a Palestinian from visiting a friend, the resulting sense of isolation might provoke them to behave more violently than they otherwise would. The basic idea is that nobody is born violent.[21] Instead, our environments prompt us to select violent strategies for protecting our interests, including staying alive.

Charles E. Cobb Jr., the former field secretary for the Student Nonviolent Coordinating Committee, reiterates this argument in his eye-opening book *This Nonviolent Stuff'll Get You Killed: How Guns Made the Civil Rights Movement Possible*. He chronicles the history of Black armed struggle in the United States, starting with slave revolts, the enlistment of enslaved soldiers in the Civil War, and self-defense in the Jim Crow South. He corrects the record on "nonviolent" civil rights activists, who frequently relied on guns to back up their peaceful tactics. Armed guards representing veterans' associations, the Deacons for Defense and Justice, and the NAACP stood watch over the sit-ins, marches, voter registration drives, and other events popularly associated with the Civil Rights Movement. Cobb recounts the remarkable story of journalist William Worthy visiting Martin Luther King Jr. shortly after King's home was bombed in 1956. As Worthy went to sit in an armchair, an activist who accompanied him intervened: "Bill, wait, wait! Couple of guns on that chair!" It turned out that the house was a veritable arsenal. King, seeming to perceive no contradiction with his espousal of nonviolence, explained that the weapons were "just for self-defense." Cobb construes King's self-defense after attempts on his life as utterly rational. Indeed, King would die by an assassin's bullet in the end. "The easiest way to understand this," writes Cobb, "is to begin with the basic fact that black people are human beings, so black people's responses to terrorist attacks are the same as anyone else's." The government wouldn't protect Black people from the Ku Klux Klan, so Black people took matters into their own hands, even while pursuing nonviolent strategies at the same time. Although they extolled the power of peaceful resistance, civil rights leaders like King did not force recruits to sign a contract disavowing violence. They knew that they needed to be morally flexible if they had any hope of surviving.

"Violent" activists were flexible, too. Despite his association with militancy, Malcolm X proclaimed in a speech, "We are peaceful people, we are loving people. We love everybody who loves us. But we don't love anybody who doesn't love us. We're nonviolent with people who are nonviolent with us. But we are not nonviolent with anyone who is violent with us."[22] Here, Malcolm X, like King, was championing self-defense as opposed to violent resistance. According to philosopher Tamara Fakhoury, violent resistance aims to injure oppressors or their property, whereas self-defense is a matter of protecting oneself by counteracting harm with a necessary degree of force.[23] What observers mischaracterize as violent resistance is often just victims fighting back when their ability to resist oppression by others means—at the ballot box, on the Congress floor, in the press, in the boardroom—is so constrained that they have no other option.

King poetically drew this distinction in a 1967 speech following a spate of racialized violence including riots in Watts, California, and Harlem, New York (the italics are mine):

> Let me say as I've always said, and I will always continue to say, that riots are socially destructive and self-defeating. I'm

still convinced that nonviolence is the most potent weapon available to oppressed people in their struggle for freedom and justice. . . . But in the final analysis, *a riot is the language of the unheard*. And what is it that America has failed to hear? It has failed to hear that the plight of the Negro poor has worsened over the last few years. . . . And so in a real sense our nation's summers of riots are caused by our nation's winters of delay. . . . Social justice and progress are the absolute guarantors of riot prevention.[24]

In *This Nonviolent Stuff'll Get You Killed*, Cobb keeps returning to the idea that oppressed people who take up arms in self-defense are not being impulsive; they are being strategic given the threats at hand. This way of thinking opens more space for dialogue between activists and their opponents: if powerholders stop vilifying activists as violent by nature, activists may be more willing to enter negotiations in good faith. Challenging the taxonomy of violent and nonviolent protesters improves science, as well. Once scholars adopted the perspective of "violent tactics, not people," they produced a wealth of research investigating which tactics work better than others, and under what conditions. The next section boils down their main discoveries into actionable takeaways.

WHY VIOLENCE USUALLY DOESN'T PAY, WHY EVEN *NONVIOLENCE* DOESN'T ALWAYS PAY, AND WHAT TO DO ABOUT IT

When was the last time you felt awe? As psychologist Dacher Keltner defines it, awe means "being in the presence of something vast and mysterious that transcends your current understanding of the world."[25] Perhaps your mind drifts to hiking on a mountain peak, hearing a rousing religious sermon, or staring with your mouth agape at a sculpture in a museum. Keltner and his colleagues posed the same question to 2,600 people around the world in twenty languages. To their surprise, the most prevalent source of awe was not nature, faith, or art. Rather, it was "other people's courage, kindness, strength, or overcoming"—what Keltner sums up as *moral beauty*.

Nonviolent protest can evoke that sort of awe. Think of Martin Luther King Jr. refusing to lay a hand on his Nazi assailant, Mahatma Gandhi on the fourteenth day of a hunger strike, or the Dalai Lama appealing tenderly to his "Chinese brothers and sisters" even after China's prolonged occupation of his Tibetan homeland. When you encounter moral beauty, your vagus nerve kicks into high gear, setting off a cascade of bodily functions. Your heartrate slows, you tear up, and you get goosebumps as if you were cold—your body's way of signaling to others that you want to draw them near. Your pituitary gland releases oxytocin, the "love hormone."[26] Conversely, watching people hurt each other triggers an array of negative emotions including anger, fear, and guilt.[27] The pulse quickens, the stomach churns, the palms sweat, and the muscles tense. Our emotional responses to peace and violence can interact: We tend to feel extra sympathetic toward nonaggressive activists who are victims of state or vigilante repression (such as civil rights protesters pummeled with fire hoses or Martin Luther King Jr. in the foregoing example).[28] We might not be wired to be peaceful or violent, but we do seem wired to admire peace over violence in our fellow humans.

For activists, this means that how others perceive you matters a lot. Nonviolence can inspire awe at your moral beauty, whereas violence—even violence that you only *appear* to initiate—can inflame resentment. White Americans panicked when the Congress of Racial Equality (CORE), which had spearheaded nonviolent direct action during the 1940s and 1950s, took a more radical turn during the 1960s. In 1964, CORE leaders announced a mass "stall-in"—they would park hundreds of cars en route to the New York World's Fair in order to force white fairgoers to pause and gaze at the urban blight that Black residents were suffering. Political theorist Erin Pineda documents how white people, desperate to "maintain the facade of their own innocence and moral standing," tore into the activists and drew false equivalences between the inconvenience of the stall-in and the racism terrorizing Black Americans. A letter to the *New York World-Telegram* chided, "If the Negro wants his rights, he should not deprive the white man of his." The *New York Times* decried CORE's "mischievous scheme" as "well calculated to do the utmost possible damage to the cause of civil rights." Obviously, a traffic jam is not genuinely violent, but this did not stop New York City's mayor from comparing the stall-in to a "gun held to the heart of the city."[29] The point here is that the mere perception of violence can unjustly hurt progressive movements. Thanks in part to such hyperbolic media coverage, the much-maligned stall-in protest never materialized. Activists seemed too afraid of a brutal crackdown.

As Twitter users asserted in response to Wasow's article, it does a double injustice to hold oppressed activists responsible for the backlash of their oppressors. CORE's planned stall-in may have "provided new ammunition for the racists," as the *New York Post* warned,[30] but it was up to racists to pull the trigger.

Nonetheless, Dacher Keltner's research informs us that humans and other animals harbor primordial affections for peaceful behavior and aversions to violent behavior. Depending on your philosophy of free will, even counterprotesters themselves are not fully in command of their own response to protests. The hard truth is that backlash—fair or not—can hobble a movement. Reams of evidence show that bystanders react more favorably toward civil resistance than to uncivil resistance, and that the support of bystanders is critical to furnish movements with recruits and allies. Political scientists Erica Chenoweth and Maria Stephan famously reported that peaceful campaigns are almost twice as likely to achieve full or partial success as their violent counterparts.[31] This, they reasoned, is because nonviolent activism has lower moral, physical, and logistical barriers to participation than violent insurgency.

Further research highlights the *electoral* benefits of nonviolence. After Martin Luther King Jr. was assassinated on April 4, 1968, the United States experienced a wave of Black-led protests, some more violent than others. Omar Wasow's viral study revealed that counties with peaceful protests saw Democratic vote share increase by up to 2.5 percent, whereas those with protester-initiated violence saw an even larger swing in the white vote toward Republicans, tipping the presidential race toward Richard Nixon.[32] This was because the news media set the public agenda by sensationalizing "race riots" with the copious use of words like *fire* and *shot*. As they say in newsrooms, "What bleeds leads." Violent protests receive far more media attention, at least in the short term, than peaceful protests.[33] Such attention is often racially biased. It's worth noting that the National Press Club did not have a Black member until 1955 and that the Gridiron Club for Washington journalists performed in blackface at dinners into the 1950s.[34]

Geographic distance may have also played a role in distorting the media narrative surrounding the 1968 protests. In stark contrast to Wasow's findings, political scientists Ryan Enos, Aaron Kaufman, and Melissa Sands found that Black-initiated violent protests *increased* support for Black communities in the wake of the 1992 Los Angeles riots.[35] Violence roiled LA after four white police officers were acquitted for the videotaped beating of Rodney King, a Black man. Enos and his coauthors found that those riots actually boosted white Angelenos' support for the Democratic Party and for referenda on liberal causes that benefited the Black community, such as public education spending. How can we square these results with Wasow's conclusion that riots hurt Democrats and racial justice causes in the aftermath of Martin Luther King Jr.'s murder? The difference in this case, versus the 1968 riots, seems to be that voters in LA were responding to *local* issues that affected their neighbors, not simply reading news articles about civil rights protests in a distant city. Voters may not have shared a racial identity with the protesters, but they could identify with abuse committed by their own police force and could see the hurt that it caused firsthand.

Wasow's study blames white newsmen writing from afar for the electoral blowback in 1968 more than it blames Black protesters—a subtlety that got lost in the 2020 Twitter fallout surrounding his article. One implication of his findings is that image-conscious activists should do whatever they can to reclaim control of the narrative about their actions, refocusing attention on their core grievances and away from violence. Social media are tools for accomplishing this (see the previous chapter for more on digital activism).

Even if science has discredited the theory that some people are intrinsically more violent than others, social psychology research indicates that people retain implicit biases when judging acts of violence. Police officers who are primed to think about violent crime become more likely to look at a dark-skinned face rather than a light-skinned face and to remember images of men as more stereotypically Black.[36] Political scientists Devorah Manekin and Tamar Mitts showed that nonviolent resistance (marching in the streets) by ethnic minorities—Black people in the United States and Ethiopian and Arab Israelis in Israel—is perceived by white observers in the US and Israel to be more violent and more in need of policing than identical resistance by majority members.[37] Describing minority protesters in hypothetical news stories, respondents wrote comments like, "They are NEVER 100% peaceful. There is always some trouble" and "Their complaints are legitimate but the protest was violent." One Israeli respondent was even blunter: "They are terrorists." A common misgiving about survey experiments is that the results might hinge on the specific wording of vignettes and questions. However, political scientists Pearce Edwards and Daniel Arnon produced similar results as Manekin and Mitts in a separate experiment: although they did not find equally strong evidence that group identity conditions people's perceptions of protester violence, they confirmed that protesters are seen to deserve tougher repression when they are from an ethnic minority.[38] This devastating finding points to an urgent role for allies. Activists from across a spectrum of races and backgrounds should speak up against the stigma that marginalized protesters endure. This must be done with care, to avoid speaking *for* marginalized people.

An anecdote from 1967 illustrates how the experiment by Manekin and Mitts plays out in the real world. On May 2 that year, Black Panthers marched on the California State Capitol to protest the Mulford Act, which would prohibit citizens from carrying loaded firearms in public without a permit. The National Rifle Association, widely known for *promoting* gun rights, backed the bill, driving home the point that the legislation was fundamentally about controlling Black people, not about enhancing public safety. The Panthers legally brandished weapons during the protest but did not fire a single shot. As Black Panther Party founder Huey Newton told the *New York Times*, "Ninety percent of the reason we carried guns in the first place was educational. To set an example . . . to establish that we had the right." Despite the bloodless nature of the march, journalists sounded the alarm: "Young Negroes armed with loaded rifles, pistols and shotguns . . . barged into the Assembly chamber," railed one article.[39] Emboldened by hysterical media, Governor Ronald Reagan signed the Mulford Act into law, and FBI Director J. Edgar Hoover announced a crusade against "black nationalist hate groups." This series of events brought to light a condition that philosopher Cornel West explains as Black people's relative inability "to represent themselves to themselves and others as complex human beings, and thereby to contest the bombardment of negative, degrading stereotypes put forward by White supremacist ideologies."[40]

My research shows that people disapprove of nonviolent Black activists even more than they are willing to admit.[41] I asked a representative sample of 2,287 Americans, "Is it disrespectful for African American athletes to kneel during the national anthem?" This question referred to athlete-activists like Colin Kaepernick who peacefully protested police brutality at the start of football games. When I posed the question directly, 47 percent of respondents answered "yes." I then used a "statistical truth serum" called a *list experiment* to indirectly estimate respondents' *true* attitudes.[42] This method involved showing each respondent one of two lists: a "treatment" version that included the sensitive item about anthem protesters or a "control" list that left out the sensitive item:

TABLE 1: Treatment and Control Lists in the Experiment

TREATMENT LIST	CONTROL LIST
The voting age should be raised to 25.	The voting age should be raised to 25.
People of the same sex should be able to legally marry.	People of the same sex should be able to legally marry.
Prayer should be allowed in public schools.	Prayer should be allowed in public schools.
It is disrespectful for African American athletes to kneel during the national anthem.	American politics is too polarized.
American politics is too polarized.	

I asked respondents to say *how many* of the statements they agreed with, not which specific ones. This allowed them to answer honestly, without fear of judgment. Because I assigned the lists at random, any difference in the average number of reported items across treatment and control groups I could attribute to different rates of believing that the protesters were disrespectful. Gauging by my list experiment, 54 percent of respondents disapproved of activists like Colin Kaepernick—7 percentage points higher than the estimate I got when I asked the question directly. In other words, *respondents were hiding 13 percent of their disapproval of the peaceful protesting of Black athletes.*

Earlier work by Wasow and others suggested that nonviolent protest is effective, but later studies including mine answered an important follow-up question: "Effective *for whom*?" While reaffirming that more extreme tactics, like destroying property, generally draw public disapproval, emerging research also underscores that marginalized folks who employ milder tactics are *judged* as dangerous or disrespectful, anyway. Marginalized protesters of color are in a double bind—damned if they do (resort to violence) and damned if they don't.

The practical upshot of this literature is that using the media to manage your public image is especially crucial if you are an activist from a marginalized identity group. Political scientist Hakeem Jefferson proposes that reframing anti-racist activism around structural inequality (e.g., the prison industrial complex) rather than individual behavior (e.g., protesters looting a store) might counteract the "respectability politics" that leads people—including some Black people—to support racialized punitive policies.[43] Combatting smear campaigns doesn't need to happen within the confines of your personal social media account; it can be a collective mission. If equipped with enough financial resources or the availability of pro bono PR professionals, social movement organizations could hire public relations firms to extinguish media fires. Imagine CORE in 1964 or Black Lives Matter in 2020 with an army of PR specialists publishing counterpropaganda in newspapers, raising awareness about structural injustice on the radio or on social platforms, and crafting punchy talking points to parry fearmongering.

Public relations, like academia, has a complicated relationship with progressive social movements, given its historical connection to corporate conservatism.[44] In a recent survey by the Annenberg Center for Public Relations, nearly half of PR professionals said they anticipate potential reactions from activist groups when they are planning an initiative, yet just 14 percent "proactively involve activist groups" in the process.[45] These statistics unveil a missed opportunity for social movement organizations and public relations firms to join forces. PR professionals are too busy producing "woke" commercials for the likes of Nike to help grassroots activists neutralize messages demonizing their activities. If you're an activist, consider taking a course on public relations at your local community college or a free course online. If you're already a PR professional, you could make a significant social impact by volunteering your services for an activist group. And if you're a journalist, be mindful of the power you wield to shape public opinions of protesters from underprivileged demographics.

I've discussed how the identity of the protester influences reactions to violent and nonviolent activism, but the identity of the observer matters, too. Manekin and Mitts's central finding, that ethnic minorities are criticized more harshly for peaceful protests than ethnic majorities, was driven almost entirely by white respondents. In a related experiment, political scientist Raynee Sarah Gutting showed that violent protests elicit worse reactions from conservatives than from liberals.[46] She also found, perhaps unsurprisingly, that people with authoritarian personalities—who prefer conformity and social order—are *not* particularly averse to violent conflict but do reject protests that target authorities like police officers. Psychologists Cátia Teixeira, Russell Spears, and Vincent Yzerbyt ran ten experiments to see how Belgian, British, and American subjects reacted to news stories about either "normative" protests (demonstrations and strikes) or "nonnormative" protests (riots and roadblocks) initiated by a low-status group such as North African immigrants in Belgium.[47] First, the authors replicated a finding from other studies: subjects felt more positively toward demonstrations and strikes than riots and roadblocks. The authors also probed into *why* people felt this way. Subjects perceived normative actions to be mainly about low-status folks protecting their own interests, whereas they saw nonnormative actions as attacks on the high-status group. It wasn't so much that the high-status subjects viewed rioters as morally depraved, but rather as threatening their community. Reactions to the protests also varied according to high-status subjects' level of identification with their in-group. That's to say, people who identify strongly with their white identity approve of riots and roadblocks much less than demonstrations and strikes, but people who do *not* identify very strongly with being white don't pay much attention to protesters' chosen tactics.

Teixeira, Spears, and Yzerbyt end their study with advice for activists. First, they stress that their results don't mean activists should jettison nonnormative tactics altogether. Crackdowns on riots and roadblocks can inspire sympathy from third parties and cultivate solidarity among marginalized people. Recall from chapter 1 that there is an advantage to disadvantage: precisely because marginalized protesters face stricter repercussions than privileged protesters, lawmakers are more likely to listen to them. Activists could mix normative and nonnormative approaches in order to achieve complementary goals: garnering sympathy, building solidarity, *and* averting the worst backlash from high-status observers. Different kinds of people might be simultaneously watching your protests and reacting in different ways; a mixed strategy can play to multiple constituents. To be clear, I am not endorsing the use of physical violence. A theme of this book is that effective tactics do not necessarily fit everybody's personal values or risk tolerance. Science can tell us what works and what doesn't, but we must look to philosophy for wisdom on the best way to live in society.[48]

Second, Teixeira, Spears, and Yzerbyt conclude that marginalized protesters can temper negative responses to their actions by deliberately focusing messages on the hardships they're experiencing. This could involve strategic communication on social media and working with PR consultants, as I mentioned before. For instance, the authors cite evidence that framing racial inequality as "Black disadvantage" instead of "white privilege" boosts support for affirmative action policies among white people.[49]

There is a caveat here. Most social science about the effects of violent and nonviolent activism concentrates on the immediate aftermath of protests—how journalists cover events the next day, or how experimental subjects respond in the seconds after reading a news article. However, activists striving for *revolutionary* change have longer time horizons than those pushing for narrower policy reforms or shifts in public opinion. Revolutionaries want to depose leaders, revise constitutions, and replace dictatorships with democracies. In earth-shattering movements like the Haitian Revolution or the Arab Spring, violence plays a different role than it does in movements like Occupy Wall Street, #MeToo, or even

Black Lives Matter, which are ambitious yet don't aim to overhaul entire political regimes. Revolutionaries confront a question that other protesters do not: If we "win" (come into power), how can we avoid being overthrown by counterrevolutions?

Political scientist Killian Clarke points out that among 123 revolutions in the world from 1900 to 2015, 98 faced counterrevolutionary challenges and 22 of those counterrevolutions succeeded at topping the new revolutionary regime.[50] The key to surviving counterrevolution, Clarke contends, is having an organized army. There are two reasons for this. First, as Chenoweth and Stephan argued before, nonviolence lowers participation costs during a revolution. This engenders a large and diverse coalition that is helpful for forcing dictators out of power but is a liability for governing afterward. Without a coercive apparatus, new leaders struggle to contain infighting and factionalism among coalition members. Second, lacking the means of coercion makes incoming leaders susceptible to armed attacks from the vengeful old guard. Consistent with this theory, Clarke's statistical analysis showed that the vast majority of the 22 ill-fated revolutionary governments came to power through nonviolent resistance. Peacefully installed regimes had a 50 percent chance of being overthrown, compared to a 10 percent chance for regimes backed by a violent guerrilla force. Clarke illustrates this pattern by comparing two revolutions in Cuba. A nonviolent uprising in 1933 ushered in a government that was toppled by a coup d'état after just one hundred days, whereas an armed insurgency in 1959 installed a regime that withstood three counterrevolutionary challenges including the US-backed Bay of Pigs invasion in 1961.

Clarke's study might seem to have little relevance for the run-of-the-mill activist who is *not* planning to overthrow a government. However, it raises a pressing concern about the long-term effects of any social movement. Even if you are not mobilizing a guerrilla army to forestall counterrevolution, it is appropriate to think ahead and ask, "What if we win? What can prevent our gains from reversing?" You might do everything "right" by limiting your use of violent tactics and mounting a meticulous PR campaign, but allies can be fickle and power configurations can change in an election cycle.

While the literature on how to consolidate protest victories is still young, existing research offers some guidance. Political scientist Paul Dosh writes that activists can succumb to a "security trap" after a major triumph. He notes how some Indigenous activists in Peru lost their motivation to keep advocating for land rights once they finally obtained their main goal after years of strife—legal titles to their property. This made Indigenous neighborhoods vulnerable to land grabs in the long run.[51]

One way for activists to safeguard their gains is by building institutions that uphold them. In the United States, the Consumer Financial Protection Bureau, the President's Emergency Plan for AIDS Relief, and the National Highway Traffic Safety Administration all arose from the efforts of grassroots activists and lobbyists to entrench their objectives for future generations. Political scientists like to say that institutions are "sticky." This means that once institutions are in place, people get used to them and form vested interests in continuing them. The initial hullaballoo around establishing an institution eventually dies down, the people who staff bureaus and agencies want to keep their jobs, and the uncertainty and headache of dissolving a regulatory body can deter even ardent libertarians from going down that road. Of course, nothing is guaranteed—Trump showed how fast one president could gut the Environmental Protection Agency—but institution building can be a bulwark against attempts to roll back activists' achievements years after protests disperse. At first glance, the army in a revolutionary regime has little in common with the National Highway Traffic Safety Administration. However, these institutions both play the same basic role of thwarting ploys to reverse change.

IS PREACHING NONVIOLENCE OUT OF TOUCH?

The overarching consensus in the scholarly literature is that violent uprisings almost never work, except in extraordinary cases of revolution. If you are like most people, this comes as good news. After the US Capitol insurrection in 2021, some bleak reports warned about an uptick in Americans' willingness to engage in political violence. However, a careful audit of the survey data revealed that those studies inflated how many people really condone extreme protest tactics. Revised figures put support for violence at no more than 6.3 percent—eight times lower than scarier estimates.[52] If you are in the 93.7 percent majority that hopes to avoid bloodshed, this chapter provided ample evidence that your preferred mode of taking a stand is also effective.

Nevertheless, the story about Omar Wasow at the beginning of this chapter showed that advising activists to protest peacefully can spur righteous indignation. How can we square activists' angry reception of Wasow's article with the fact that people overwhelmingly agree with its conclusion—that civil resistance is the best policy, either strategically or morally? Answering this question is important because the recommendations emerging from empirical research are only useful insofar as activists are amenable to implementing them. If the exhortation to "give peace a chance" is politically out of touch, then social scientists are wasting their breath.

I designed an exploratory study to untangle this puzzle of why activists would take offense at research that is basically consistent with prevailing views on violent protest. I wanted to know whether activists and scientists *generally* talk differently about empirical evidence, or whether the Wasow affair was an anomaly. Wasow's paper might have been uniquely divisive due to its timing around George Floyd's murder. If so, then we don't need to worry much about a rift between activists and the scholars who study them. But if activists and scholars are constantly talking past each other, then scholars have more work to do to translate their findings effectively.

I scraped the Twitter histories of 103 activists and 84 scientists, amounting to 464,047 tweets. The activists were diverse, including household names like environmentalist Greta Thunberg and Black Lives Matter founder Alicia Garza, along with less familiar people working on issues ranging from Indigenous rights to disability rights. The scientists were also an eclectic bunch, spanning physics, genetics, social sciences, and other fields. I used a statistical technique[53] to detect whether activists and scientists use the words *evidence* and *science* differently. Sure enough, they do. Broadly speaking, scientists use those words to discuss specific studies and findings, without explicitly connecting them to real-world social causes. In contrast, activists are less interested in scholarly details and more interested in how evidence and science *apply* to their causes. The differences in word use remained even when I compared scientists to the subset of activists who work on climate change—those we might expect to be the most sympathetic to "hard science."

Bridging this divide between scholars and activists is the chief reason I wrote this book. Now, armed with the knowledge in these pages, you too can build bridges. The evidence that I've presented may help you to individually become a more effective activist, but it has even greater potential to make a difference if you spread the word. Wasow inferred in his study that an entire presidential election outcome would have flipped if civil rights protests had been less violent in 1968. Manekin and Mitts substantiated the hunch that some activists already have—that ethnic minorities are disproportionately condemned for nonviolent protests and bear the burden of managing their public image. Teixeira, Spears, and Yzerbyt showed us how activists can strategically choose violent or nonviolent tactics according to their audience, so as to mitigate negative reactions. Clarke validated the importance of building institutions after a victory to stop reforms from backsliding. Keltner observed in surveys and in the laboratory how witnessing the compassion of others activates physiological states of awe. Imagine if activists in the past had this knowledge at their fingertips and interpreters to translate it into plain language. How much more successful could they have been?

How you spread the word about this knowledge is vital. David Shor learned this the hard way by hastily tweeting about Wasow's paper and sparking a backlash to a study that might have advanced the cause of racial justice. We can learn from this cautionary tale: when sharing empirical insights with fellow activists—say, about the relative effectiveness of nonviolent versus violent protest—don't just post links to papers; also try, as diplomatically as possible, to accentuate how the research can serve specific causes and communities. Otherwise, the science may sound out of touch.

Here's a recap of the evidence from this chapter and how it can inform movements:

- It's a myth that some people are inherently violent and others are peaceful; instead, *tactics* may be violent or peaceful. Convey this message in negotiations with power-holders, who are often quick to villainize activists.
- Humans can't help but feel awe toward peaceful protests and disgust toward violent protests; it's in our evolutionary makeup. Activists can gain an edge by developing a psychological strategy with this in mind.
- What is fair is not always effective. An "eye for an eye" consistently backfires on protesters. Some activists will continue making the radical choice to use force,[54] but those who hope to win recruits, public approval, and favorable votes should refrain from violence except when self-defense absolutely requires it.
- Violent repression initiated by authorities generates sympathy for protesters. Activists can use media to call attention to any repression they experience.
- Society judges protesters from marginalized groups more harshly than protesters from powerholding groups, even when they are behaving peacefully. Public relations campaigns can reduce backlash to peaceful protests—for example, by framing protests as helping aggrieved people instead of attacking privileged people.
- While it is not activists' moral responsibility to manage the feelings of their aggressors, it is strategic to consider who is watching you protest.

- Activists who achieve policy victories can protect their gains by setting up institutions that are difficult to roll back.
- Sharing research about protest tactics can rub other activists the wrong way if it lacks the proper context. Highlight how the research can serve particular people and causes.

4. "THE PEOPLE UNITED WILL NEVER BE DEFEATED!"

The Secrets of Successful Coalitions

On June 24, 2022, the United States Supreme Court handed down its ruling in *Dobbs v. Jackson Women's Health Organization*, overturning the 1973 landmark case of *Roe v. Wade* that protected abortion access under the right to privacy. Although 61 percent of Americans think that abortion should be legal in all or most circumstances,[1] abortion is one of the most polarizing political issues in the country, with liberals overwhelmingly supporting it and conservatives overwhelmingly opposing it.[2] Activists on both sides of this issue have taken extreme, sometimes violent, measures to defend their positions (see the previous chapter on perceptions and outcomes of violent and nonviolent resistance). Physicians and clinics that provide abortions have been targeted with murders, assaults, kidnappings, and vandalism.[3] Attacks are so frequent that sociologists classify anti-abortion extremism as a domestic terrorist threat.[4] Meanwhile, pro-choice groups have fought back. In 2022, an anti-abortion "pregnancy crisis center" in North Carolina had its windows smashed and graffiti scrawled on its walls reading "If abortions aren't safe then you aren't either."[5] Investigators linked the attack to the militant pro-choice organization Jane's Revenge, which that same year claimed credit for firebombing a pregnancy center in Wisconsin.[6]

Against this backdrop of fierce opinions and extreme activism, it is no wonder that public reactions to *Dobbs v. Jackson* were intense. Anti-abortion activists wept tears of joy outside the Supreme Court Building, while psychologists grappled with a rash of mental illness plaguing pro-choice Americans. Family therapist Claudia Parada lamented to the *Los Angeles Times*, "It's not normal to have power and autonomy taken from you and your body. Many folks have felt dissociated, at a loss and overwhelmed."[7] Concern Health, a counseling services provider, issued a guidebook on "coping with the emotional fallout" of the court's ruling.[8] It advised patients to "focus on what you can control," "arm yourself with the facts," "take action," and "lean on others." Although this book is not a mental health manual, it follows those same principles of taking action on urgent issues and controlling what we can with the best evidence-backed tactics. The current chapter takes up Concern Health's last recommendation, to lean on others. It's about coalitions—that is, people with various motives merging their efforts to bring about change. We'll cover how coalitions strengthen movements, how they form, and how to hold them together.

The events preceding and following the *Dobbs* decision are an ideal laboratory for studying the ingredients of effective coalitions, as they allow us to compare coalitions of very different makeups and outcomes. Drawing on my fieldwork at both pro-choice and anti-choice rallies, I'll explain why the lack of cohesion in the progressive women's coalition disadvantaged abortion rights advocates vis-à-vis abortion rights opponents. I'll offer tips on how to convey a cohesive set of demands and how to balance cohesion with the goal of assembling a diverse, intersectional movement. We'll explore the importance of *bridge builders* in forging and maintaining coalitions. You'll learn how to recruit bridge builders into your movement or become one yourself. And because building bridges—also known as "allyship"—can involve misunderstandings and hurt feelings, I'll address what to do if you accidentally offend others within your coalition so that you can move forward together. But before we get to the secrets to coalitional success, I will briefly clarify what coalitions are and why they matter.

TEAMWORK MAKES THE DREAM WORK

How can you mobilize a movement around defending the Constitution when most people in your country a) have never even read the Constitution and b) have more pressing concerns on their minds, like putting food on the table? This was the dilemma facing leaders of the Senegalese social movement Y'en a Marre ("Fed Up") in 2011. Senegal's president at the time, Abdoulaye Wade, was running for a third term, claiming that the constitutional rule limiting a president to two five-year terms didn't apply to him because he took office the year before the new constitution was adopted. Wade's opponents were having none of it. Not only did Wade's third-term bid reek of authoritarianism, but Wade had also neglected to fix chronic development problems, such as persistent power blackouts in the capital city of Dakar.

In one middle-class Dakar neighborhood, a group of friends consisting of three journalists and three rappers founded Y'en a Marre. They planned to hold a protest each month until Wade backed down. The musicians of the group wrote a song that they performed at rallies:

> *Abdoulaye! Don't push it!*
> *I swear! Don't push it!*
> *Abdoulaye, stay true to your word.*
> *I swear! Don't push it!*
> *[He] who plays with the constitution finds us along his way.*
> *Who can stop these youths determined to have a better future? . . .*
> *We are ready to roll with the punches to block your way.*[9]

Thousands of Senegalese answered Y'en a Marre's call to protest, flooding the streets and blanketing the city in anti-Wade graffiti. Even more remarkable than the initial mobilization was how long Y'en a Marre's leaders managed to *sustain* their movement to tackle Senegal's long-term economic and political woes. Years after Wade lost the 2012 election to Macky Sall, Y'en a Marre continued organizing community events to register voters, teach job skills, and moderate dialogues between citizens and legislators.

Other opposition movements that rose up in 2011 fizzled out once the imminent threat of Wade's third term faded. I phoned a leader of one such movement for an interview in 2015, but he had clearly moved on to other business. "I'm not involved with [activism] anymore," he barked before hanging up.

Why did Y'en a Marre stake out a lasting political presence in Senegal, winning the Ambassador of Conscience Award from Amnesty International and earning kudos from Barack Obama, whereas similar movements disbanded or even became co-opted into the government once the protests of 2011 died down?

The answer is that the leaders of Y'en a Marre were master coalition builders.[10] They realized early on that they could not fill the streets just with "their" people, meaning middle-class professionals. The movement's main spokesperson, Fadel Barro, was an accomplished journalist, and other founding members had already achieved commercial success in the rap group Keur Gui. All of Y'en a Marre's top leaders made comfortable livings in the private sector, so they did not have to worry about meeting their basic economic needs. This allowed them to devote their time to reading the constitution, recording protest music, and organizing rallies. And because they weren't on the government payroll, they were free to criticize the president.

However, most Senegalese people were not so privileged. In 2011, while Y'en a Marre was taking shape in the manicured suburbs, much of the population languished in urban slums and the agrarian hinterland. More than 67 percent of Senegalese earned less than $3.20 per day, and 38 percent earned less than $1.90.[11] Almost half of adults were illiterate, so they could not read the constitution if they wanted to.[12] Senegal, like many African countries, has an emerging but still small middle class (only about a third of the population, by conservative estimates).[13] Due to severe inequality, even high-growth years bring scant benefits to citizens at the bottom of the income distribution, who struggle just to subsist. We learned in chapter 1 that tiny crowds are unlikely to change history. In order to summon crowds large enough to defeat a stubborn autocrat, the leaders of Y'en a Marre knew they could not rely entirely on well-to-do folks like themselves; they needed to reach across class lines and build a coalition with the poor. The middle class could *launch* a movement, but only the lower classes (small-scale farmers and informal urban workers) could make a movement viable.

Barro, the journalist cofounder, was explicit about this coalition-building strategy, saying, "When [a rural person] comes to Dakar and you talk to him about the Constitution, he has no idea what you're talking about. To him, the Constitution has nothing to do with the people, it's a matter for the intellectuals, it's not his concern."[14] Knowing that the average citizen was more preoccupied with making ends meet than saving democracy, Barro artfully framed the origin story of Y'en a Marre in material, not ideological, terms: "We were there on the 16th during a 20-hour power outage. We told ourselves, 'Folks can't continue to just sit back and watching this excess, this injustice, without doing anything.' And that same night we drafted a declaration calling on all of Senegal's driving forces, the youth, the street vendors, the workers, the executives, etc. from all sides to join us so that together we could take this step forward and overturn the political class."[15]

That fateful decision, to rally Senegalese "from all sides," distinguished Y'en a Marre from more ephemeral opposition movements such as Le Mouvement 23 Juin ("The June 23 Movement"), which primarily concentrated on "elite" political issues like Article 27 of the constitution and the Constitutional Court's decision to authorize Wade's candidacy. Y'en a Marre had more to offer "the everyman" than highfalutin democratic ideals. It blended defending the constitution with bread-and-butter initiatives like vocational training and fighting for a lower cost of living. The movement's middle-class organizers set up hubs in the countryside called *esprits* to reach people beyond the coastal capital. Rousing hip-hop anthems, rapped in the national language of Wolof rather than colonial tongue of French, put an exclamation mark on Y'en a Marre's populist ethos. The resulting alliance between middle-class protest leaders and lower-class protest joiners left durable marks on national—and even international—politics. Y'en a Marre spokespeople toured other countries, including Burkina Faso and the Democratic Republic of Congo, disseminating their approach to mobilizing the masses. That approach rested on sharing resources: the middle class had privileged access to the media and finances, while the lower classes brought numbers to the streets that could really make a dictator tremble. Following Y'en a Marre's model, a wave of social movements sprang up across sub-Saharan Africa in the early twenty-first century—an "African Spring" to match the "Arab Spring" happening at the same time.[16]

Y'en a Marre is a quintessential *coalition*, which political scientists define as "the joint use of resources to determine the outcome of a decision in a mixed-motive situation."[17] The word *coalition* stems from the Latin words *cum* (with) and *alere* (nourish). Members of a coalition do not just march alongside each other; they nourish each other logistically, financially, and morally. Scholars have traditionally studied coalitions in legislatures—how lawmakers from different political parties pool their votes for passing (or defeating) bills, controlling budgets, and running the government. More recently, researchers have adapted the literature on legislative coalitions to understand how groups of activists join forces to effect change.

The first step was to recognize that most social movements and protests are not, despite appearances, about a single issue. Instead, they are assemblages of diverse people with diverse goals. A "pro-democracy" protest could be about democracy, unemployment, and a dozen other things all at the same time. Sudanese "bread riots" in 2018 were about much more than food prices; rioters were also demanding the overthrow of the ruling party and the restoration of peace and justice. As anthropologist Nisrin Elamin and political scientist Zachariah Mampilly asserted, "Framing this uprising as spontaneous riots against rising bread prices also obscures the ways working-class Sudanese have mobilized against the regime, particularly in smaller towns, which have been hit hardest by recent austerity measures following decades of political neglect and repression."[18] The sociologist Dana Fisher conducted a survey at the 2017 March for Our Lives, nominally a "gun control" rally in Washington, DC.[19] Although prominent organizers were teenage survivors of school shootings, Fisher's survey revealed that only about 13 percent of the crowd was nineteen years old or younger, and that many of the middle-aged rally goers had concerns besides gun violence: 57 percent of survey respondents said they were protesting about "social welfare," 49 percent said "Donald Trump," and 54 percent said "peace" in general. Just 27 percent stated that gun violence was their primary reason for protesting. Movements can bring people together who do not have much in common. As *New Yorker* journalist Adam Gopnik wrote in a retrospective on revolutions, "There were plenty of blue bloods on the sansculottes side of the French one, at least at the beginning, and the American Revolution joined abolitionists with slaveholders."[20]

Uniting activists of heterogeneous interests can strengthen social movements. There are three reasons why. The first is simply mathematical: you can grow a larger movement by adding people from different backgrounds than you can by mobilizing a narrower constituency. For example, feminists *plus* environmentalists make for a bigger crowd than feminists by themselves. Movements that forgo coalition building leave a lot of people power on the table. Political scientist Bryn Rosenfeld estimated that ninety thousand more people would have participated in pro-democracy demonstrations after Russia's 2011 parliamentary election if state-sector professionals had joined their private-sector counterparts in the streets.[21]

Some social causes directly affect so few people that they can garner widespread support *only* with reinforcement from allies.

LGBTQ+ people, for instance, make up a minor fraction of the population (just 7.1 percent in the United States as of 2021, up from 3.5 percent in 2012).[22] And yet, the LGBTQ+ movement has made significant strides in terms of public recognition, workplace protections, marriage equality, and other civil rights. Coalitions like PFLAG (Parents and Friends of Lesbians and Gays)[23] are decisive elements of its success, multiplying the power of queer folks themselves by the number of their loved ones. PFLAG was founded in 1973 by Jeanne Manford, a prim and otherwise conservative mother of a gay son who defiantly marched in a precursor to New York City's Pride Parade while carrying a sign that read, "PARENTS OF GAYS: UNITE IN SUPPORT FOR OUR CHILDREN."[24] This was a time when many parents would rather learn that their child was a murderer than homosexual. By 1979, PFLAG had opened chapters in cities across the United States and held packed conferences with workshops on political organizing, legislation, and estate planning for queer couples. In 2013, Barack Obama posthumously awarded Jeanne Manford the Citizens Medal for her unwavering allyship.

A second reason why coalitions help movements is that different groups supply different resources. Y'en a Marre's cross-class coalition in Senegal was just one example. Another is the coalition that formed between Korean immigrants and African Americans in the aftermath of the Los Angeles Riots in 1992. While the news media highlighted conflicts between these two groups, sociologist Angie Chung documents how Asian and Black Angelenos collaborated to establish the Koreatown and West Adams Public Safety Association, a multiracial nonprofit overseeing community policing.[25] Korean immigrants contributed financial resources to the project, whereas African Americans contributed their extensive organizational skills accumulated over generations of neighborhood movement making.

A third reason to care about coalitions, as I foreshadowed in chapter 1, is that the size of a crowd is not the sole factor shaping how powerholders react to a protest; *who* is in the crowd also matters. Some categories of protesters send stronger signals than others that a crowd means business. Those categories include the following:

1. People who haven't protested before, because they provide new information about a powerholder's popular legitimacy.
2. Marginalized people, because they take great risks to protest, and thus have more credible grievances than privileged folks.
3. Defectors from the powerholder's own camp, because they reveal that the emperor has no clothes.

When any of these groups—new demographics, marginalized people, or defectors—joins a movement, it enters a coalition with the rest of the participants. Coalition building in social movements tends to occur on an informal basis, whereas legislative coalitions often have official names such as Jaunā Vienotība ("New Unity") in Latvia or Benno Bokk Yaakaar ("United in Hope") in Senegal.

Ample evidence indicates that coalitions can help social movements win concessions. For instance, activists in New York successfully fended off a merger between secular and Catholic hospitals that would have ended reproductive services, by forming a broad-based coalition of concerned citizens. Rather than framing their cause as an attack on the conservative Catholic Church, reproductive rights advocates strategically emphasized wider issues such as access to healthcare, religious freedom, and patient privacy that could appeal to Catholics and non-Catholics alike.[26] In contrast, German daycare workers who went on strike in 1989 came up empty-handed after feminists and the labor movement failed to reach common ground.[27]

These examples suggest that building a coalition should be a no-brainer for any social movement. However, coalitions do not guarantee victory. Many coalitions succeed, but we are about to see that plenty fall short of their goals or collapse completely. In the next sections, we'll examine what sets apart the successes from the failures so that we can harvest strategies from the former and avoid repeating the missteps of the latter.

A TALE OF TWO PROTESTS

Dana Fisher, the sociologist who surveyed protesters' motivations at the March for Our Lives, fielded a similar survey at the Women's March on Washington on January 21, 2017, the day after Donald Trump's inauguration.[28] Eight enumerators fanned out across the 575,000-strong crowd,[29] asking marchers why they attended. Although the sample was only 516 people, the enumerators selected respondents at random to collect an unbiased set of answers. As one might expect, 85 percent of respondents were women. Surprisingly, though, just 53 percent said that women's rights was their main reason for marching. Many respondents cited other motivations, some only loosely related to women's issues: general equality (42 percent), reproductive rights (23 percent), the environment (23 percent), social welfare (22 percent), racial justice (19 percent), LGBTQ+ rights (17 percent), politics/voting (17 percent), and immigration (15 percent). The Women's March, one of the largest one-day mobilizations in history, was touted as a coalition of unprecedented size and breadth. The participants evinced a wide range of goals, the movement's cochairs were racially and professionally diverse, and the Women's March website listed more than four hundred organizational partners.

Unfortunately, the coalition was short-lived. Jewish women accused one of the Women's March cochairs, Tamika Mallory, of bigotry after she attended a gathering associated with Louis Farrakhan, the Nation of Islam leader who had made anti-Semitic remarks in the past. Angie Beem, president of the Washington state chapter of the Women's March, dissolved her chapter over the incident. "They're anti-Semitic," she said about the national organizers. "I mean, they claim they aren't. But they are. They're being racist."[30] Black and Latina activists also felt sidelined, grumbling that they never had a say in planning the march.[31] Racial discord was exacerbated by fake Russian social media accounts deliberately created to split the movement. Russian trolls falsely claiming to be Black American women posted messages like the following: "White feminism seems to the be most stupid 2k16 trend," "Ain't got time for your white feminist bullshit," and "Why black feminists don't owe Hillary Clinton their support."[32] Another fissure opened between women who wanted to keep marching in the streets and those who preferred taking a more institutional route of mobilizing voters and electing Democrats to office. Just a year after observers celebrated the Women's March as a triumph of coalition building, the original organization had shattered into spin-offs such as March On and March On the Polls.[33] Gender and sexuality scholar Benita Roth puts this case into historical perspective, explaining that feminists in the United States have a track record of retreating into culturally homogeneous groups and deprioritizing coalition building. The instinct to "organize one's own" rather than partner with diverse others is the Achilles' heel of the fractured women's movement.[34]

We can't draw a direct causal arrow from the breakup of the Women's March to the Supreme Court's rollback of abortion rights in 2022, but it is noteworthy how cohesive the anti-abortion coalition was in comparison. A coalition is cohesive when its members agree on a goal.[35] Cohesion is a lot like solidarity, where activists aspire to a common vision of social change.[36] The movement to roll back *Roe v. Wade* was a paragon of cohesion.

A few years prior to attending the Women's March, I attended what might be considered the *anti*-Women's March. Officially called the March for Life, this was a rally of anti-abortion activists in Washington that takes place annually on the anniversary of *Roe v. Wade* (it still happens, even after the court reversed *Roe*). My objective was the same as Dana Fisher's at the Women's March: to understand protesters' motivations. However, my methods were ethnographic instead of quantitative. I embedded myself with activists, attending a suburban church service with protest goers in the morning, before accompanying them on a train to the city for the main protest. I spent the rest of the day shadowing marchers as they processed through the National Mall. I also observed conferences and speeches that activists held around the march.

During my hours of observations, I saw hardly any posters or slogans that strayed from a "pro-life" message. If a naïve person were to suddenly teleport into the middle of the March for Life, they would instantly be able to identify the core demand: ban abortion. They would also notice clusters of marchers from church groups. Scholars have found that religious organizations help to create "bonds of loyalty cemented through spiritual cohesion."[37] Religion is what sociologists call a "cross-cutting cleavage"—an identity or interest that overlaps among groups that diverge on other identities or interests. For example, a working-class Christian and a wealthy Christian might look past their class differences because they view themselves as Christian first. Cross-cutting cleavages foster interdependence among groups that would otherwise oppose each other, thereby "sewing" coalitions together.[38] Because people often hold tightly to their religious beliefs, religion is an especially strong cross-cutting cleavage that can smooth over differences of ethnicity, class, language, or lineage.[39] The French sociologist Émile Durkheim wrote that "a religious society cannot exist without a collective *credo* and the more extensive the *credo* the more unified and strong is the society."[40]

The secular Women's March had no such glue to patch the cracks in its coalition. This might explain why the coalition crumbled and why one of its marquee causes, reproductive rights, took a momentous blow in *Dobbs v. Jackson*. Only *some* participants in the Women's March cared first and foremost about defending abortion access; a few even identified as pro-life.[41] The coalition took on too many goals, ultimately splitting over which should take priority and whose interests ought to be "centered." An iconic protest chant goes, "The people united will never be defeated!" The Women's March never fully united, and it suffered a dramatic defeat.

MAKE YOUR COALITION MIND-FRIENDLY

Cognitive science shows us why the lack of a cohesive message turned out to be a fatal flaw for the Women's March coalition. Cohesive messages, which stick to the main point, are easier for our brains to comprehend than scrambled messages, which stray from the main point.[42] Think back to the last time you read a poorly written article, where the paragraphs meandered away from topic sentences and ideas were haphazardly sprinkled throughout the text. It probably made your head hurt, especially if the article was on a subject that was unfamiliar to you. Your headache resulted from *cohesion gaps*, which occur when pieces of text have little overlap and force you to fill in the connections with your own knowledge.[43] Research shows that cohesive texts are more persuasive than aimless texts because they are less taxing for the brain to process.[44]

Protests are a kind of text: powerholders "read" them—through signs, chants, apparel, and social media posts—and then decide whether to give protesters what they want. Powerholders can't grant demands that they can't understand. The Women's March, with its sundry stakeholders and grievances, was much less mind-friendly than the March for Life, with its unambiguous message. Republican politicians knew exactly what to do to appease their constituents: write state laws restricting abortion and seat judges who would overturn *Roe v. Wade*. Democratic politicians had no equivalent guidelines; their constituents were demanding the kitchen sink.

The divergent outcomes of the Women's March and the March for Life are consistent with the hypothesis that *more cohesive demands make an activist coalition more likely to win concessions*. However, it's easy to cherry-pick cases to support a theory. After attending the Women's March and the March for Life, I wanted more conclusive evidence before advising readers to invest a ton of energy in uniting their coalitions around a central message. By "conclusive," I mean a) generalizable and b) causal: Do cohesive demands correspond with better outcomes across many protests, not just the two I happened to attend in Washington? And if so, does crowd cohesion actually *cause* success, or just correlate with it? Conclusive studies didn't exist yet, so I became my own detective.[45]

To produce generalizable evidence, I compiled a database of ninety-seven protests in Europe and the Americas between 2009 and 2014. The protests were nominally about a host of issues, from climate change and gay pride to pensions and corruption. However, we've seen that it's difficult to tell what a protest is really about just by the protest's name, especially when the event is orchestrated by a coalition of different groups. As we saw in Dana Fisher's surveys, activists who attend a "gun control" rally or a "women's march" might be there for all sorts of reasons. Luckily, a consortium of European researchers surveyed participants at each of these ninety-seven protests on why they had attended. I just needed to aggregate the responses into a measure of crowd cohesion. To do that, I used artificial intelligence that transformed raw survey responses (e.g., "Stop with the contemporary way of consuming, working, and producing!") into a cohesion score for each protest ranging from 0 (least cohesive demands) to 1 (most cohesive demands). I then used news reports to code the outcome of each protest in terms of whether protesters won their nominal demands or not within three years. For example, a protest in the Czech Republic billed as "End of the Godfathers" called on government officials to be held accountable for organized crime. The prime minister resigned and was charged with bribery after the protest, so I coded that protest as winning a concession.

My statistical results confirmed that more cohesive protests, where attendees largely agreed on their goals, were more likely to win concessions even after I controlled for crowd size, violent tactics, and other confounding variables. I ran simulations showing that raising a protest's cohesion score from 0.6 (the average) to 0.8 corresponds with an increase in the probability of obtaining concessions from 20 percent to 40 percent. These results reassured me that my anecdotal observations from the Women's March and the March for Life were not anomalies; they reflected a systematic trend whereby activist coalitions that unify their message are more likely to win than those that demand the kitchen sink.

I now had generalizable evidence, but the question remained: Was the relationship between crowd cohesion and protest success causal, or just a correlation? I had reason to suspect that it was not causal. For one thing, there might be something about the context of a protest's unfolding, such as good communication infrastructure, that helps people assemble cohesive crowds *and* communicate clear demands to policymakers. In that case, I might have found a statistical link between cohesion and concessions because a third factor was causing them both. Another concern was the pesky chicken-or-the-egg problem: Maybe powerholders who are already rather accommodating give activists the political freedom to organize effectively. If so, then a high likelihood of concessions might cause cohesive crowds and not the reverse.

To solve these issues, I turned to the scientific gold standard for causal inference: a randomized controlled trial. I could not practically or ethically randomize the demands of activists in the real world and see how their protests turned out. So instead, I randomized the demands of hypothetical protesters in an online survey experiment. I ran my experiment on South African respondents, because South Africa had recently experienced many large protests around themes such as educational access (the #FeesMustFall and #RhodesMustFall movements), workers' rights, environmental protections, and more. I showed respondents images of protesters waving signs and randomized whether messages on the signs had a high-cohesion score or a low-cohesion score. Figure 2 shows high-cohesion and low-cohesion protests about education. The experiment also included protests about labor and environmentalism.

The survey read, "In recent years, South Africans have taken to the streets in protests like the one depicted in the image below. Government officials have debated how to respond, but granting the protesters' demands will cost money. Imagine that officials have decided to hold a referendum on raising taxes to give the protesters what they want. To grant the protesters' demands, would

FIGURE 2: Experimental Treatments in the South Africa Experiment

HIGH-COHESION DEMANDS (COHESION SCORE = 0.79)	LOW-COHESION DEMANDS (COHESION SCORE = 0.53)
We demand education! / Reform universities! / Fund education for all! / #FeesMustFall	We demand education! / Decolonize learning! / Justice for support staff! / Listen to youth!

you vote to increase taxes on families like yours?" After analyzing the responses of all 1,051 respondents, I found that receiving the high-cohesion treatment significantly increased the odds that a taxpayer would support protesters at a cost to themselves. A typical survey respondent (a Black man with a secondary school education and a modest income) had a 21 percent probability of voting for the tax hike under the low-cohesion condition and a 29 percent probability under the high-cohesion condition. I was increasingly convinced that cohesive demands really are a critical ingredient of coalitional success.

I did one more analysis to make sure my experimental results translated beyond the laboratory. I compared two real-world protests that were very similar except in terms of crowd cohesion: Take Back Parliament and Occupy London. Both protests took place in London around the same time (2010 and 2011, respectively), were nonviolent, and had comparable turnout and organizations behind them. Both were coalitions of interest groups. However, these protests could not have been more different in terms of how activists voiced their demands.

Anyone who stumbled into a Take Back Parliament rally would immediately know what the activists were demanding: replacing Britain's winner-take-all electoral rules with a more proportional system of allocating seats in Parliament. Organizers distributed standard signs with clear slogans like "Fair votes now!" and "A referendum on fair votes now!" This strategy helped to harmonize the crowd's message, even though protesters hailed from various interest groups like the Electoral Reform Society, Greenpeace, the New Economics Foundation, Operation Black Vote, and the feminist Fawcett Society. Protesters were also *visibly* cohesive: many wore purple, a throwback to the women's suffrage movement.

Occupy London, an offshoot of Occupy Wall Street, was a hodgepodge of grievances compared to Take Back Parliament. What began as a movement vaguely about seeking economic justice for "the 99 percent" devolved into a cacophony of demands for health services, employment, education, welfare, global tax justice, ending wars and arms dealing, climate change solutions, and regulatory reform. One bystander told me that he walked by a sign calling on authorities to legalize skateboarding. Authorities understandably had a difficult time deciding how to respond to the Occupy protests. Members of Parliament complained about protesters' "incoherent goals," which impeded even sympathetic lawmakers from deciding a course of action. A national survey on Occupy London elicited responses such as, "The manner of protest . . . dilutes and confuses the intrinsic message which may well have a lot of justification and considerable public support."[46] Simply put, Occupy London was not very mind-friendly.

One would be hard-pressed to pinpoint any tangible concessions that materialized from Occupy London. By contrast, Take Back Parliament won a historic referendum on electoral rules. Even though the final vote was against adopting a more proportional system of counting votes, the referendum placed electoral reform high on the political agenda and was therefore a major victory on the path to fairer democracy.

Combined with the quantitative evidence from my experiment, the qualitative evidence from these British case studies finally assured me that activists should try their best to get everyone in their coalition on the same page about their goals. There is abundant proof that demanding one clear concession, like activists did at the March for Life and Take Back Parliament, really is more effective than demanding a jumble of concessions, like at the Women's March or Occupy London.

So, what can activists do with this robust evidence? Fortunately, it can be quite easy to increase cohesion in a coalition. One idea is for rally organizers to hand out standard posters. Looking around me at the 2017 Women's March, I sensed that no two posters were alike. The handmade signs were creative, poignant, and sometimes funny ("Girls just wanna have fun . . . damental rights," "You will die of old age; our children will die from climate change," "My pussy wants world peace," "Make America gay again"). However, they reduced cohesion in the crowd. The more uniform posters at Take Back Parliament were relatively boring, but they got the main message across loud and clear.

Another cohesion-enhancing tool is the "people's microphone." This is a way to amplify core messages at a protest without an electronic sound system. Someone starts by saying, "mic check!" Protesters in proximity reply, "Mic check!" to indicate that they are paying attention. The first speaker then says a phrase, and the crowd repeats it in unison. With more repetitions, the phrase starts rippling through the crowd until everyone can hear it and many voices synchronize into one, like this:

> Speaker 1: Mic check!
> Small group: Mic check!
> Speaker 1: Living wages now!
> Small group: Living wages now!
> Larger group: Living wages now!
> Even larger group: Living wages now!

Some activists, including Angela Davis, criticize this practice for silencing valid dissent in a diverse crowd. The objective of the people's mic, after all, is to suspend difference by drowning out alternative messages.[47] Protesters tend to feel alienated when a dominant voice tries to speak on behalf of a large coalition with diverse opinions.[48] Hence, it is important for whoever initiates the people's mic to be mindful of how well their message represents the will of the whole crowd, especially the less privileged people within it.

Other tactics can hold coalitions together in between protest events, during the everyday work of coordinating a social movement. At organizing meetings, you can remind fellow activists of their cross-cutting cleavages—what they have in common despite their mixed demands. Perhaps members of your coalition are racially diverse but are all working-class, or maybe they are economically diverse but practice a common religion. If there is no preexisting cross-cutting cleavage, it is possible to cultivate cohesion by planning opportunities for activists to socialize on a regular basis. Political scientist Robert Putnam famously argued that joining civic organizations, even recreational ones like bowling leagues, can strengthen trust and reciprocity among people of different backgrounds.[49] Neurobiologist Robert Sapolsky gives a striking illustration of this argument from the US Civil War:

> In the Battle of Gettysburg, Confederate general Lewis Armistead was mortally wounded while leading a charge. As he lay on the battlefield, he gave a secret Masonic sign, in hopes of being recognized by a fellow Mason. It was, by a Union officer, Hiram Bingham, who protected him, got him to a Union field hospital, and guarded his personal effects. In an instant the Us/Them of Union/Confederate became less important than that of Mason-non-Mason.[50]

Yet another tactic for enhancing cohesion is to give talking points to coalition members so that they don't contradict each other when speaking to powerholders, the press, and the public. Greenpeace is a network of environmental activists comprising at least twenty-six independent organizations, each with their own specific interests and cultures, across fifty-five countries on six continents. To cohere its far-flung affiliates, the Greenpeace website provides a toolkit for writing op-eds, complete with talking points such as, "Plastic industry surrogates have stepped up their lobbying efforts against reusable bags" and "In fact, the most relevant study from the National Institutes of Health, CDC, UCLA, and Princeton University shows that [COVID-19] can live on plastic surfaces longer than others—a convenient point for the industry to ignore in its PR push."[51] These ready-made statements encourage editorialists to stay on the message of reducing plastic waste, rather than digressing to other issues. Admittedly, not all activists are willing to put in the time to write a full op-ed. For the "slacktivists" in your coalition, you could designate an official hashtag. #BlackLivesMatter is a well-known example of a hashtag helping to unite a coalition (see chapter 2 for more about online protest).

It is also worthwhile to ponder how *not* to build a cohesive coalition. Some activists, particularly movement founders, may be tempted to deny membership to anyone who does not toe the official line. In the nineteenth century, a hardline wing of the American temperance movement required activists to strictly reject liquor, both politically and personally. Any member of the Prohibition Party, the Women's Christian Temperance Union, or the International Organization of Good Templars who so much as questioned the goal of constitutional prohibition or drank a sip of alcohol was a traitor to the movement.[52]

The instinct to purify a coalition is understandable; as political scientist Christian Davenport warns, factions can "kill a movement from the inside."[53] However, it is misguided to cohere an activist coalition by purging nonconformists because purity tests can shrink a coalition below the size needed for impact.

Legislative scholars once thought that it was irrational to form a coalition any bigger than necessary to win a vote. An "oversized" coalition, they reasoned, would force coalition members to divide the spoils of winning (money, power, or policies) among more people, thus shrinking the benefits to each individual.

But this theory is outdated. In practice, oversized coalitions frequently form in both legislatures and social movements. The updated wisdom is that large, "big tent" coalitions are beneficial when no one knows exactly how many coalition members are necessary to win a campaign, or when maintaining bargains among coalition members is difficult.[54] These are often the conditions in social movements, where there are no formal rules on what it takes to win and no infrastructure for maintaining a "party line." Most social movements cannot afford to impose purity tests. If you are an activist, therefore, it is strategic to err on the larger side and accept as many allies as you reasonably can into your coalition. Extra members are an insurance policy against adversaries and dropouts. For instance, a green coalition could slightly relax its ideological boundaries to accept moderate environmentalists (even if it would never admit people from the far opposite end of the ideological spectrum, like fascists).

Choosing an inclusive name for your coalition can signal your openness to newcomers. Sociologist Jonathan Coley profiled an organization called the Bridge Builders, which sought to "bridge the gap between LGBT and Christian communities" at a Christian university in Tennessee.[55] And sociologist Amin Ghaziani studied how some LGBTQ+ organizations traded names highlighting a specific in-group (e.g., Lesbian and Bisexual Women's Task Force) for names

> **EXERCISE:** Can you think of a more inclusive name for a social movement that you support?

Besides revising their own ideologies, leaders of social movement organizations can watch for ideological shifts occurring in *other* organizations that present opportunities for new coalitions to form. Sometimes, unlikely partners can morph into close allies.

The American Federation of Labor and Congress of Industrial Organizations (AFL-CIO) is a labor federation made up of two groups, the AFL and the CIO, which used to routinely butt heads over philosophy, jurisdictions, membership rules, policy goals, and personality differences. In the 1930s and 1940s, several merger attempts broke down. But in the 1950s, the AFL began embracing emerging welfare reforms such as public wealth redistribution and legislation to protect all workers, thus bringing it more in line with the CIO. This ideological convergence finally allowed the two groups to enter a coalition in 1955. A committee tasked with preparing the pact "discovered that on virtually all major issues, the two organizations had adopted policies which were in all respects either identical or very similar."[57] Today, the AFO-CIO is the largest trade union federation in the United States, comprising sixty national and international unions that represent more than twelve million workers including teachers, municipal employees, and meatpackers. It is a political force to be reckoned with, raising funds for Democratic candidates, registering voters, and canvassing. For the 2010 midterm elections, the AFL-CIO sent 28.6 million pieces of mail and staffed call centers in twenty-six states.[58] Four years later, more than 100,000 volunteers for the AFL-CIO's Pennsylvania chapter knocked on doors in a massive get-out-the-vote drive.[59] With a supersized membership, a coalition is more politically imposing and can survive losing a supporter here and there. The AFL-CIO juggernaut became possible because of an ideological shift in the AFL.

Numbers, we must remember, are not all that matter. A coalition's *diversity* is also one of its main advantages for signaling that it is not just a fringe uprising, but a revolt by a formidable cross section of society. Political scientist Sirianne Dahlum analyzed anti-regime protest campaigns from 1900 to 2013 and found that socially diverse campaigns were more likely to overthrow authoritarian regimes and to establish democracies, even after controlling for protest size.[60] We saw in chapter 1 that a coalition is all the mightier if it includes defectors from the target's own circle.

Powerholders who ignore or suppress diverse coalitions risk grave political repercussions, especially when activism surrounds hot-button issues that the public is watching closely.[61] American government officials could write off resistance to the Vietnam War when protesters were predominantly "flower children" flashing the peace sign. However, once thousands of Vietnam veterans converged on the White House in 1971 to oppose the war in which they had fought, the writing was on the wall for military leaders. The counterculture *became* the culture, tilting public relations in favor of the anti-war movement.

Granted, communicating cohesive demands *while* preserving a coalition's size and diversity is no easy feat. Strange bedfellows can unite around a common message, but this requires foresight, patience, and sometimes forgiveness. The following sections turn to intersectional coalitions and how to make them work.

IS A "RAINBOW COALITION" IDEALISTIC?

As deputy chairman of the Black Panther Party, Fred Hampton was already a card-carrying radical. But in 1969, he came up with an idea that was radical even by the standards of the Panthers: to start a multicultural partnership with the Puerto Rican–led Young Lords and the white-led Young Patriots and Students for a Democratic Society. He called it the Rainbow Coalition. Promoting interracial solidarity was an uphill battle in the 1960s, as it is today. Nevertheless, Hampton saw it as a necessity: "We got to face some facts. That the masses are poor, that the masses belong to what you call the lower class, and when I talk about the masses, I'm talking about the white masses, I'm talking about the black masses, and the brown masses, and the yellow masses, too."[62]

The Rainbow Coalition was intersectional before legal scholar Kimberlé Crenshaw coined the term in 1989.[63] Intersectionality refers to how multiple identities combine to produce modes of privilege and marginalization. Hampton acknowledged that people experience race-based and class-based oppression simultaneously. Members of the Rainbow Coalition would stay active in their racially specific organizations while also fighting capitalism across the color line.

Unfortunately, the Rainbow Coalition never had a chance to realize its intersectional vision. FBI agents infiltrated Hampton's Chicago chapter of the Black Panther Party, which they suspected of plotting to overthrow the government. With the presumed blessing of the Nixon administration, local police shot Hampton to death in his apartment while he was sleeping next to his pregnant fiancée.[64] He was twenty-one years old.

Because the Rainbow Coalition barely got off the ground before authorities demolished it, we can only speculate whether it would have succeeded. However, a recent study offers some hints.

Political scientists Tabitha Bonilla and Alvin Tillery Jr. ran an experiment to test the potential for an intersectional movement to win popular support.[65] They focused on Black Lives Matter, which carries on the legacy of the Rainbow Coalition by presenting itself as intersectional. As of this writing, the movement's website declares:

> We are expansive. We are a collective of liberators who believe in an inclusive and special movement. We also believe that in order to win and bring as many people with us along the way, we must move beyond the narrow nationalism that is all too prevalent in Black communities. We must ensure that we are building a movement that brings all of us to the front. We affirm the lives of Black queer and trans folks, disabled folks, undocumented folks, folks with records, women, and all Black lives along the gender spectrum.[66]

Bonilla and Tillery wanted to know: Does framing Black Lives Matter as intersectional boost or reduce support for the movement? To find out, they randomized descriptions of the movement in a survey of 849 consenting African American participants. One description framed the movement in nationalist terms (BLM believes "in elevating the experiences of Black people as a distinct nation within a nation. . . ."). A second version used a feminist frame (BLM believes "in elevating the experiences of the most marginalized Black people, especially women. . . ."). And a third version used an LGBTQ+ frame (BLM believes "in elevating the experiences of the most marginalized Black people, especially those who identify as queer, trans, gender nonconforming, and intersex. . . .").

The authors measured the effects of each description by asking respondents questions such as, "Do you support the goals of Black Lives Matter?" and "How much, if at all, do you generally trust the leaders of Black Lives Matter?"

The results, they found, depended on the identities of respondents. Most notably, the feminist and LGBTQ+ frames *reduced* support for BLM among Black male subjects. One could conclude from Bonilla and Tillery's results that intersectional coalitions, despite sounding like a good idea, can actually weaken coalitions.

This sounds dismaying, but there is still hope for intersectional coalitions to flourish within the constraints that Bonilla and Tillery illuminated. The solution that I propose has two components: targeting and sequencing.

Targeting means knowing your audience. For example, when trying to recruit in predominantly male settings, Black Lives Matter organizers could downplay their feminist and LGBTQ+ agendas even if those remain integral to their mission. Smaller movements could try the same strategy when recruiting at local neighborhood councils, schools, or labor union meetings. The rule of thumb is to ask yourself, "What identity frame resonates most with this audience in front of me?"

Sequencing has to do with how coalition leaders plan campaigns. Leaders might center one subgroup at a time to maintain cohesion at any single protest but guarantee that each subgroup gets its day in the spotlight. For example, a rally this week could emphasize Black women's rights, and a demonstration next week could spotlight queer Black folks. This approach lets organizers "have their cake and eat it too" by harnessing the support-generating power of narrow identity frames that we saw in Bonilla and Tillery's study, while also ensuring that no identity group (or interest group) is left behind. Although it is never easy to wait one's turn, sequencing might have spared the Women's March from falling apart by making all of its affiliates feel heard. Rainbow coalitions are feasible; they just need to be crafted with patience and care.

BRIDGE BUILDING 101

The sun had set on the crowd and I was starting to shiver. It was November 10, two days after the 2016 US presidential election. I had joined thousands of other protesters in Minneapolis to express our anger about Donald Trump's victory over Hillary Clinton. I doubt that any of us believed our actions would change the outcome of the election, but protesting offered us catharsis and a chance to express the people's will (Clinton had won the popular vote but lost the electoral vote). We stood in the street for hours, listening to speeches. Demonstrators of diverse ages and races chanted slogans like "Not my president," "Love trumps hate," and, most bluntly, "Fuck Trump!"

Suddenly, I heard voices shouting, "TO THE FREEWAY!" The crowd began winding its way toward the Interstate 94 onramp and, eventually, onto the busy freeway. Fearing for my safety, I went home and spent the rest of the night glued to live video footage of the continuing march. I watched activists stand their ground in front of oncoming vehicles and shut down traffic for miles. At one point, a truck driver tried to breach the human wall. Intrepid protesters jumped onto the truck's hood. When another vehicle started moving toward the crowd, a protester hit its mirror. The driver fired pepper spray. Police finally dispersed the rally, and miraculously nobody was injured or arrested.

Occupying I-94 is a symbolic tradition among left-leaning activists in the twin cities of Minneapolis and Saint Paul. Protesters occupied it again in 2020, during the George Floyd uprisings. The Minnesota Department of Transportation built I-94 in the 1950s by bulldozing a vibrant African American community called Rondo. Construction workers demolished approximately three hundred businesses and six hundred homes to make way for the freeway. Not only did this devastate Black neighborhoods; it segregated the surrounding areas racially and economically. According to census data, residents north of I-94 are 21 percent white, whereas residents south of I-94 are 48 percent white. The median annual family income in what remains of Rondo is almost $20,000 less than in other parts of Saint Paul.[67] When activists shut down the freeway, they force people to confront the legacy of institutional racism and inequality.

There is no way to erase historical injustices, but some Minnesotans have advocated for a partial remedy: building a huge cap, or "land bridge," over the below-grade freeway to reconnect neighborhoods to the north and south. The bridge would be wide enough to accommodate new housing, parks, shops, and office space for nonprofit organizations. It would be a meeting place for residents of different races to cocreate a healthier, integrated community. The planned bridge acknowledges that powerful social movement coalitions outlast a single night of protest; they link the fates of aggrieved communities and allies for the long haul, until real change is achieved.

If occupying I-94 is symbolic, so is the proposed land bridge. Coalitions need *bridge builders* to connect people across social fault lines. As educational studies scholar Thor-André Skrefsrud explains, bridges "represent an opportunity to explore what lies on the other side of the expanse," whether the expanse is physical or cultural.[68]

It can be difficult, however, to initiate communication between groups that have remained separate for a long time. Mutual suspicion and "empathy gulfs"[69] can get in the way of forging a coalition that lifts everyone up. That's why effective bridge builders often have one foot in each of the worlds they want to connect. They can identify with, and authentically give voice to, the grievances and ambitions of people on both sides.

In *Coalitions Across the Class Divide*, community organizer Fred Rose recounts how peace activists formed a coalition with labor unions in Maine. This was an improbable alliance, because many peace activists came from middle-class families and began their activist journeys in college, where they had the luxury of taking classes on "post-material" issues like world peace, feminism, and environmentalism. By contrast, the typical labor union member was blue-collar, concerned with material issues like wages and workplace safety, and might not have attended college at all.

However, a small subset of peace activists grew up in union homes. As first-generation college students, they stayed rooted in the blue-collar culture of their parents, even while exploring post-material activism at school.

There were also students like Tom, a kid who grew up middle-class but made friends with union activists while he was supporting a labor strike at his university. After graduating, Tom got a job at the Amalgamated Clothing and Textile Workers Union. Although it took some time for him to fit in on the factory floor, labor organizing was a "natural extension" of his student organizing.[70]

Both types of bridge builders—peace activists with working-class backgrounds and union activists with middle-class back-

> **EXERCISE:** Consider whether you have any hybrid identities that you can marshal to bridge groups of activists. People with mixed class backgrounds, multiracial heritage, dual citizenship, and fluency and multiple languages are in an ideal position to serve as ambassadors between the different communities they represent. You may possess gifts as an activist that you didn't realize you had.

WHEN ALLIES MESS UP: COALITIONAL HEALING

Early in this chapter, I defined coalitions as "the joint use of resources to determine the outcome of a decision in a mixed-motive situation."[72] In the parlance of contemporary activism, we could think of coalition members as *allies*. *Allyship* refers to how people with certain advantages (money, power, or privilege) help less advantaged people, often out of a mix of altruistic and self-interested motivations.[73]

Allies seldom intend to exploit, but folks on the receiving end of allyship sometimes come to feel exploited, marginalized, or misunderstood—like the Jewish women who felt ostracized within the Women's March organization. Hurt feelings, in turn, threaten to tear coalitions apart.

Diverse coalitions are especially susceptible to these problems because members who are relatively privileged—whether due to their race, class, gender, citizenship, or something else—may inadvertently replicate the very social hierarchies they are trying to dismantle. "White people often come to these protests and they want to lead them and they want to be screaming the loudest and they want to throw things at police," said Benjamin O'Keefe, a Black political organizer involved with the George Floyd protests in 2020. The sensitive ally's doctrine, condensed, is *listen + shut up + read*.[74]

Friction like this is a feature of coalitions, not a bug. Recall that coalitions are fundamentally about sharing resources, and that social movements with broad-based coalitions tend to be stronger than movements without them. This means that some coalition members will necessarily have more, and different, advantages than others. And they may, as a function of their privilege, fail to empathize with fellow activists or behave in ways that are tone-deaf or even offensive. Black Lives Matter founder Alicia Garza wrote in *The Purpose of Power*, "We can't be afraid to establish a base that is larger than the people we feel comfortable with. . . . We have to reach beyond the choir and take seriously the task of organizing the unorganized— the people who don't already speak the same language, the people who don't eat, sleep and breathe social justice."[75] The goal is not to eliminate intra-coalitional resource disparities and cultural differences but to navigate them sensitively. It is primarily the job of more privileged activists to do this work, but less privileged activists also have a role to play. Within reason, they can give allies who make honest mistakes the chance to do better. Some disagreement within coalitions is healthy and productive; it opens space for difficult, yet important, conversations about how to improve. A seasoned activist once told me, "If you aren't messing up, you aren't doing the work." Only by hearing your comrades' concerns can you begin to address them. And conversely, only by voicing your own concerns can you help your allies to do better by you.

Psychologists remind us that humans have an innate tendency to return negative behavior—intentional or unintentional—with more negative behavior. Even chimpanzees maintain strong social norms of reciprocity and punishment.[76] This evolutionary inclination can set off a vicious cycle whereby a victim exacts revenge, the original offender perceives the revenge as worse than their own transgression, *they* take revenge, and so on. As a result, allies too often wind up fighting each other instead of their true rivals. For instance, a gay YouTuber accidentally "liked" an Instagram post from a Trump supporter at the Capitol insurrection, prompting a deluge of verbal attacks from progressive activists. Commenting on the incident, transgender cultural critic Natalie Wynn questioned whether attacking allies who mess up is the best use of energy in a social movement. "I think it's often well-meaning allies of a cause [who get attacked]. . . . You can cause more damage to a person with less power than a person with more power. So it can feel more productive to attack less powerful people. Although, in fact, I would argue that's not really productive."[77] Martin Luther King Jr. likewise flagged the danger of revenge cycles. "The old law of an eye for an eye leaves everybody blind," he wrote.

To keep communities from self-destructing, humans throughout history have devised antidotes for the natural yet counterproductive tendency to strike back at those who offend us. Activists can fall back on these same technologies to prevent coalitions from crumbling when interpersonal conflicts inevitably bubble up.

We don't tend to think of forgiveness as a technology, but historically speaking that is what it is. Technology is simply the application of knowledge for practical ends. Forgiveness rituals emerged through millennia of people trying to resolve their differences in practical, reproducible ways. In some Christian sects, a priest prostrates before the congregation and members prostrate in return, mutually requesting forgiveness for their sins. Ablution ceremonies—the washing of body parts or possessions—are common in many faiths. Repentance and forgiveness customs are often religious, but they don't need to be. Karen Wyatt is a hospice physician who has counseled patients on their deathbeds about letting go of resentments.[78] She recommends making a sacrifice (say, of time or money) to release blame from the past, writing lists of your grievances and then burning them, or planting a "forgiveness garden" to represent the nurturing of healthy relationships.

People across cultures intuitively understand what psychologists have empirically shown: that forgiveness interrupts the revenge cycle by making our thoughts and behaviors more positive, or "prosocial."[79] Forgiveness tends to follow an apology, which redirects attention away from the harm and onto the transgressor's human flaws. It is a process of empathizing with people who behave in hurtful ways that we know, under different circumstances, we might behave ourselves.

No one is *entitled* to forgiveness, but Rabbi Danya Ruttenberg stresses that healing can happen even if forgiveness never comes. The offending party can still repent, which in the Jewish tradition of *t'shuvah* means "coming back to where we are supposed to be, returning to the person we know we're capable of being—coming home, in humility and with intentionality, to behave as the person we'd like to believe we are."[80]

Psychologists have observed that forgiveness is easier when people are in close relationships.[81] We are more willing to forgive an intimate partner than an anonymous internet troll. Therefore, anything that coalition organizers can do to foster close relationships among members—spending time together face-to-face, engaging in social activities not directly related to activism—can help a coalition weather internal strife.

If we accept the starting premise of this chapter, that coalitions of diverse people are important for helping social movements succeed, then activists mustn't let the best be the enemy of the good when including allies in their efforts. If you do coalition work in any deep and sustained way, you will almost certainly offend someone at some point, and someone will offend you. However, cutting off ties with coalition partners who commit microaggressions (or even mesoaggressions) can doom the coalition altogether.

Macalester College, where I teach, offers Allies Training in which students, faculty, and staff learn that it is impossible to be a perfect ally because we are humans—prone to bias, with brains not too evolutionarily distant from those of chimpanzees. "Allyship is a process, not an identity," the facilitators advise. In other words, allyship is not a badge that you wear after attending a rally to congratulate yourself on being a good person. It is not a shirt that says "This is what a feminist looks like," nor is it a Black Lives Matter lawn sign. The *ally* label certainly does not insulate you from criticism. Allyship requires constant renewal. It is an interminable project of taking risks, making mistakes, reflecting, learning, apologizing, and forgiving. It is personal growth for the common good.

Activism is emotionally intense, even in "normal" times when allies are getting along relatively well. I hope the tools in this section give you more confidence to heal emotional injuries when they happen, so that your coalition can resume fighting together, stronger than before.

We've covered a lot of ground in this chapter. Here are some highlights that you can incorporate into your activist playbook:

- Coalitions allow social movement organizations to share resources, including people power. If you are working on a cause that affects a small minority of people, then you might succeed *only* by partnering with others.
- Make your message clear. You can do this by handing out standard posters to protesters, using the people's mic, publishing a mission statement, distributing talking points, or creating a unifying hashtag.
- Encourage organization members to get to know each other! Try team-building exercises, and hold events

outside of meetings and protests to help everyone bond and realize their shared goals.
- Avoid ideological purity tests. Give everyone the benefit of the doubt, allow room for listening and growing, and focus on the core message.
- Choose a name for your coalition that signals your openness to joining forces with others (e.g., Pride Alliance instead of Lesbian and Bisexual Women's Task Force).
- Watch for ideological shifts happening in other organizations, which can present opportunities to bring new partners onboard.
- Intersectional coalitions can work best with a dual strategy of *targeting* and *sequencing*. Targeting involves speaking directly to specific identity groups, such as men or queer people. Sequencing means giving each identity group or interest group in the coalition its day in the spotlight. This keeps messages cohesive without sidelining anyone in the long run.
- Try to recruit bridge builders into your coalition, or become one yourself. People with hybrid identities can serve as translators and liaisons between communities.
- Practice forgiveness, of others and yourself, when interpersonal conflicts arise. Hurt feelings are an unavoidable part of coalition work, but forgiving each other interrupts destructive cycles of resentment and revenge.

5. MONEY TALKS

Fundraise Like a Pro...
Without Losing Your Soul

You know your social movement has "made it" when critics start asking to see the books. Like publicly traded companies or leading electoral campaigns, prominent movements inevitably face financial scrutiny. Keen to unmask high-profile activists as hypocrites, detractors accuse movement leaders of enriching themselves with charitable donations. Such allegations have embroiled major campaigns like the Women's March and Black Lives Matter.[1] The subtext of the accusations is, "Where can millions of dollars be going if not into the pockets of organizers?"

But when organizers show their receipts, it becomes clear just how expensive it is to run a mass movement. Under public pressure, the Women's March organization released its tax forms for 2017, the year it held its historic march on Washington following Donald Trump's election. The records showed that copresident Tamika Mallory and assistant secretary Linda Sarsour earned salaries of $70,570 and $69,927, respectively—hardly exorbitant for heads of national nonprofits. Three other full-time staffers split $100,000 among themselves. Rather than padding the pockets of leaders, most of the budget went toward logistics, including $413,092 for event fees and $154,613 to transport, house, and feed thousands of protesters.[2] And because senior leaders like Mallory and Sarsour received credible threats to their safety, some of the money paid for licensed security firms to protect them. Defending her movement against critics, Women's March chief operating officer Rachel O'Leary Carmona underscored the price of mounting a large and inclusive campaign (the italics are mine):

> The power of the Women's March is in our people. . . . There are a lot of false rumors going around that our work is well-resourced: It isn't. We ensure every national event we host, and every protest, is accessible to all women regardless of disability or income. *True accessibility and intersectionality aren't cheap.* But we make it work—our chapter leaders, our members, and our staff pull off incredible work with few resources.[3]

Veteran social movement organizers know firsthand how fast budgets can balloon. When Senegalese citizens took to the streets in 2011 to denounce bad economic conditions and President Abdoulaye Wade's bid for a third term in office (see the previous chapter for the full story), all that reporters could see on the surface was crowds swarming Senegal's capital city. However, investigative research by political scientist Leila Demarest revealed significant resource mobilization behind the scenes. Demarest unearthed internal documents from the Organization Commission of Le Mouvement 23 Juin ("The June 23 Movement") listing expenses such as 3,000 minibuses to move protesters from suburbs to central Dakar ($92,000), 10,000 T-shirts to give out at rallies ($17,000), a sound system ($1,500), and posters ($1,500).[4] That adds up to $112,000, a hefty sum in a country where the average household income in 2011 was about $1,400 (compared to about $50,000 in the United States).[5]

Even if you are planning a small local protest and not a national revolution, financial constraints can get in the way of pulling off a successful event, meaning one that is a) large enough to attract attention and b) accessible to diverse stakeholders. Recall from earlier chapters that large, diverse crowds signal to powerholders that a broad-based coalition is serious about achieving change.

Social movements often begin with abstract ideals like justice, equality, accountability, or democracy. To be sure, activists tend to be rich in the "moral resources" of solidarity, empathy, and legitimacy.[6] However, even the most idealistic and morally endowed activists eventually must admit that money is also a necessity. As eminent social movement scholars Bob Edwards and John McCarthy put it, "No matter how many other resources a movement mobilizes it will incur costs and someone has to pay the bills."[7] You probably didn't get into activism because you care a lot about money. But this book is about making activism *work*—about really being heard. And whether we like it or not, money talks.

The details of mobilizing a movement can be very material indeed. I once stood in a seemingly interminable line to use the portable toilet at a protest, debating with myself whether I should just leave to find a restroom someplace less crowded. I wondered how much bigger the crowd might have grown, and how much longer the protest could have lasted, if participants had been better able to take care of their human needs to eat, drink, stay warm, and relieve themselves. And, having spent hundreds of my own dollars to fly from Minnesota to Washington, DC, for the event, I asked myself how many people never made it to the protest in the first place for want of personal resources. A quick Google search informed me that renting a single portable toilet in Washington can cost between $180 and $680 per day. No wonder the go-to tool of activists these days is not the megaphone, but the phone bank. How can small grassroots movements hope to afford $680 toilets, along with the innumerable other payments—for permits, microphones, transport, publicity, etc.—required to put on what amounts to a free concert? And how can activists raise necessary funds without "selling out" and losing sight of their core moral objectives?

This chapter is the most pragmatic of all the chapters in this book. It will leave you with evidence-backed strategies to pay the bills of your activist campaigns, without losing your soul in the process. I will first walk you through a brief history of social movement fundraising, as some old-school methods remain useful today. The history books also offer some cautionary tales about the ambiguous relationship between activists and philanthropists. Next, we'll explore the promises and pitfalls of a new-school fundraising method: internet crowdfunding. I'll then discuss why "selling" a social movement to donors is surprisingly similar to selling breakfast cereal to shoppers: I'll explain how I borrowed cutting-edge market research techniques to engineer high-impact fundraising appeals for progressive activists. Finally, this chapter will dissect the psychology of charitable giving and outline how you can leverage it to boost the bottom line of your social movement. You will learn, among other things, why it's a smarter idea to hold a charity run than a bake sale and why reminding people of social traumas from the past can inspire more activism for a better future.

HISTORY LESSONS: FROM POOR PEOPLE'S MOVEMENTS TO "RADICAL CHIC"

When I teach courses on social movements, I often kick off the semester with an informal two-question poll. First, I ask students to raise their hands if they are pissed off about something—anything—in the world right now. It could be pollution, war, racism, economic inequality, or a bundle of issues. Invariably, everyone shoots a hand into the air. Feel free to play along: raise your hand right now if you are angry about some aspect of the status quo.

I then say, "Keep your hands up if you have protested about that concern—whether by marching, signing a petition, writing a letter, or something else—in the past twelve months." Even at the politically engaged college where I teach, I watch most hands go down, looks of mild shame on students' faces. If you lowered your hand, too, you are not unusual. As we saw in chapter 1, grievances are ubiquitous whereas protest participation is rare (although there is variation across countries).

This simple experiment confirms a fact that now seems intuitive but was once revolutionary in the study of activism: social movements require resources, not just grievances. Resource mobilization theory took academia by storm when sociologists John McCarthy and Mayer Zald introduced it in the 1970s.[8] McCarthy and Zald corrected theories that had long emphasized only psychological causes of protest. According to resource mobilization theory, social movements do not spontaneously spring from moral indignation. Rather, they take shape with much effort, through organizations that channel money and labor toward staging protests, communicating with the press, hiring lawyers, composing strategy memos, and other costly activities. McCarthy and Zald observed structural shifts occurring within social movement organizations (SMOs) in the mid-twentieth century. SMOs were beginning to look less like disorganized masses yelling in the street and more like streamlined operations making strategic appeals to deep-pocketed philanthropists.

This shift was pronounced in the United States, which emerged from World War II as an economic superpower. Combined with expanded social welfare under the New Deal, a booming economy injected white middle-class Americans with unprecedented disposable income and leisure time to spend on social causes—think political clubs where men fraternized after work and cocktail party fundraisers in the burgeoning suburbs.[9] For most of Western history (and still in many developing countries), *classical SMOs*, as McCarthy and Zald termed them, derived their strength from the direct participation of constituents who would immediately benefit from the movement's success: workers supported labor movements, farmers supported farmers' movements, women supported women's movements, African Americans supported civil rights movements, and so on. But in postwar America, nascent *professional SMOs* increasingly drew on the financial support of "conscience adherents" who were *not* the primary beneficiaries of the movements' success and who participated mostly at an arm's length. No longer was activism just for the marginalized—a last resort when other channels of influence, such as voting, were closed off; activism became a pastime for the upwardly mobile. Joining the board of a social movement organization, holding a fundraiser, or attending a meeting was a chance for the well-to-do to hobnob, enlarge their political clout, and soothe their consciences in between bouts of conspicuous consumption.

For some well-heeled conscience adherents, donating to activist groups was also a fashion statement—a way to distinguish themselves from "ordinary" elites who indulged in more humdrum amusements like yachting or breeding show poodles. Helping the downtrodden—or, more precisely, *being seen* to help—lent the liberal upper class a "radical chic" image and a concomitant savior complex. Journalist Tom Wolfe coined the phrase "radical chic" in a 1970 *New York* magazine article about a swanky dinner party that the illustrious composer Leonard Bernstein and his wife hosted to raise money for the Black Panthers' legal defense fund.[10] Wolfe assumed Bernstein's internal voice, satirizing how he imagined the distinguished host to have planned the soirée:

> Wonder what the Black Panthers eat here on the hors d'oeuvre trail? Do the Panthers like little Roquefort cheese morsels wrapped in crushed nuts this way, and asparagus tips in mayonnaise dabs, and *meatballs petites au Coq Hardi*, all of which are at this very moment being offered to them on gadrooned silver platters by maids in black uniforms with hand-ironed white aprons. . . . The butler will bring them their drinks.

One invitee was Mrs. Lee Berry, the wife of a Panther who was arrested for allegedly conspiring to bomb New York City police stations. Mr. Berry was handcuffed in the Veterans Administration Hospital while recovering from an epileptic seizure, a condition he acquired while serving in Vietnam. Mrs. Berry mostly kept quiet during her evening at the Bernsteins' Park Avenue apartment, uneasily nibbling on canapés in a sumptuous salon while her husband's physical and legal health hung in the balance. At one point, she found herself consoling a woman who said the Panthers' philosophy "scared her." When a *New York Times* reporter asked Mrs. Berry if the opulence impressed her, she replied, "These are not the things I want to fulfill me as a person—all these material things. I know it's not envy. But I do wonder that one segment of the population has so much and the others don't have hot water and heat."[11]

Cringing at awkward scenes like this, scholars and activists debated whether the professionalization and fetishization of SMOs was a good thing. The optimistic take was that increased buy-in from conscience adherents like the Bernsteins signaled larger, more socioeconomically diverse coalitions (see chapter 4 on the importance of coalitions) and infused grassroots movements with much-needed resources and credibility. Movements that once would have scraped by on the margins, shouting into the void and struggling to pay the bills, could now staff formidable bureaucracies of managers, publicists, lawyers, and lobbyists to spar with the political establishment on its own turf. By rubbing shoulders with society bigwigs, activists could gain overdue access to the halls of power.

The more pessimistic outlook was that professionalization and radical chic culture set SMOs down a slippery slope to co-optation. Conscience adherents were, by definition, outsiders of a movement who could never fully grasp the adversity of the oppressed. A bleeding-heart businessman in San Francisco might write a check to the Natural Resources Defense Council, but he could not authentically raise a fist in solidarity with poor communities that grappled daily with the consequences of living downstream from a hazardous waste dump. The Bernsteins, even with selfless motives, would always remain laughable white saviors. As sociologist Ira Silver argued, attempts to "buy an activist identity" usually just reproduced class differences.[12] What activists really needed, contended social scientists Hahrie Han, Elizabeth McKenna, and Michelle Oyakawa, was an independent source of resources that did not depend on access to elites.[13] Only that would afford activists the autonomy, flexibility, and resilience to hold powerholders accountable.

Twentieth-century American donors paid effusive lip service to progressive causes, but their basic interest presumably lay in upholding the class, gender, and racial hierarchies that furnished their wealth and status to begin with. They were also constrained by the US tax code, which barred tax-exempt 501(c)(3) organizations from "substantial political activity." Philanthropists would help less privileged folks to a degree, pessimists conceded, but they would inevitably shy away from controversy and discourage radical reforms such as tougher business regulations or tax hikes on the rich. When a consortium of philanthropic foundations pledged to financially back the Voter Education Project in 1962, Black journalist Louis Lomax objected, "[They] are out to defang the civil rights movement."[14] Skeptics like Lomax feared that wealthy patrons would gentrify and ultimately undercut grassroots movements, the purported advantages of professionalization be damned. As SMOs hired more "experts" and cashed generous checks, they risked crowding out—and selling out—the very people on whose behalf they were ostensibly fighting.

Voices from the left and the right have converged on their mutual disdain for social movement philanthropy. While left-wing critics continue to bemoan the hijacking of grassroots movements by the middle and upper classes, right-wing critics decry the supposed liberal agenda of corporate do-gooders. Vivek Ramaswamy, a Republican entrepreneur and 2024 US presidential candidate, distilled this paranoia in his book *Woke, Inc.: Inside Corporate America's Social Justice Scam*. Pointing to examples like Nike's racial justice initiatives, Ramaswamy lambastes "environmental, social, and governance investing," known as E.S.G., as a cabal of private business leaders and Democratic politicians plotting to destroy society.[15] Ramaswamy and other "anti-woke" commentators entreat consumers to boycott companies that endorse progressive causes. The Claremont Institute, a conservative think tank, maintains a Black Lives Matter Funding Database with the tagline, "Americans deserve to know who funded BLM riots."[16] The implicit message from the right is that social movement philanthropy is working *too* well, emboldening left-wing activists and their elite puppeteers.

Whether philanthropy helps or hurts social movements is not just a matter of opinion; it is an empirical question. So, what does the evidence say? The quick answer is that philanthropy is a double-edged sword: it both blunts movements' ambitions *and* enforces movement's achievements. Here's how that works.

Patronage blunts movements' ambitions through what sociologist Herbert Haines termed "the radical flank effect," whereby donors shift money from radical activists to more moderate activists in the same movement or different movements.[17] Haines noticed that violent civil rights protests in the 1950s and 1960s not only spurred white backlash (see chapter 3); they also prompted a flood of donations to less militant Black organizations such as the Voter Education Project, which focused on registering voters and paying civil rights attorneys. There is evidence for the radical flank effect both within and across social movements. Sociologists J. Craig Jenkins and Craig Eckert estimated that 51.5 percent of all grants to Black activist groups in the 1960s went to professional (read: moderate) SMOs like the National Committee Against Discrimination in Housing, instead of classical (read: radical) SMOs like the Congress of Racial Equality. The share going to professional SMOs rose to 69.3 percent in the 1970s.[18] Financial contributions to all Black activist groups peaked in 1973 as those groups collectively started embracing more contentious goals such as school integration and affirmative action. Already disapproving of urban riots in the 1960s, squeamish trustees of charitable foundations began eyeing safer investments. In 1980, the broad African American movement received less than a third of the funding that it received in 1970.[19] Meanwhile, donations to environmentalist, women's rights, and consumer rights organizations crept upward. Some donors took their money overseas, turning their attention away from messy American politics to the "simpler" task of combatting poverty in the developing world.

The net result of the radical flank effect was to replace grassroots militants with smooth talkers in suits. Civil rights SMOs did not entirely abandon their original goals or tactics, but historical accounts show that they lost rank-and-file members, scaled back their direct actions, and took on a more corporate air. There were approximately 265 major civil rights protests across the United States in the 1960s, but just 83 in the 1970s. During the same period, the National Association for the Advancement of Colored People (NAACP) hemorrhaged members and survived mainly by dint of staffers sitting behind desks at the NAACP headquarters, their salaries paid with foundation grants.[20]

For other movements, an influx of donations in the 1980s and 1990s was a mixed blessing, boosting operating capacity but diluting radical ambitions. In 1984, delegates from twenty women's organizations assembled in Washington, DC, at a joint meeting of the National Black United Fund and the National Committee for Responsive Philanthropy. They conceived a mutual aid system that became the Women's Funding Network (WFN), with the mission of achieving "equality, justice, and power for all." The organizers immediately felt the tension between economic and social goals. They deliberately avoided references to "feminism" in their public statements, which they worried would sound too radical for risk-averse donors. The majority of WFN board members were white professionals. Women who attended WFN conferences in the 1990s complained about being asked to participate in diversity trainings, preferring to practice their leadership and fundraising skills. The cost of even attending their conferences was prohibitive for some people. As a consequence, more than 84 percent of attendees at the 1998 conference identified as middle class and above, with 9 percent reporting to have inherited wealth.[21]

On the one hand, the WFN was, and is, instrumental to women's causes. By the year 2000, the network boasted ninety-four member funds and over $30 million in annual grantmaking.[22] During the COVID-19 pandemic, the WFN dedicated a multimillion-dollar Response, Recovery, and Resilience Collaborative Fund and set up 610 Women's Economic Mobility Hubs. These efforts extended housing and childcare to more than seven thousand children and provided job training to over nine thousand women.[23]

In a survey, 59 percent of women who received WFN grants said their projects would have been impossible without the support.[24]

On the other hand, given the WFN's uneven record on diversity and inclusion, it is questionable how much the WFN has mitigated society's inequities rather than mirroring them. The WFN also appears to be taking its cues from above rather than from below. It partners with the Bill and Melinda Gates Foundation, one of the largest charitable foundations in the world with a $53.3 billion endowment as of 2022.[25] While the Gates Foundation and its peer foundations have probably done much good for humanity,[26] they are not immune to criticism for violating the autonomy of grantees, voters, and taxpayers. "[Academics], activists, and the policy community live in a world where philanthropists are royalty—where philanthropic support is often the ticket to tackling big projects, making a difference, and maintaining one's livelihood," writes Frederick Hess, a political scientist and director of education policy studies at the American Enterprise Institute. The desire to remain in foundations' good graces imposes "an amiable conspiracy of silence" around touchy subjects that might offend donors.[27]

Proving that money is power, philanthropists have shaped not just individual SMOs, but entire *organizational fields*—arenas in which "participants take one another into account as they carry out interrelated activities."[28] An organizational field demarcates what activists consider legitimate behavior. For example, environmental foundations devised systems in the 1990s for certifying sustainable forests. A new Forest Stewardship Council would define responsible forestry practices and accredit inspectors to award an official stamp of approval on forest products. Grassroots activists subsequently started boycotting noncertified products and protesting against retailers that sold them. The Rainforest Action Network, a grassroots campaign cofounded by radical environmentalist Mike Roselle, was once preoccupied with lobbying the United Nations to halt deforestation in the Amazon and demanding that Brazil's president recognize Indigenous rights. Its best-known victory, in

1987, was convincing Burger King to cancel $31 million of beef contracts in environmentally sensitive Central America. Suddenly, with the creation of forest certification protocols, the Rainforest Action Network switched to urging consumers not to buy tropical hardwood unless it was "independently certified using the Forest Stewardship Council principles." As sociologist Tim Bartley explains, environmentalists' evolving market-based goals would have been unthinkable if foundations had not first established the forest certification *field*.[29] Activists thought they were acting autonomously, but in truth they were following the lead of powerful foundations.

Environmentalists' pivot from political lobbying to consumer awareness is a case of *mission drift*, where a movement strays from its initial objectives, often under explicit or subtle donor pressure.[30] Young SMOs, like the early WFN, are especially vulnerable to mission drift because they have not yet established a reliable funding base. The challenge, then, is to establish a funding base and then use your newfound financial capabilities to make good on your original aims. Historically, this has been easier said than done due to the compromises that securing start-up money often requires.

Activists have field-tested various approaches to paying the bills while staying true to their core missions. One approach is to prohibit donors from sitting on SMO boards. Since its founding in 1974, the Haymarket People's Fund has provided grants "to almost every major social justice movement in New England." In 2022, it distributed $904,000 to fifty-two groups working on issues ranging from anti-racism and education justice to housing rights and immigrant welfare.[31] Haymarket differs from other SMOs in one critical regard: donors to the Fund, who tend to be white and affluent, *do not* have a say in allocating money. Instead, the grantmaking panel consists of diverse grassroots volunteers who "are actively involved in working for change on a daily basis in their own communities and know where resources are needed the most."[32] Haymarket seeks not only to mold a just society, but also to embody that vision in the way it functions.

As sociologist Susan Ostrander details in her book *Money for Change*, Haymarket's innovative structure has helped to prevent some of the mission drift that befalls other SMOs with privileged people at the helm. However, it has also had some negative side effects. One member of Haymarket's grantmaking panel said of the relationship between donors and activists, "It feels like we're very separate. I feel like there's this god up there that drops the money, and we spend it. I've never met the donors."[33] Segregating donors from activists inadvertently produced a climate of secrecy: Activists aren't sure exactly where the money is coming from and feel like they must shoulder all the responsibility for running the fund. Donors likewise express feelings of estrangement from the people they want to assist.

Another option for avoiding mission drift is to simply refuse all outside donations, or at least those from dubious sources. In 2022, the Florida state legislature passed House Bill 1557, colloquially called the "Don't Say Gay" Bill, which banned public schools from having classroom discussions about gender identity and sexual orientation. This put pressure to respond on the Walt Disney Company, which operates many theme parks and resorts in Orlando, Florida. Disney CEO Bob Chapek waited weeks before speaking out against the legislation and promising to donate money to LGBTQ+ groups. When he finally did, some activists thought the gesture was too little, too late. The Human Right Campaign, America's largest LGBTQ+ civil rights organization, called out Chapek and refused the donation. Its press release said:

> The Human Rights Campaign will not accept this money from Disney until we see them build on their public commitment and work with LGBTQ+ advocates to ensure that dangerous proposals, like Florida's Don't Say Gay or Trans bill, don't become dangerous laws, and if they do, to work to get them off the books. . . . While Disney took a regrettable stance by choosing to stay silent amid political attacks against LGBTQ+ families in Florida—including hardworking families employed

by Disney—today they took a step in the right direction. But it was merely the first step.[34]

The Human Rights Campaign, being so well established, could afford to decline Disney's money on principle. But turning down funding is not a viable option for upstart social movements trying to get off the ground and claim their first victories. Money—*a lot* of money—is often necessary not just to win concessions, but also to prevent them from being rolled back.

Deferred Action for Childhood Arrivals, or DACA, is a policy that allows undocumented immigrants to remain in the United States and apply for work permits if they were brought to the country as children. Barack Obama enacted DACA in 2012, even though his administration had been on course to deport more non-citizens than any prior administration. Activists undoubtedly played a decisive role in making Obama more sympathetic to the plight of immigrants. After Congress failed to pass a comprehensive immigration reform bill called the DREAM Act in 2010, activists known as "Dreamers" delivered eighty-one thousand petitions to the Senate, staged rallies, and launched media campaigns featuring the personal narratives of brave Dreamers willing to risk deportation by telling their stories.[35] Two years later, DACA marked a triumph for the immigrant rights movement.

However, the fight was only just beginning. Republicans vowed to reverse Obama's policy and had their best shot when Donald Trump took office in 2016. Trump's plan to repeal DACA triggered lawsuits culminating in a Supreme Court case. Fighting to preserve DACA in the courts demanded enormous resources for legal expenses and mobilizing a new wave of nationwide protests. Businesses and private citizens scrambled to pay renewal fees for "DACAmented" people before October 5, 2017, when the Trump administration said it would stop processing applications. Massachusetts businesses pooled $65,000 for this purpose; Rhode Island residents chipped in $125,000; the Mission Asset Fund in San Francisco raised more than $2.5 million.[36]

These concerted efforts worked. The Supreme Court ruled on June 18, 2020, to block the rescission of DACA, and Joe Biden issued an executive order reinstating DACA in 2021. We can't compare this to any observable alternate universe where the immigration movement received fewer resources, but it is fair to surmise that DACA would have faced a steeper uphill battle without copious donations of money, time, and legal expertise to back up the earnest activism of Dreamers themselves. The well-funded, well-organized crusade to save DACA illustrates a general point made by sociologists J. Craig Jenkins and Abigail Halci: "In terms of addressing legal and political advocacy, professionalization and the movement philanthropy in which it is rooted have provided resources which have helped implement and ensure enforcement of many of the changes secured initially by grassroots protests."[37]

Dreamers had one major advantage that earlier generations of activists lacked: the internet. Funding a social movement without losing your soul has never been easier thanks to crowdfunding, which allows activists to raise money directly from the grassroots while reducing their reliance on elite donors. MoveOn.org first put political crowdfunding on the map by raising $250,000 in just five days soon after it began accepting credit card donations in 1999, to help elect Democratic candidates and later to support the anti-war movement in the wake of the 9/11 attacks. MoveOn then mobilized $58 million for Democrats in the 2004–6 election cycle, sealing its reputation as a fundraising powerhouse.[38] MoveOn's advocacy director took the group's crowdfunding model global, advising GetUp!, an Australian progressive movement, on building a similar a campaign. GetUp! now commands as much money as some mainstream political parties. It raised more than $12 million in 2018, mostly from donations of less than $100.[39] Crowdfunding has become a trusted weapon for grassroots movements and established political parties alike. Today, almost anyone can start a crowdfunding campaign using platforms such as GoFundMe, FundRazr, and Fundly. That said, making it succeed is another question altogether. For every campaign raking in millions, there are countless others that sputter out before meeting their modest targets of a few thousand, or even a few hundred, dollars. The next section will unpack the science of fruitful online crowdfunding. Your campaign might not become the next MoveOn or GetUp!, but the advice I lay out can put you in a better position to pay the bills of your movement.

CROWDFUNDING A MOVEMENT

As I write this book, immigrant rights, in the United States and elsewhere, are still under attack. The US Citizenship Act of 2021 would have undone many of Trump's restrictive policies on visas and border control, as well as creating a pathway to permanent residence for eleven million undocumented immigrants. That bill died in committee, however, forcing immigration advocates and their allies in Congress to regroup yet again. They set about crafting new legislation such as the American Dream and Promise Act, which was less comprehensive than the US Citizenship Act but would enshrine DACA into federal law. Activist groups scrambled to raise money for DACA recipients, who remained in legal limbo while the legislative process lumbered on. For example, the Coalition for Humane Immigrant Rights of Los Angeles (CHIRLA) posted the crowdfunding campaign depicted in figure 3.

Would you donate to CHIRLA's fundraiser? If so, how much? Let's do an experiment: Read the ad in figure 3 carefully, and then write down the amount you would give, from zero dollars to all the money you have in the bank. I promise not to judge you.

Whatever your decision, what do you think led you to make it? If you would readily give $10, $50, or even the full $495 to cover someone's DACA application fees, is it because the opportunity to "make dreams come true" fired you up, sending a rush of empathic hormones through your nervous system? Or did reading that DACA "remains the only protection that these young people have" fill you with a sense of urgency that you could only assuage by reaching for your credit card?

Conversely, suppose you (or your evil twin) would *not* donate to CHIRLA, or would donate very little. You might be stingy even

FIGURE 3: CHIRLA Crowdfunding Campaign

DACA TRUST FUND

You can make dreams come true! Help us protect thousands of young immigrants who depend on Deferred Action for Childhood Arrivals (DACA) to live and work freely in this country. As this pandemic looms above us, many of our DACAmented individuals have been hit hard by the loss of family members and income. Your donation will help DACAmented folks be able to obtain resources that can help them ahead.

After many challenges, the Deferred Action for Childhood Arrivals (DACA) program is back to its orginal state from 2012. The Dream and Promise Act of 2021 will ensure that DACA beneficiaries become legal permanent residents and eventually citizens of this country. While it passed the House of Representatives this past week, it is still not the law of the land. DACA remains the only protection that these young people have. The inability to pay the government fee of $495 can not be the barrier to their only available protection.

Help a DACA recipient by making a donation in support of their application fees!

With the impact of Covid on work and finances, it is difficult for DACA recipients to cover their application fees. Your gift today will help cover a portion or the full $495 the U.S. Department of Citizenship and Immigration Services (USCIS) charges to keep these young people from facing deportation.

Make a real difference with a doncation, big or small. Thank you for stepping in for immigrant youth!

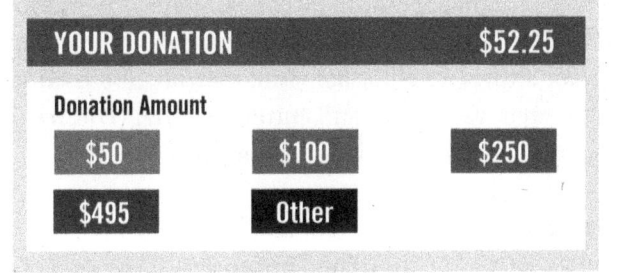

| YOUR DONATION | $52.25 |

Donation Amount

| $50 | $100 | $250 |
| $495 | Other | |

Adapted from https://www.chirla.org/get-involved/donate-support/trustfund.

despite having money to spare and agreeing with CHIRLA's goals. Perhaps you're reading this book beside the marble fireplace in your mansion, humming along to the *Hamilton* soundtrack ("Immigrants, we get the job done!") . . . but would *still* not pitch in to support undocumented immigrants. What about the ad could have turned you off? Was it CHIRLA's boldness to make $50 the default donation amount, or to preselect the option to tack on a $2.25 processing fee? "The audacity!" you scoff, indignant that activists would so brazenly try to squeeze every red cent from your hard-earned paycheck. Some tiny detail of the ad, even one as subtle as the boldface text, might have subliminally made you feel like someone was yelling at you. "Immigration police could be banging on an undocumented person's door *right now*," your subconscious thinks, "but three exclamation points in one ad are just too much for my exhausted neurons to process." I'm sure you've never spoken those words out loud, or even silently to yourself. If you're reading this book, then I assume no thought could be further from your sincere views.

However, scientists know that our brains tend to react to stimuli instinctively, beyond our full awareness, in ways that alter our altruistic and selfish behaviors.[40] Activists are wise to remember that, and to use this knowledge to their strategic advantage while running crowdfunding campaigns. Let's look at some recent social science on how to design a campaign that makes donors open their wallets instead of running for the hills. Much of this research has examined crowdfunding on popular platforms such as GoFundMe and Kickstarter. These platforms are commonly, though not always, used for activism; they are also used to raise money for creative projects and entrepreneurial ventures. Below, I've organized key findings into four themes:

- **Fundraising goals:** Finance scholars Saif Ullah and Yulin Zhou analyzed 27,117 crowdfunding projects, 33 percent of which ended up fully funded and 67 percent of which failed to meet their goals.[41] Corroborating other studies,[42] they found that successful projects, which reached their fundraising goals, requested $11,616 on average, whereas the failed projects asked for $95,333 on average. Ullah and Zhou interpreted this disparity to mean that inflated targets scare donors away. Asking for more money than donors think you need risks making you come across as incompetent or corrupt. Do your research on how much money you realistically need and then ask for that—no less, no more.
- **Audience and timing:** Unsurprisingly, friends and family often make the most generous donors. As we learned in chapter 1,

close-knit communities have stronger norms of reciprocity that can overcome temptations to free ride on other people's contributions. In one crowdfunding campaign, local investors (who also tended to be friends and family of the requester) gave $196 on average compared to $74 on average for more distant investors.[43] However, it's important not to limit your campaign only to friends and family, because there are many more people outside your personal network than in it. Although friends and family are more generous, donations from distant investors can eventually add up to more money than you receive from people you know. Target friends and family early to kickstart your campaign, and then expand your advertising to more far-flung audiences. Experimental evidence shows that later funders follow the lead of early funders.[44] Strangers don't normally give you the benefit of the doubt right away, but they will be more willing to support your campaign if others have already vouched for it. This is known as the "bandwagon effect" or "herding behavior."[45]

- **Length of the ad:** The evidence here is mixed. Ullah and Zhou found that each additional word in a project description is "detrimental" to funding outcomes because the length of the description affects the donors' first impressions: succinct, straightforward descriptions require less patience to read—they are more mind-friendly, to use a phrase from chapter 4. However, a different team of scholars found that a higher word count *increased* the odds of a campaign succeeding, theoretically because longer descriptions provide more information to potential backers.[46] Surprisingly, longer descriptions can improve funding rates even when the extra text centers on *risks* of the project. Apparently, donors appreciate thorough and honest details.[47] What should activists do with this competing evidence on description length? One approach is to tailor your ad to your target audience. If you are courting donors who you suspect might have short attention spans when reading text (workers juggling

multiple jobs, multitasking parents of young kids, people with less access to education), then keep your description short and sweet. If you are courting donors with graduate degrees and plenty of leisure time on their hands, go wild with elaborate descriptions.
- **Content and style of the ad:** Images and videos make fundraising ads more enticing than text alone,[48] especially if the images contain people. Business and information scholars Lauren Rhue and Lionel Robert Jr. used image classification software to analyze the emotions in people's facial expressions in thirty-two thousand GoFundMe campaigns.[49] They found that happy expressions raised more money than neutral or sad expressions. Interestingly, adding joyful text *reduced* contributions, suggesting that people react differently to emotions expressed in images versus text. Multiple studies have also shown that regularly updating your ad content is one of the most efficient ways to boost your campaign because it shows that you are actively engaged with your project.[50] In one study, projects with more than one update increased their odds of meeting their goals by 51.3 percent.[51]

Research on effective crowdfunding is in its infancy. There's still a lot we don't know about the subtle signals that crowdfunding ads send to would-be donors. Future studies might examine the effects of bold text, fonts, specific words, and other details. Nevertheless, the evidence we have so far is a great start. Try designing your next crowdfunding campaign using the best practices outlined above.

WHY FUNDING A SOCIAL MOVEMENT IS LIKE SELLING BREAKFAST CEREAL

We can unlock additional secrets on successful crowdfunding from the real pros at getting people to open their wallets: market researchers. "Hold on," a left-leaning reader of this book might interject. "Are you seriously recommending a capitalist solution to social injustices? Didn't Audre Lorde teach us that the master's tools will never dismantle the master's house?" I will grant that using market research tools to raise money for a social movement is not exactly a radical revolution. If you want to dismantle the master's house (i.e., overturn capitalism), this section will leave you unsatisfied. However, pending a revolution, I humbly assert that the proverbial master's house is actually a really nice house; the problem is that it has a master, and people don't have equal access to it. If activists can learn to wield the tools that for-profit companies routinely use (and occasionally abuse) to shake down consumers, then activists can redirect money into worthy causes instead of CEOs' bank accounts.

Profiteering market researchers are exceptionally eager to exploit cutting-edge statistical and experimental methods to gain a competitive edge. One of the most powerful tools in their arsenal is a *conjoint experiment*. If you live in an area with a supermarket, think about shopping in the cereal aisle. How do you make your selection from dozens of options? Until recently, cereal companies had no choice but to guess which attributes of their products moved the most merchandise. They would choose ingredients they hoped consumers would like, haphazardly slap a cute cartoon character on the box, ask an intern to write a product description, print the labels in an arbitrary font, and run some rudimentary supply-and-demand calculations to set a price.

Eventually, though, market research got more sophisticated. A cereal company with a decent marketing budget would run an experiment on test subjects, randomizing different product designs and then asking survey respondents to say how likely they were to purchase the products, and for how much. The trouble with this approach was that researchers couldn't tell *which* specific attributes—the ingredients, the image on the box, the price, or something else—drove consumers' choices. The is called the "compound treatment" problem. Maybe a consumer would buy the cereal because she loved its protein content, but she would have paid even more for it had the box displayed an adorable panda instead of a charismatic tiger. There was no way to know, because typical experiments bundled many attributes together, preventing market researchers from fine-tuning individual attributes to maximize profits.

A *conjoint* experiment improves on a typical experiment because it unbundles the attributes of a product. "Conjoint" means "joined together," referring here to joining multiple experiments into one. Researchers randomize not an entire cereal box, but *each attribute* they want to test. This works like a slot machine, where each reel is controlled by a separate random number generator determining which symbol (such as cherries, a bell, or a horseshoe) will appear to the gambler. Likewise, when subjects in a conjoint experiment evaluate how much they'd pay for hypothetical boxes of cereal, random number generators have already determined which ingredients, which cartoon character, which price, and so forth get displayed. For example, a subject is presented with a cereal containing ten grams of protein, selected at random from three possible values: one gram, five grams, or ten grams. This subject sees a box with a picture of a panda, but another subject might see a tiger, a frog, or a bunny—also displayed at random. By running the conjoint experiment on many people, researchers can infer which attribute values, on average, cause consumers to pay more for cereal, and then design their product accordingly. Not unlike cereal manufacturers, activists are in the sales business. Their "product" is a social movement, and their "customers" are prospective donors.

It wasn't long before political scientists repurposed the conjoint experiments developed by market researchers to study political phenomena, such as which attributes of electoral candidates (e.g., gender, experience, party) affect voter preferences or which attributes of immigrants (e.g., country of origin, education level, profession) affect the odds of a successful visa application.[52] Following suit, I used a conjoint experiment to test which attributes of social movements attract the most donations.[53]

I ran my experiment on 1,552 self-identified American Democrats who were otherwise representative of the national population.

I randomized different attributes of hypothetical Democratic social movements and asked respondents to say how much they would donate to each movement. Readers will recognize some of these attributes from previous chapters. They included the movement's priorities (ranging from highly mixed to very cohesive), its social media policy (that is, how much organizers control activist communication), its activities (how many protests activists are expected to attend per year), its dominant strategy (peaceful or violent), and its membership size (100, 1,000, or 5,000 members). Figure 4 shows a sample of what subjects saw on the survey.

I found that a movement whose main focus is electing Democrats brings in, on average, $5.56 more in donations per person contacted, compared with one whose members disagree on their priorities. This increase can add up to sizable returns for social movements with millions of donors. ActBlue, a nonprofit technology company that provides online fundraising services to Democratic electoral campaigns, collected more than $700 million in donations by the third quarter of 2019, with an average individual

FIGURE 4: Sample Vignette from the Experiment

	MOVEMENT 1	MOVEMENT 2
PRIORITIES	Members support other liberal causes, not only electing Democrats.	Electing Democrats is the main focus.
SOCIAL MEDIA POLICY	Movement leaders must pre-approve any posts about the movement.	Members are free to post whatever they want.
ACTIVITIES	Members are encouraged to attend one protest per year.	The norm is attending monthly protests.
STRATEGY	Lawful, nonviolent tactics.	Violent when deemed necessary.
SIZE	1,000 members.	1,000 members.

contribution of just $30.50—an amount comparable to the average donation among subjects in my study ($37.46).[54] In contrast, subjects were extremely reluctant to donate to violent movements: "I WOULD NOT WANT TO BE A PART OF ANY MOVEMENT THAT SANCTIONS VIOLENCE," wrote one respondent in the comments section of the survey. The results of my conjoint experiment thus complement the evidence in chapters 3 and 4 on the benefits of peaceful protest and cohesive coalitions. They show that nonviolence and cohesion are *lucrative* activist strategies, besides being prudent tactics in general. Other attributes of social movements, such as size and commitment expectations, did not have as big an effect on intended donations.

USE PSYCHOLOGY TO BOOST YOUR BOTTOM LINE

To many activists on the frontlines, it is self-evident why their causes matter. Someone who has spent years pursuing humane immigration laws, free elections, or clean oceans doesn't need to be convinced to devote more time, money, or both to making that change happen. Casual donors, however, may need extra encouragement before giving to a cause. In this last section of the chapter, we'll check out some insights from psychology to boost your movement's bottom line.

Make Donors Sweat

For most mortals, running the Boston Marathon in 2:58:46 would be a major achievement. But the iconic race was just one leg of an epic journey for Rob Pope of Liverpool, England. Pope quit his job as a veterinarian to run across the United States more than four times (a distance of about 15,600 miles, or 600 marathons), following the route traveled by the title character of the movie *Forest Gump*.[55] He recruited donors to sponsor his trek and raised roughly £38,000 for organizations supporting world peace, women's rights, the homeless, the environment, and endangered species. Pope was inspired by his mother, who died of cancer. Before she passed away, she asked Pope to "Do one thing in your life that makes a difference." Running for worthy causes was Pope's way of honoring his promise. It was a deeply personal, 422-day, thoroughly exhausting form of activism.

Could Pope have raised tens of thousands of pounds for charity *without* putting himself through that physical ordeal? Possibly, but empirical evidence suggests that he would have been less motivated to fundraise and less generous without the *martyrdom effect*. The martyrdom effect refers to how people become more altruistic when they have to suffer to raise money—either because the discomfort makes them ascribe greater symbolic meaning to their contributions, or because experiencing pain brings people psychologically closer to those facing hardship. Behavioral scientists Christopher Olivola and Eldar Shafir conducted an experiment to test whether people would donate more to charity if they participated in an easy event (a picnic) or a strenuous event (a five-mile run).[56] The charity in question delivered relief to victims of a tsunami in Southeast Asia. Participants who worked up a sweat at the run gave significantly more money on average ($23.87) than those who kicked back at the picnic ($13.88). In a supplemental experiment, subjects donated almost a dollar more on average if they first submerged their hands in painfully cold water for 60 seconds, compared to subjects in a control group. The upshot? It's better to host a foot race or an obstacle course than a picnic or a bake sale for your next fundraiser. Take it from Rob Pope: no pain, no gain (for a good cause).

The martyrdom effect demonstrates the power of psychology to shape people's giving patterns. I'll highlight three other psychological strategies that can boost the bottom line of your social movement: involve stakeholders in your fundraising campaign, identify clear "victims," and frame campaigns around salient historical events.

Involve Stakeholders

When Mike Krzyzewski, the legendary Duke basketball coach, took over as head coach of the US men's national basketball team in 2005, he knew he'd have to think outside the box to carry his athletes to Olympic glory in Beijing in 2008. Team USA had been struggling to repeat the success of the fabled "Dream Team" that brought home gold in 1992. Now, the country needed a "Redeem Team." Bronze medals at the 2004 Olympics and the 2006 world championships were especially embarrassing for NBA stars on the squad, who were accustomed to fans worshipping them like gods. Apparently, the individual standouts that the USA Basketball governing committee cobbled together from different professional teams did not play *as a team* while wearing the stars and stripes. At international competitions, their rivals had noticeably more experience practicing together. Players from Argentina, Lithuania, and Greece navigated the court in balletic synchrony, and their egos didn't clash. Krzyzewski (or "Coach K," as players called him) resolved to mold Team USA into a unit worthy of the name "team." He wouldn't suppress players' egos, but rather put those egos to work for the nation. Any coach could fill a playbook with, well, plays. Coach K had the wisdom to also pack his playbook with strategies for building esprit de corps *off* the court.

Besides the standard weight sessions, drills, and scrimmages, summer training camp in Las Vegas featured a busy schedule of bonding exercises and inspirational speeches. One memorable day, the towering athletes filed into a conference room, greeted by a decorated Green Beret accompanied by a group of wounded warriors, including Major Scotty Smiley. When Smiley was serving in Mosul during the Iraq War, a car bomb exploded and shot shrapnel through his eyes and skull. Maimed but indomitable, Smiley continued serving as the army's first blind active-duty officer. Addressing his players, Coach K, himself an army veteran, underscored Smiley's sacrifice for his brothers in arms: "All of a sudden, you recognize that there is a car bomb coming toward your unit, which might take out your unit. What would you do? What would you do? What he did was stay above, and he took out that car bomb, and as a result, helped save the men in his unit."[57] As captured in the 2022 documentary *The Redeem Team*, the normally macho basketball stars were visibly touched by the story, tears welling in their eyes. The flag on the shoulder of their uniform took on a deeper meaning. Team USA boarded the plane to Beijing physically and mentally prepared to strive for a higher cause—to do their nation proud and honor the sacrifices of heroes like Smiley. After clinching a redemptive gold medal, Coach K brought back Smiley in subsequent years to motivate new crops of players. Team USA went on to win gold at the next three Olympics.

In *The Science of Giving*, social psychologists Rebecca Ratner, Min Zhao, and Jennifer Clarke conjecture that people will contribute more to a cause if they respect someone who has a personal stake in that cause.[58] Under such circumstances, *not* contributing makes people feel guilty about dishonoring the stakeholder's experience. To back up this theory, the researchers showed experimental subjects a public service announcement. In one version, actor Cicely Tyson mentioned losing her sister to lung cancer. In another version, actor Brooke Shields warned about the health risks of smoking without mentioning any personal links to the cause. Subjects who saw the Cicely Tyson ad were more likely to send a card to their friends asking them to quit smoking, compared to subjects who saw the Brooke Shields ad. Even though Tyson herself did not suffer from smoking-related illness, her close relationship to an ill person elicited sympathy—and action—from viewers.

Likewise, Major Smiley was not directly involved in the sport of basketball, but he nevertheless had a personal stake in the success of the Redeem Team. His willingness to sacrifice for his nation compelled the players to bring their A game to the Olympics in the name of national pride. The guilt from slacking off and failing to win the gold—of letting a wounded warrior down—would have been unbearable. Coach K could not have instilled this commitment on his own. It took someone like Smiley, with his poignant personal story, to trigger a game-changing psychological response.

By extension, involving stakeholders in your fundraising campaign can move donors to give more time, money, and effort. Seeking pledges for an environmental cause? Invite a nurse to your fundraiser to speak about treating patients with pollution-induced asthma. Soliciting donors to underwrite a protest against mass incarceration? Publicize the testimonies of parents with incarcerated children. Of course, ask for the stakeholders' consent before using their stories. There is a fine line between strategizing and tokenizing.

Identify a Clear "Victim"

The moral philosopher Peter Singer articulated one of the most famous thought experiments in applied ethics:

> On your way to work, you pass a small pond. On hot days, children sometimes play in the pond, which is only about knee-deep. The weather's cool today, though, and the hour is early, so you are surprised to see a child splashing about in the pond. As you get closer, you see that it is a very young child, just a toddler, who is flailing about, unable to stay upright or walk out of the pond. You look for the parents or babysitter, but there is no one else around. The child is unable to keep his head above the water for more than a few seconds at a time. If you don't wade in and pull him out, he seems likely to drown. Wading in is easy and safe, but you will ruin the new shoes you bought only a few days ago, and get your suit wet and muddy. By the time you hand the child over to someone responsible for him, and change your clothes, you'll be late for work. What should you do?[59]

Singer's question, "What would you do?" is probably easier for you to answer than Coach K's question of whether you would leap onto a car bomb to protect your fellow soldiers. Even if you would not immediately risk your own life in a spontaneous act of valor, maybe you would not hesitate to sacrifice something as trivial as your shoes to save a drowning child.

If you *would* wade into the pond, would you also donate money to save a child on the other side of the world—one of the ten million who, according to the UNICEF figures that Singer cites, die each year from poverty-related, preventable causes like malaria, diarrhea, and malnutrition? GiveWell, a nonprofit that assesses the cost-effectiveness of charities, estimates that $4,500 could save a life in Guinea by funding a mosquito net distribution program through the Against Malaria Foundation.[60] Would you donate even a portion of that amount? Singer dares the rich and not-so-rich among us to reflect on all of the discretionary purchases we make in our daily lives: lattes, restaurant meals, concerts, trendy clothing. Added up, that money could be put to more ethical—i.e., life-saving and life-enhancing—uses. Singer doesn't mince words: "Is it possible that by choosing to spend your money on such things rather than contributing to an aid agency, you are leaving a child to die, a child you could have saved?" Your geographic proximity to a dying child, he maintains, is inconsequential.

I don't bring up Singer's thought experiment to guilt-trip you. Instead, I am interested in *why* more people do not donate to urgent causes and how activists can surmount psychological barriers to giving. One reason why people seem so ready to rescue a child drowning right in front of them yet timid about donating to children's charities is that the pond scenario has a clear victim that you know your actions will help. In the split second it takes for you to decide you'll wade into the pond, your mind can imagine hugging the child, seeing the relief on the child's face, and hearing the gratitude in the parents' voices. But if you send an electronic payment to the typical charity, you have little idea of where that money goes. It could pay for a mosquito net that protects a child from malaria, but maybe the net will wind up being used instead as a fishing net or a wedding dress (as has been known to happen).[61] Worse, your donation could pay for the holiday trip of an NGO bureaucrat or even get captured by a corrupt official. The uncertainty of where your money goes deters you from giving.

Similar to involving stakeholders, pinpointing a clear beneficiary of your campaign can encourage generosity. Psychologists call this the *identifiable "victim" effect*. I put "victim" in quotes because people who experience adversity often reject the label as disempowering. Some find the very concept of charity demeaning and tarnished by saviorism.[62] At the same time, evidence shows that victim narratives are extremely powerful. Behavioral scientists Cynthia Cryder and George Loewenstein cite Procter and Gamble's 2006 marketing campaign for Pampers disposable diapers.[63] Called "1 Pack = 1 Vaccine," the collaboration with UNICEF promised consumers that each sale would deliver a tetanus vaccine to a specific baby. This campaign significantly out-earned another campaign that used the slogan "1 pack will help eradicate newborn tetanus globally." The second campaign was less effective because it didn't allow consumers to imagine their dollars going directly to a baby in need—the equivalent of the child drowning in a pond. Piles of studies back up this anecdote:[64] College students who are asked to share any portion of ten dollars share more when they know the recipient's name, hometown, major, and hobbies. Physicians provide more attentive care when treating individual patients as opposed to writing policies for whole populations of patients. People attribute greater intelligence and personality to a single animal than to larger groups of animals—hence why a lone ant crawling across your picnic blanket is cute, whereas a full-on ant attack is upsetting. Subjects donated nearly twice as much to Oxfam when the fundraising ad included more detailed information on who would benefit from the money and how.

In short, naming "victims" and stating precisely how funds will support them can raise more money than making vague appeals for donations to a cause. Ideally, fundraising teams will include members of the beneficiary community, rather than activists unilaterally dropping in to "save" people. Inclusivity and collaboration can go a long way toward avoiding saviorism, while still allowing activists to harness the power of the identifiable "victim" effect.

Frame Campaigns Around Historical Events

Movements are fighting for police reform around the world, from Black Lives Matter in the United States to the #EndSARS campaign in Nigeria (SARS refers to the notoriously abusive Special Anti-Robbery Squad). These efforts are not just altruistic; they are also self-interested. That's because activists themselves often endure police repression in the form of tear gas, rubber bullets, arrests, and even heavy artillery. In 2020, Ugandan security forces killed forty-five people during unrest surrounding the detention of opposition leader Bobi Wine.[65] That same year, French police beat protesters who were trying to stop them from dismantling a migrant encampment.[66] Local civilian police forces have become more militarized over time.[67] Native Americans defending their water rights against the Dakota Access Pipeline in 2017 faced "an array of para-military police vehicles including BearCats, Humvees, and mine-resistant ambush protected vehicles."[68] In 2020, Black Lives Matter protesters were met with National Guard soldiers in fatigues. Crowd control becomes deadly when troops who are trained to use maximum force against a foreign enemy fail to show restraint against domestic demonstrators.[69]

Raising enough money to keep police reform movements afloat is a matter of life and death. The trouble is, public enthusiasm for police reform usually spikes after a dramatic incident but then wanes before real reform can occur. In Minneapolis, where an officer murdered George Floyd, the city council initially seemed responsive to protester demands to defund the police. However, the council's resolution to "end policing as we know it" soon collapsed once public opinion shifted.[70] Less than a year after the French interior minister announced a probe into "shocking" police clashes, French lawmakers passed a bill expanding police powers.[71] In otherwise progressive cities, mayoral candidates have run, and won, with tough-on-crime platforms.[72] How can activists sustain public investment—both monetary and moral—in their reform work after the shock of a violent incident fades into memory?

Research that I conducted with my fellow political scientists Kai Thaler and Eric Mosinger suggests that activists can sustain support for police reform, and potentially for other causes, by applying the psychology of *historical frames*. A frame, generally speaking, is a way of interpreting events in our lives. Your therapist might advise you to frame a misfortune as an opportunity: you can choose to interpret getting laid off from work as an excuse to finally apply for a dream job. Analogously, my coauthors and I hypothesized that activists could get people to donate more money to organizations that promote police reform by framing police violence as not just a flash in the pan, but as a chronic problem across history. We tested this hypothesis by running a survey experiment in Chile, which in 2019 and 2020 experienced nationwide uprisings about a host of economic and political grievances. During the protests, an estimated thirty-one people died, three thousand were injured, and twenty thousand were arrested. Eyewitnesses overwhelmingly blamed the *carabineros*, Chile's national law enforcement.[73] The crackdowns echoed repression under the brutal regime of General Augusto Pinochet in the 1970s and 1980s.

Would reminding Chileans that history was repeating itself make them more willing to invest in police reform efforts, even months after the most intense police clashes had subsided? To find out, we told some survey respondents, "During the recent uprisings, the *carabineros* committed many acts of violence against unarmed protesters, including beating, blinding, and even killing some protesters." Other respondents saw the same message but with a historical frame tacked on the end: "During the recent uprisings, the *carabineros* committed many acts of violence against unarmed protesters, including beating, blinding, and even killing some protesters, reminding some people of violence committed by security forces under the Pinochet regime." We then said, "Imagine you had 40,000 pesos you were planning to donate to a cause or causes you care about. How much, if any, money would you donate to the Comisión Chilena de Derechos Humanos, which focuses on documenting and advocating for accountability for state violence and human rights violations?" We found that the historical frame increased intended donations among left-wing Chileans and older Chileans who had experienced the Pinochet dictatorship firsthand.[74] Right-wing and younger Chileans did not respond as strongly to the historical frame, probably because they were either not going to support police reform anyway (in the case of right-wingers) or had no personal memory of suffering under Pinochet (in the case of young people). Our results indicate that historical frames can boost fundraising, but that it's important to direct frames at people with whom they are likely to resonate.

Fundraising is inconvenient at best, soul crushing at worst. To finance your activist campaign without losing sight of your core mission, keep these evidence-backed tips in mind:

- Seek donations from large foundations if you must, but crowdsourcing is a better option for maintaining political autonomy and grassroots relationships.
- Successful crowdfunding ads have:
  - realistic goals
  - images of happy people
  - frequent updates
  - early buy-in from friends and family
  - shorter descriptions, unless you are confident that your audience has a long attention span (like if you are writing a targeted campaign for donors who are already interested in your cause)
- Movements that are nonviolent and have cohesive goals draw more donations than those that are violent and can't agree on their goals.
- Make donors sweat—host a running race for a fundraiser instead of a bake sale. People are more generous when they must suffer for the opportunity to give.
- Involve stakeholders in your campaign and identify clear "victims."
- Remind potential donors how current injustices repeat past injustices, while staying mindful of how historical frames resonate with different audiences.

CONCLUSION

ACTIVISTS ARE NOT ROBOTS

Something that makes protests so thrilling is that they tend to occur in close succession, building energy until their combined power upends the world as we know it. In that regard, protests are like a series of seismic disturbances under the sea, merging to form an awesome tsunami: A street vendor in Tunisia self-immolated in 2010, and suddenly the Arab Spring swept North Africa and the Middle East. Within days after the French Revolution of 1848, popular revolts ricocheted throughout Europe in what became known as the Springtime of the Peoples. Prior to that, the American Revolution of 1765–91 unfolded within a cascade of upheavals, including the Haitian Revolution of 1791–1804 and the French Revolution of 1789–99. Protests are not, typically, isolated events. Rather, to quote political scientist Kurt Weyland, they "make waves."[1]

One theory for why protests become wave-like will sound obvious to anyone reading this book: protests are inspiring. A disaffected Egyptian sees a viral video of demonstrations in Tunisia and starts imagining the possibilities of a democratic revolution at home. A teenager in suburban Texas gets fired up watching Greta Thunberg address the United Nations and decides to start an environmental movement at her high school. Weyland, the political scientist, recounts how activists throughout history have used heuristics, or cognitive shortcuts, to learn from the precedents of mass movements elsewhere: Tunisia was the blueprint for revolution in Egypt, France provided a template for politics in nineteenth-century Prussia, Occupy Wall Street spun off into Occupy London and Occupy Nigeria, and so on. This learning process explains why protests, strikes, and democratic transitions become contagious.[2]

But mass uprisings, as dramatic as they might be, are not the end of the story. This book is concerned with what waves of contention leave in their wake: How healthy will Egyptian democracy be many decades removed from the Arab Spring? What will policing practices look like generations after Black Lives Matter mobilized twenty-six million people? Will school walkouts impact environmental policies in time to prevent irreversible climate change? I mentioned in the book's introduction that protests worldwide are failing at record rates. Gaze back at social movements from the past, and you will notice more setbacks than triumphs. An overlooked reason for this discouraging trend is that historically, protesters have had less information on how to win than their opponents.

Weyland points out that most revolutionaries behave rashly, springing into action at the first provocation. They are like my students pleading "How can we sit in this classroom staring at datasets when there's a struggle in the streets right now?" In contrast, counterrevolutionaries *are* studying datasets, as well as consulting political advisors and reading history books about how other leaders managed to suppress rebellions. They spend months, even years, meticulously plotting ways to restore order. This method demands a degree of patience that activists can seldom afford. A dictator who sees a revolution break out in a neighboring country might be tempted to crack down on domestic demonstrators immediately, but aides advise him (most dictators are men) to bide his time and monitor public opinion until the perfect moment to strike. Even monarchs, not usually known for their humility, deferred to experts while crafting their responses to nineteenth-century European insurrections:

> While [King Friedrich Wilhelm IV of Prussia] sought to project unassailable authority in public, behind closed doors he was far from enforcing conformity and allowed for surprisingly strong and direct criticism. In fact, he often solicited candid assessments and independent advice from his confidants, who embraced divergent viewpoints, offered conflicting counsel, and frequently "pushed" the monarch directly.[3]

Consequently, as revolutions diffuse across cities and countries "like a raging torrent," counterrevolutions transpire slowly "through a long trickle of suppression, taking hold first here, then there...."[4] Revolutionaries, as a group, are passionate and act from the gut; counterrevolutionaries are methodical and act according to empirical evidence on which tactics have worked before. This caution gives counterrevolutionaries the strategic advantage and may be why protests that initially show so much promise frequently produce disappointing results in the long run.

I wrote this book to shift the informational advantage to activists who might not have the luxury of poring over data, reading stacks of history books, and hiring aides. The preceding chapters offered a quick-and-dirty overview of scientific research on how to win campaigns for social and environmental justice. Consider me your personal strategist.

LIMITATIONS OF THIS BOOK

I am confident that the peer-reviewed evidence I've laid out represents some of the most reliable information that exists on effective and ineffective protest tactics. However, as an activist *and* a scholar, I am acutely aware that models and equations are not the final word on the best way to protest.

One caveat to everything in this book is that statistical models are great for estimating *average* effects but cannot perfectly predict whether a given tactic will work in a particular situation. To some extent, protesting is always a roll of the dice. We saw plenty of evidence in chapter 4 that cohesive protest demands are more persuasive than mixed demands, but there is a non-zero chance that mixing demands will work for you. Analogously, a clinical trial can confirm that a drug cures an illness on average across thousands of patients, but that drug isn't guaranteed to cure *you*. Activists must avoid the pitfall of taking such uncertainty as license to simply wing it. Rejecting science will only lead activists back to where they began, in the dark about which tactics to choose and at a serious disadvantage against their calculating rivals. This would be like snubbing all medicine because you once experienced negative side effects from a pill.

Another caveat to what I've written in these pages is that science cannot definitively answer questions of morality. Experiments clearly indicate that violent protests cause backlash, and yet, as we saw with the saga of Omar Wasow's study in chapter 3, admonishing protesters to lay down their bricks and stop looting stores can sound like unfairly blaming the victim when protesters are themselves on the receiving end of violence. As Wasow proposed, an "eye for an eye" in response to repression may not be strategic, but it may be moral. Occasionally, the most effective tactics according to the evidence are not the ones that activists deem ethically acceptable or "authentic." The philosopher Charles Taylor acknowledged that the difference between right and wrong is "not a matter of dry calculation" but is "anchored in our feelings." He concludes, "Morality has, in a sense, a voice within."[5] Keep this in mind before lecturing your comrades on "optimizing" their activism with science. Although intellectual study has played an important role in social movements throughout history, the Indigenous rights activist and Nobel Peace Prize laureate Rigoberta Menchú cautions bookish types against condescending to activists with other kinds of skills: "Before, everyone used to think that a leader had to be someone who knew how to read, write, and prepare documents. . . . 'You peasants are stupid, you don't read or study.' And the peasants told them: 'You can go to hell with your books. We know you don't make a revolution with books, you make it through struggle.'"[6]

It might be true that you can't make a revolution only with books. But books (and articles) can be valuable complements to activists' experiential knowledge. To repeat a refrain from the introduction, just because you are close to something doesn't mean you understand all of its complexities. Astrophysicist and science communicator Neil deGrasse Tyson reminds us that the scientific method was invented in the first place to guard against our biased intuitions about how the world works. "If you show up at a conference and the best evidence for your research is that you saw it happen, we will show you the exit door," he quips.[7] Rest assured, embracing a data-driven approach to protest doesn't mean losing your empathy. The philosopher Bertrand Russell wrote that the mark of a civilized person is the ability to look at a column of numbers and weep.

I HAVE THE TOOLS; NOW WHAT SHOULD I BUILD?

Congratulations! You have a full toolbox to build a winning social movement. But what kind of movement should you build? Now for a final caveat. Science can help activists choose effective tactics, but it cannot decide for us which causes to support. This book lent you an arsenal of data-backed strategies, but where should you direct them? Toward saving the whales? Raising wages? Ending racism? Abolishing nuclear weapons? Safeguarding democracy? Time and resources are limited, so unfortunately you may need to prioritize.

Data can only partially answer the question of how to "do good better."[8] Organizations like GiveWell calculate how many lives are saved or enhanced per dollar donated to various charities, but those calculations are mute about whose lives matter most or which aspects of well-being should receive more weight. You may find the very idea of placing a dollar value on life and well-being off-putting. Nevertheless, "effective altruists" pride themselves on dispassionate giving and activism in order to make the biggest positive impact. They don't do what most of us do, which is default to combatting the most visible or personal problems—homelessness in your city, underpaid teachers at your child's school, the cancer that afflicted a close relative, a child drowning in a pond directly in front of you. Instead, effective altruists apply four objective criteria for choosing which problems should receive their attention: *scale* (how much the problem affects lives in the short and long terms), *neglectedness* (how many resources are already going toward the problem), *tractability* (how easy it is to measure progress toward a solution), and *personal fit* (how likely you, specifically, are to make a big difference on this issue). Based on these criteria and crunching some numbers, the philosopher and effective altruist par excellence William MacAskill identifies the following high-priority causes: extreme poverty, US criminal justice reform, international labor mobility, factory farming, climate change, and "other global catastrophic risks" including nuclear war, pandemics, and bioterrorism.[9] If you aren't devoting your activism to one of those causes, you could "do better," according to utilitarian calculations.

However, critics worry that this extreme brand of applied utilitarianism precludes solidarity, stinks of saviorism, and breeds zealotry. Maybe, counters journalist Larissa MacFarquhar, we *should* have a greater moral responsibility to defend our own communities, nations, or families as opposed to complete strangers.[10] Perhaps we should follow our hearts and not let numbers dictate how we go about our activism. To do otherwise, contends MacFarquhar, runs so counter to evolutionary social norms as to be suspicious, and even repulsive—in short, not fully human. Peter Singer, who wrote the famous thought experiment about the kid drowning in the pond (see chapter 5) and who inspired many effective altruists, complicated his own ethical prescriptions by rushing to nurse his mother when she fell ill with Alzheimer's disease; he might have saved more lives by redirecting money from his mother's care to the Against Malaria Foundation. Even for this poster child of utilitarianism, the primordial drive to care for "one's own" was overpowering. The philosopher Bernard Williams said about Singer, "One of the reasons his approach is so popular is that it reduces all moral puzzlement to a formula. You remove puzzlement and doubt and conflict of values, and it's in the scientific spirit. People seem to think it will all add up, but it never does, because humans never do."[11]

Only you can ultimately decide how to channel your activism. You might let utilitarianism guide you, or you might turn to alternative philosophies or the teachings of your religion. But once you do choose your cause, I hope the advice in this book can help you advance that cause more effectively. Protest and social movements have long been the last resort for people to advocate for themselves and others when formal routes to power, such as voting or running for office, are closed to them. However, advocating is not enough. To truly achieve justice, advocates must win. Armed with an understanding of what strategies broadly work, all that's left to do is *put that knowledge to work* for the issues you care about.

ACKNOWLEDGMENTS

This book opened with a confession: I am a professional scientist and an amateur activist. I recognize the boldness of writing a book about making social movements succeed when I have spent most of my life outside of them. I am grateful to the veteran activists who welcomed me into their communities, as both a researcher and an aspiring ally. Academics and other "elites" have not always been kind to grassroots activists. Too often, we have failed to take them seriously or hijacked their movements. But interacting with protesters and organizers while researching this book made me optimistic that scholars and activists can make amends, share resources, and learn from each other. I have been fortunate to meet several generous, patient activists who let me into their worlds. I hope this book will forge stronger links between the ivory tower and people power.

I thank the friends and colleagues who nudged me out of the ivory tower and encouraged me to write my first book for a general audience. Eric Mosinger suffered through innumerable rough drafts and steered me around intellectual obstacles. Julie Dolan connected me with the fabulous literary agent Jennifer Thompson at Nordlyset. Jennifer was instrumental in finding my manuscript a home at Beacon, where my editor, Haley Lynch, guided it to publication with the utmost expertise and enthusiasm. It is uncool in academia to say that writing one's book was anything but torture, but writing this book was a joy at every stage with Haley as my coach, cheerleader, and sounding board. Thanks also to Molly Woodward for copyediting.

I incubated this project in a new class that I taught at Macalester College, "Protest Hacking," which I developed with a grant from the Mellon Foundation. Macalester has a storied history of student activism. One thing that attracted me to my job was learning that student protesters had occupied the president's office the year before I applied; what better place to study activism than in the heat of the action? Teaching "Protest Hacking" to a group of passionate, politically engaged undergraduates—especially in the wake of the George Floyd uprisings, which unfolded just down the road from campus—offered inspiration and healthy pushback against my wonkier ideas or problematic assumptions about how activism works in the trenches. I thank the entire class for unforgettable discussions and feedback on my drafts: Celia D'Agostino, Fitz Fitzpatrick, Tsion Hatte, Life Kunene, Gustavo Marchant Allende, Ally Mueller, Lena Pak, Joseph Polyak, Alessandra Rosa Policarpo, and Ellie Spangler.

I wrote much of this book during a sabbatical fellowship at Sciences Po Bordeaux. I extend my gratitude to the Franco-American Fulbright Commission and my Sciences Po hosts for their financial and moral support throughout those nine months. I conducted the core empirical research for chapter 4 during a previous sabbatical fellowship at the Notre Dame Institute for Advanced Study. Thanks to my NDIAS cohort, facilitators, and research assistants.

This book and the years of scholarship on which it is based would not have been possible without the career-long mentorship of Pierre Englebert, as well as the love, humor, and encouragement of my partner, Eric Sammuli, and the rest of my family.

READING GUIDE

Tips and Inspiration for Activists by Activists

Stacey Abrams, *Our Time Is Now: Power, Purpose, and the Fight for a Fair America* (New York: Picador, 2021).

Saul D. Alinksy, *Rules for Radicals: A Practical Primer for Realistic Radicals* (New York: Vintage Books, 1971).

adrienne maree brown, *Emergent Strategy: Shaping Change, Changing Worlds* (Chico, CA: AC Press, 2017).

Alicia Garza, *The Purpose of Power: How We Come Together When We Fall Apart* (New York: One World, 2020).

Amika George, *Make It Happen: How to Be an Activist* (New York: HarperCollins, 2021).

Vanessa Holburn, *How to Be an Activist: A Practical Guide to Organising, Campaigning and Making Change Happen* (London: Robinson, 2020).

In This Together Media, *Nevertheless, We Persisted: 48 Voices of Defiance, Strength, and Courage* (New York: Ember, 2018).

Greg Jobin-Leeds and AgitArte, *When We Fight We Win! Twenty-First-Century Social Movements and the Activists That Are Transforming Our World* (New York: The New Press, 2016).

Maureen Johnson, ed., *How I Resist: Activism and Hope for a New Generation* (New York: Wednesday Books, 2018).

Nick Licata, *Becoming a Citizen Activist: Stories, Strategies & Advice for Changing Our World* (New York: Penguin Random House, 2015).

Courtney E. Martin, *Do It Anyway: The Next Generation of Activists* (Boston: Beacon Press, 2010).

Elizabeth McKenna and Hahrie Han, *Groundbreakers: How Obama's 2.2 Million Volunteers Transformed Campaigning in America* (New York: Oxford University Press, 2014).

Hillary Rettig, *The Lifelong Activist: How to Change the World Without Losing Your Way* (New York: Lantern Books, 2006).

Sophia Rückriegel and Kilian Rückriegel, *How to Be a Social Activist: How to Play, Launch, and Support Social Change in Your Community and Our World* (New York: Geiger & Weis, 2022).

The Ruckus Society, *Action Strategy: A How-To Guide*, https://ruckus.org/training-manuals/the-action-strategy-guide (2000).

Randy Shaw, *The Activist's Handbook: Winning Social Change in the 21st Century* (Berkeley: University of California Press, 2013).

Micah White, *The End of Protest: A New Playbook for Revolution* (Toronto: Afred A. Knopf Canada, 2016).

Alice Wong, *Year of the Tiger: An Activist's Life* (New York: Vintage Books, 2022).

NOTES

INTRODUCTION

1. Eric Mosinger et al., "Civil Resistance in the Shadow of the Revolution: Historical Framing in Nicaragua's Sudden Uprising," *Comparative Politics* 54, no. 2 (2022): 253–77, https://doi.org/10.5129/001041522X16281740895086.

2. Max Fisher, "Even as Iranians Rise Up, Protests Worldwide Are Failing at Record Rates," *New York Times*, September 30, 2022, https://www.nytimes.com/2022/09/30/world/middleeast/iran-protests-haiti-russia-china.html.

3. Nicholas Eubank and Adriane Fresh, "Enfranchisement and Incarceration After the 1965 Voting Rights Act," *American Political Science Review* 116, no. 3 (2022): 1–16, https://doi.org/10.1017/S0003055421001337.

4. Helen Pluckrose and James Lindsay, *Cynical Theories: How Activist Scholarship Made Everything about Race, Gender, and Identity—and Why This Harms Everybody* (Durham, NC: Pitchstone Publishing, 2020), 115.

5. Samuel Brannen et al., *The Age of Mass Protests: Understanding an Escalating Global Trend*, Center for Strategic & International Studies Report, March 2, 2020, https://www.csis.org/analysis/age-mass-protests-understanding-escalating-global-trend.

6. Deborah G. Martin, Susan Hanson, and Danielle Fontaine, "What Counts as Activism? The Role of Individuals in Creating Change," *Women's Studies Quarterly* 35, nos. 3/4 (2007): 79.

7. Lisa Mueller, *Political Protest in Contemporary Africa* (New York: Cambridge University Press, 2018).

8. Naomi Oreskes, *Why Trust Science?* (Princeton, NJ: Princeton University Press, 2019), 132.

9. On tactical identities, see James M. Jasper, "The Emotions of Protest: Affective and Reactive Emotions in and around Social Movements," *Sociological Forum* 13, no. 3 (1998): 415, https://www.jstor.org/stable/684696.

10. William MacAskill, *What We Owe the Future* (New York: Basic Books, 2022).

11. Howard White, "The Twenty-First Century Experimenting Society: The Four Waves of the Evidence Revolution," *Palgrave Communications* 5, no. 47 (2019): 1–7, https://www.nature.com/articles/s41599-019-0253-6.

12. Sasha Issenberg, *The Victory Lab: The Secret Science of Winning Campaigns* (New York: Crown, 2012).

13. Jonas Hjort et al., "How Research Affects Policy: Experimental Evidence from 2,150 Brazilian Municipalities," NBER Working Paper Series no. 25941 (2019): 1–59, http://www.nber.org/papers/w25941.

14. Dean Karlan and Jacob Appel, *More Than Good Intentions: How a New Economics Is Helping to Solve Global Poverty* (New York: Dutton, 2011).

15. William Easterly, *The Tyranny of Experts: Economists, Dictators, and the Forgotten Rights of the Poor* (New York: Basic Books, 2013).

16. Jerry A. Muller, *The Tyranny of Metrics* (Princeton, NJ: Princeton University Press, 2018).

17. Michael C. Desch, *Cult of the Irrelevant: The Waning Influence of Social Science on National Security* (Princeton, NJ: Princeton University Press, 2019).

18. Cathy O'Neil, *Weapons of Math Destruction: How Big Data Increases Inequality and Threatens Democracy* (New York: Crown, 2016).

19. Ellen Messer-Davidow, *Disciplining Feminism: From Social Activism to Academic Discourse* (Durham, NC: Duke University Press, 2002).

20. Erica Chenoweth and Maria J. Stephan, *Why Civil Resistance Works: The Strategic Logic of Nonviolent Conflict* (New York: Columbia University Press, 2012); Sharon Erickson Nepstad, "Nonviolent Resistance Research," *Mobilization* 20, no. 4 (2015): 415–26, https://doi.org/10.17813/1086-671X-20-4-415.

21. Omar Wasow, "Agenda Seeding: How 1960s Black Protests Moved Elites, Public Opinion and Voting," *American Political Science Review* 114, no. 3 (2020): 649, https://doi.org/10.1017/S000305542000009X.

22. Edward O. Wilson, *Consilience: The Unity of Knowledge* (New York: Vintage Books, 1998), 199.

23. Lisa Mueller, "Crowd Cohesion and Protest Outcomes," *American Journal of Political Science* (forthcoming), https://doi.org/10.1111/ajps.12725; Lisa Mueller, "United We Stand, Divided We Fall? How Signals of Activist Cohesion Affect Attraction to Advocacy Organizations," *Interest Groups & Advocacy* 10 (2021): 1–18, https://doi.org/10.1057/s41309-020-00108-7.

24. Cynthia Peters, "Knowing What's Wrong Is Not Enough: Creating Strategy and Vision," in *Rhyming Hope and History: Activists, Academics, and Social Movement Scholarship*, ed. David Croteau et al. (Minneapolis: University of Minnesota Press, 2005), 45.

25. Peter J. Hotez, "Anti-Science Extremism in America: Escalating and Globalizing," *Microbes and Infection* 22, no. 10 (2020): 505–7, https://doi.org/10.1016/j.micinf.2020.09.005.

26. Jake Horton, "Does US Really Have the World's Highest COVID Death Toll?" BBC, May 12, 2022, https://www.bbc.com/news/61333847.

27. Oreskes, *Why Trust Science?*, ix.

28. Matthew Motta, "The Polarizing Effect of the March for Science on Attitudes Toward Scientists," *PS: Political Science & Politics* 51, no. 4 (2018): 782–88, https://doi.org/10.1017/S1049096518000938.

29. Robert J. Brulle, "Critical Reflections on the March for Science," *Sociological Forum* 33, no. 1 (2017): 255–58, https://doi.org/10.1111/socf.12398.

30. Neil deGrasse Tyson, *Starry Messenger: Cosmic Perspectives on Civilization* (New York: Henry Holt, 2022), 86–87.

31. Aristide R. Zolberg, "Moments of Madness," *Politics and Society* 2, no. 2 (1972): 183–207, https://doi.org/10.1177/003232927200200203.

32. Stefan Stürmer and Bernd Simon, "Pathways to Collective Protest: Calculation, Identification, or Emotion? A Critical Analysis of the Role of Group-Based Anger in Social Movement Participation," *Journal of Social Issues* 65, no. 4 (2009): 681–705, https://doi.org/10.1111/j.1540-4560.2009.01620.x.

33. James M. Jasper, *The Emotions of Protest* (Chicago: University of Chicago Press, 2018).

34. Jasper, *Emotions of Protest*, 7.

35. Olúfẹ́mi O. Táíwò, *Elite Capture: How the Powerful Took Over Identity Politics (And Everything Else)* (Chicago: Haymarket Books, 2022).

36. William MacAskill, *Doing Good Better: How Effective Altruism Can Help You Make a Difference* (New York: Gotham Books, 2015).

37. Nicholas Wade, "Scientists Cite Fastest Case of Human Evolution," *New York Times*, July 1, 2010, https://www.nytimes.com/2010/07/02/science/02tibet.html.

38. Judson Brewer, *Unwinding Anxiety: New Science Shows How to Break the Cycles of Worry and Fear to Heal Your Mind* (New York: Avery, 2021).

39. Richard Flacks, "The Question of Relevance in Social Movement Studies," in *Rhyming Hope and History: Activists, Academics, and Social Movement Scholarship*, ed. David Croteau et al. (Minneapolis: University of Minnesota Press, 2005), 7.

40. Julie Ellison and Timothy K. Eatman, "Scholarship in Public: Knowledge Creation and Tenure Policy in the Engaged University," *Imagining America* 16, no. 1 (2008), https://surface.syr.edu/ia/16.

41. Ralph Ranalli, "Erica Chenoweth Illuminates the Value of Nonviolent Resistance in Societal Conflicts," Harvard Kennedy School, Summer 2019, https://www.hks.harvard.edu/faculty-research/policy-topics/advocacy-social-movements/paths-resistance-erica-chenoweths-research.

42. Roderick Kefferpütz, "China's Digital Dictatorship Goes Global," *Towards Data Science*, November 5, 2018, https://towardsdatascience.com/chinas-digital-dictatorship-goes-global-bee6b093ff9b.

43. Andrea Kendall-Taylor, Erica Frantz, and Joseph Wright, "The Digital Dictators: How Technology Strengthens Autocracy," *Foreign Affairs*, March/April 2020, https://www.foreignaffairs.com/articles/china/2020-02-06/digital-dictators.

CHAPTER 1: "HUNDREDS OF FLOWERS, ABLOOM"

1. My grandaunt, Peggy Tang Strait, recorded this family history in a self-published memoir, *Unbound: Memories of an Immigrant Daughter*.

2. Louisa Lim, "Painful Memories for China's Footbinding Survivors," NPR, March 19, 2007, https://www.npr.org/2007/03/19/8966942/painful-memories-for-chinas-footbinding-survivors.

3. Dorothy Ko, *Cinderella's Sisters: A Revisionist History of Footbinding* (Berkeley: University of California Press, 2005), 9.

4. Alison R. Drucker, "The Influence of Western Women on the Anti-Footbinding Movement 1840-191," *Historical Reflections* 8, no. 3 (1981): 179–99, https://www.jstor.org/stable/41298767.

5. Fan Hong, *Footbinding, Feminism and Freedom: The Liberation of Women's Bodies in Modern China* (London: Frank Cass, 1997), 91.

6. Qiu Jin, translated by Yilin Wang, "Reflections: Written During Travels in Japan," *Hotazel Review*, https://hotazelreviewlit.org/two-poems-by-qiu-jin/.

7. Rachel Keeling, "The Anti-Footbinding Movement, 1872–1922: A Cause for China Rather Than Chinese Women," *Footnotes* 1 (2008): 11–19, https://journal.lib.uoguelph.ca/index.php/footnotes/article/view/3837.

8. Herbert Kohl, *She Would Not Be Moved: How We Tell the Story of Rosa Parks and the Montgomery Bus Boycott* (New York: The New Press, 2005), 12.

9. Herbert Kohl, "The Politics of Children's Literature: What's Wrong with the Rosa Parks Myth," in *Rethinking Our Classrooms, Volume 1*, ed. Wayne Au, Bill Bigelow, and Stan Karp (Milwaukee: Rethinking Schools, 2007), 171.

10. Michael Hardt and Antonio Negri, *Assembly* (Oxford: Oxford University Press, 2017), 21.

11. William M. Arkin, "Exclusive: Classified Documents Reveal the Number of January 6 Protestors," *Newsweek*, December 23, 2021, https://www.newsweek.com/exclusive-classified-documents-reveal-number-january-6-protestors-1661296.

12. Diana Fu, *Mobilizing Without the Masses: Control and Contention in China* (New York: Cambridge University Press, 2018).

13. Stephania Taladrid, "The Post-Roe Abortion Underground," *New Yorker*, October 10, 2022, https://www.newyorker.com/magazine/2022/10/17/the-post-roe-abortion-underground.

14. Data are from Christian Haerpfer et al., "World Values Survey: Round Seven–Country-Pooled Datafile Version 4.0," 2022, https://www.worldvaluessurvey.org/WVSDocumentationWV7.jsp.

15. "Stress in America," American Psychological Association, March 2022, https://www.apa.org/news/press/releases/stress/2022/march-2022-survival-mode.

16. Sharon Lurye, "Global Survey Shows Young People Are Anxious Yet Hopeful," *US News & World Report*, January 24, 2022, https://www.usnews.com/news/best-countries/articles/2022-01-24/u-n-survey-young-people-are-anxious-yet-hopeful.

17. Samuel Brannen et al., *The Age of Mass Protests: Understanding an Escalating Global Trend*, Center for Strategic & International Studies report, March 2,

2020, https://www.csis.org/analysis/age-mass-protests-understanding-escalating-global-trend.

18. Cheryl W. Thompson, "Fatal Police Shootings of Unarmed Black People Reveal Troubling Patterns," NPR, January 25, 2021, https://www.npr.org/2021/01/25/956177021/fatal-police-shootings-of-unarmed-black-people-reveal-troubling-patterns.

19. Larry Buchanan, Quoctrung Bui, and Jugal K. Patel, "Black Lives Matter May Be the Largest Movement in US History," *New York Times*, July 3, 2020, https://www.nytimes.com/interactive/2020/07/03/us/george-floyd-protests-crowd-size.html.

20. Ashley Westerman, Ryan Benk, and David Greene, "In 2020, Protests Spread Across the Globe with a Similar Message: Black Lives Matter," *Morning Edition*, NPR, December 30, 2020, https://www.npr.org/2020/12/30/950053607/in-2020-protests-spread-across-the-globe-with-a-similar-message-black-lives-matt.

21. Susanne Lohmann, "The Dynamics of Informational Cascades: The Monday Demonstrations in Leipzig, East Germany, 1989–91," *World Politics* 47, no. 1 (1994): 42–101, https://www.jstor.org/stable/2950679.

22. Craig R. Whitney, David Binder, and Serge Schmemann, "How the Wall Was Cracked," *New York Times*, November 19, 1989, https://www.nytimes.com/1989/11/19/world/wall-was-cracked-special-report-party-coup-turned-east-german-tide-clamor-east.html.

23. Travis B. Curtice and Brandon Behlendorf, "Street-Level Repression: Protest, Policing, and Dissent in Uganda," *Journal of Conflict Resolution* 65, no. 1 (2021): 166–94, https://doi.org/10.1177/0022002720939304.

24. Maria Angélica Bautista, Felipe González, Luis R. Martínez, Pablo Muñoz, and Mounu Prem, "The Geography of Repression and Opposition to Autocracy," *American Journal of Political Science* (2021), https://doi.org/10.1111/ajps.12614.

25. Arturas Rozenas and Yuri M. Zhukov, "Mass Repression and Political Loyalty: Evidence from Stalin's 'Terror by Hunger,'" *American Political Science Review* 113, no. 2 (2019): 569–83, https://doi.org/10.1017/S0003055419000066.

26. Jennifer Pan and Alexandra A. Siegel, "How Saudi Crackdowns Fail to Silence Online Dissent," *American Political Science Review* 114, no. 1 (2020): 109–25, https://doi.org/10.1017/S0003055419000650.

27. Maya Wang, *Hong Kong Repression's True Cost*, Human Rights Watch report, February 24, 2021, https://www.hrw.org/news/2021/02/24/hong-kong-repressions-true-cost.

28. Sunniva Rose, "EU Expands Sanctions on Iran Over Repression of Protests," *The National*, November 14, 2022, https://www.thenationalnews.com/world/2022/11/14/eu-to-expand-sanctions-on-iran-over-repression-of-protests.

29. Vjosa Isai, "Canada Protests: A New Blockade Threatens Supply Chain for Carmakers," *New York Times*, February 9, 2022, https://www.nytimes.com/live/2022/02/09/world/canada-trucker-protest.

30. Laura Osman and David Fraser, "Winter 'Freedom Convoy' Blockages Cost Billions to Canada's Economy, Inquiry Hears," *North Shore News*, November 16, 2022, https://www.nsnews.com/politics/winter-freedom-convoy-blockades-cost-billions-to-canadas-economy-inquiry-hears-6113785.

31. Zack Beauchamp, "The Canadian Trucker Convoy Is an Unpopular Uprising," *Vox*, February 11, 2022, https://www.vox.com/policy-and-politics/22926134/canada-trucker-freedom-convoy-protest-ottawa.

32. Erica Chenoweth and Maria J. Stephan, *Why Civil Resistance Works* (New York: Columbia University Press, 2011), 39.

33. For a review, see Charles Butcher and Jonathan Pinckney, "Friday on My Mind: Re-Assessing the Impact of Protest Size on Government Concessions," *Journal of Conflict Resolution* 66, nos. 7–8 (2022): 1320–55.

34. Andreas Madestam, Daniel Shoag, Stan Veuger, and David Yanagizawa-Drott, "Do Political Protests Matter? Evidence from the Tea Party Movement," *Quarterly Journal of Economics* 128, no. 4 (2013): 1653, https://doi.org/10.1093/qje/qjt021.

35. Butcher and Pinckney, "Friday on My Mind," 1320–55.

36. Erica Chenoweth, Andrew Hocking, and Zoe Marks, "A Dynamic Model of Nonviolent Resistance Strategy," *PLoS ONE* 17, no. 7 (2022): e0269976, https://doi.org/10.1371/journal.pone.0269976.

37. Almira Tanner, "The Rule of 3.5% Has Been Broken. What Does This Mean for DxE?" *Direct Action Everywhere*, February 11, 2021, https://www.directactioneverywhere.com/theliberationist/chenoweth-blog.

38. Thomas Apolte, "Mass Protests, Security-Elite Defection, and Revolution," *Journal of Comparative Economics* 50 (2022): 981–96, https://doi.org/10.1016/j.jce.2022.07.001.

39. Aaron Morrison, "Race Double Standard Clear in Rioters' Capitol Insurrection," AP, January 7, 2021, https://apnews.com/article/congress-storming-black-lives-matter-22983dc91d16bf949efbb60cdda4495d.

40. LaGina Gause, "Revealing Issue Salience via Costly Protest: How Legislative Behavior Following Protest Advantages Low-Resource Groups," *British Journal of Political Science* 52, no. 1 (2022): 259–79, https://doi.org/10.1017/S0007123420000423.

41. Maciej Cegłowski, "Observations on Technology Use in Hong Kong Protests," *Idle Words* (blog), 2019, https://idlewords.com/talks/hk_stanford.html.

42. Paul Mozur, Muyi Xiao, and John Liu, "'Breach of the Big Silence': Protests Stretch China's Censorship to Its Limits," *New York Times*, November 30, 2022, https://www.nytimes.com/2022/11/30/business/china-protests-censorship-video.html.

43. Paul Schuler and Mai Truong, "Connected Countryside: The Inhibiting Effect of Social Media on Rural Social Movements," *Comparative Politics* 52, no. 4 (2020): 647–69, https://doi.org/10.5129/001041520X15743805571380.

44. Leonard Bursztyn, Davide Cantoni, David Y. Yang, Noam Yuchtman, and Y. Jane Zhang, "Persistent Political Engagement: Social Interactions and

the Dynamics of Protest Movements," *American Economic Review: Insights* 3, no. 2 (2021): 240, https://doi.org/10.1257/aeri.20200261.

45. James Rufus Koren, "Paid Protesters? They're Real—and a Beverly Hills Firm That Hires Them Stands Accused of Extortion in a Lawsuit," *Los Angeles Times*, October 21, 2018, https://www.latimes.com/business/la-fi-crowds-extortion-20181021-story.html.

46. Aaron Couch and Emmet McDermott, "Donald Trump Campaign Offered Actors $50 to Cheer for Him at Presidential Announcement," *Hollywood Reporter*, June 17, 2015, https://www.hollywoodreporter.com/news/politics-news/donald-trump-campaign-offered-actors-803161.

47. Carole Fader, "Fact Check: Were Activists at Charlottesville Paid?" *Florida Times-Union*, October 21, 2017, https://www.jacksonville.com/story/news/reason/2017/10/21/fact-check-were-activists-charlottesville-paid/15362775007.

48. Marin Austin, "Concerned Citizens Turn Out to Be Political Theater," NBC Los Angeles, February 18, 2016, https://www.nbclosangeles.com/news/local/concerned-citizens-turn-out-to-be-political-theater/2021439.

49. Koren, "Paid Protesters?"

50. Stefan Stürmer and Bernd Simon, "Pathways to Collective Protest: Calculation, Identification, or Emotion? A Critical Analysis of the Role of Group-Based Anger in Social Movement Participation," *Journal of Social Issues* 65, no. 4 (2009): 701, https://doi.org/10.1111/j.1540-4560.2009.01620.x.

51. Elisabeth Jean Wood, *Insurgent Collective Action and Civil War in El Salvador* (New York: Cambridge University Press, 2012).

52. Anselm Hager, Lukas Hensel, Johannes Hermle, and Christopher Roth, "Group Size and Protest Mobilization across Movements and Countermovements," *American Political Science Review* 116, no. 3 (2022): 1051–66, https://doi.org/10.1017/S0003055421001131.

53. Roy F. Baumeister and Mark R. Leary, "The Need to Belong: Desire for Interpersonal Attachments as a Fundamental Human Motivation," *Psychological Bulletin* 117, no. 3 (1995): 497–529, https://doi.org/10.1037/0033-2909.117.3.497.

54. Gwyneth H. McClendon, "Social Esteem and Participation in Contentious Politics: A Field Experiment at an LGBT Pride Rally," *American Journal of Political Science* 58, no. 2 (2014): 279–90, https://www.jstor.org/stable/24363485.

55. Allison P. Anoll, "What Makes a Good Neighbor? Race, Place, and Norms of Political Participation," *American Political Science Review* 112, no. 3 (2018): 494–508, https://doi.org/10.1017/S0003055418000175.

56. Bernd Beber and Christopher Blattman, "The Logic of Child Soldiering and Coercion," *International Organization* 67, no. 1 (2013): 65–104, https://doi.org/10.1017/S0020818312000409.

57. Patricia Funk, "Social Incentives and Voter Turnout: Evidence from the Swiss Mail Ballot System," *Journal of the European Economic Association* 8, no. 5 (2010): 1077–1103, https://www.jstor.org/stable/25700915.

58. Stephen Knack, "Civic Norms, Social Sanctions, and Voter Turnout," *Rationality and Society* 4, no. 2 (1992): 137, https://doi.org/10.1177/1043463192004002002.

59. Stephen Knack, "Civic Norms, Social Sanctions, and Voter Turnout," *Rationality and Society* 4, no. 2 (1992): 139, https://doi.org/10.1177/1043463192004002002.

60. This term is not politically correct in every context, but some people use it to refer to themselves. For a thorough discussion, see Jennifer L. De Maio and Daniel N. Posner, "Terms Matter: The Use of 'Tribe' in African Studies," in *Re-Membering Africa: Critical Dimensions of African Studies*, ed. Jennifer L. De Maio, Suzanne Scheld, and Tom Spencer-Walters (Lanham, MD: Lexington Books, 2023), 17–29.

61. James Habyarimana, Macartan Humphreys, Daniel N. Posner, and Jeremy M. Weinstein, "Why Does Ethnic Diversity Undermine Public Goods Provision?" *American Political Science Review* 101, no. 4 (2007): 709–25, https://doi.org/10.1017/S0003055407070499.

62. William MacAskill, *Doing Good Better: How Effective Altruism Can Help You Help Others, Do Work that Matters, and Make Smarter Choices About Giving Back* (New York: Avery, 2016), 85.

63. Shannon Ho and Phil McCausland, "How Instagram Became a Destination for the Protest Movement," NBC News, June 28, 2020, https://www.nbcnews.com/tech/tech-news/how-instagram-became-destination-protest-movement-n1232342.

CHAPTER 2: THE TRUTH ABOUT SLACKTIVISM

1. Katy Steinmetz, "Oxford's 2014 Word of the Year Is Vape," *Time*, November 17, 2014, https://time.com/3590093/oxfords-2014-word-of-the-year-is-vape.

2. Maeve Shearlaw, "Did the #bringbackourgirls Campaign Make a Difference in Nigeria?" *The Guardian*, April 14, 2015, https://www.theguardian.com/world/2015/apr/14/nigeria-bringbackourgirls-campaign-one-year-on.

3. Amnesty International, "Nigeria: Abducted Women and Girls Forced to Join Boko Haram Attacks," April 14, 2015, https://www.amnesty.org/en/latest/news/2015/04/nigeria-abducted-women-and-girls-forced-to-join-boko-haram-attack.

4. Jumoke Balogun, "Dear World, Your Hashtags Won't #BringBackOurGirls," *The Guardian*, May 9, 2014, https://www.theguardian.com/world/2014/may/09/nigeria-hashtags-wont-bring-back-our-girls-bringbackourgirls.

5. Brooke Auxier and Colleen McClain, "Americans Think Social Media Can Help Build Movements, But Can Also Be a Distraction," Pew Research Center, September 9, 2020, https://www.pewresearch.org/fact-tank/2020/09/09/americans-think-social-media-can-help-build-movements-but-can-also-be-a-distraction.

6. As a group, conservatives are less likely to engage in hashtag activism because their mistrust of Big Tech and mainstream media increasingly pushes

them off major platforms and into right-wing communities such as Parler and Gab. See Deen Freelon, Alice Marwick, and Daniel Kreiss, "False Equivalencies: Online Activism from Left to Right," *Science* 369, no. 6508 (2020): 1197–1201, https://www.science.org/doi/10.1126/science.abb2428.

7. Anjali S. Bal et al., "Do Good, Goes Bad, Gets Ugly: Kony 2012," *Journal of Public Affairs* 13, no. 2 (2013): 202, https://doi.org/10.1002/pa.1475.

8. Tom Watson, "The #StopKony Backlash: Complexity and the Challenges of Slacktivism," *Forbes*, March 8, 2012, https://www.forbes.com/sites/tomwatson/2012/03/08/the-stopkony-backlash-complexity-and-the-challenges-of-slacktivism/?sh=3536d21d45cd.

9. Don Caldwell, "Want to Be Taken Seriously? Don't Be Fake. Be Consistent," *Adweek*, July 18, 2020, https://www.adweek.com/creativity/brands-need-to-be-careful-not-to-exploit-a-cause-and-be-accused-of-slacktivism.

10. Lara Robertson, "How Ethical Is Nike?" *Good on You*, June 29, 2022, https://goodonyou.eco/how-ethical-is-nike.

11. David Clark Scott, "Everyday Heroes: 11 Tales of American Heroes," *Christian Science Monitor*, April 16, 2012, https://www.csmonitor.com/USA/Society/2012/0416/Everyday-heroes-11-tales-of-American-heroes/Wesley-Autrey-the-subway-hero.

12. Cara Buckley, "Man Is Rescued by Stranger on Subway Tracks," *New York Times*, January 3, 2007, https://www.nytimes.com/2007/01/03/nyregion/03life.html.

13. Doug Lederman, "Are Elite College Courses Better?" *Inside Higher Ed*, November 9, 2015, https://www.insidehighered.com/news/2015/11/09/study-questions-whether-elite-college-courses-are-higher-quality-others.

14. Yusuke Tsugawa et al., "Association between Physician *US News & World Report* Medical School Ranking and Patient Outcomes and Costs of Care: Observational Study," *BMJ* 362 (2018): k3640, https://doi.org/10.1136/bmj.k3640.

15. S. Michael Gaddis, "Discrimination in the Credential Society: An Audit Study of Race and College Selectivity in the Labor Market," *Social Forces* 93, no. 4 (2015): 1451–79, https://doi.org/10.1093/sf/sou111.

16. Olivia M. Jochi, "Welcome to the Harvard of Online Dating," *Harvard Crimson*, April 9, 2021, https://www.thecrimson.com/flyby/article/2021/4/9/flyby-the-league.

17. Jeff Spross, "America's Bizarre, Backwards Worship of the Ivy League," *The Week*, November 10, 2015, https://theweek.com/articles/587790/americas-bizarre-backwards-worship-ivy-league.

18. Amotz Zahavi, "Mate Selection—A Selection for a Handicap," *Journal of Theoretical Biology* 53, no. 1 (1975): 205–14, https://doi.org/10.1016/0022-5193(75)90111-3.

19. Andrew W. Delton and Theresa E. Robertson, "The Social Cognition of Social Foraging: Partner Selection by Underlying Valuation," *Evolution and*

Human Behavior 33, no. 6 (2012): 715–25, https://doi.org/10.1016/j.evolhumbehav.2012.05.007.

20. Colin Camerer, "Gifts as Economic Signals and Social Symbols," *American Journal of Sociology* 94 (1988): S180–S214, https://www.jstor.org/stable/2780246.

21. A. Michael Spence, "Time and Communication in Economic and Social Interaction," *Quarterly Journal of Economics* 87, no. 4 (1973): 651–60, https://www.jstor.org/stable/1882035.

22. Catherine Kim, "Minneapolis Mayor Is Booed Out of a Rally for Rejecting Calls to Defund the Police," *Vox*, June 7, 2020, https://www.vox.com/2020/6/7/21283089/minneapolis-mayor-protests-frey-booed-rally-defund-police.

23. Mark R. Leary, "Motivational and Emotional Aspects of the Self," *Annual Review of Psychology* 58 (2007): 329, https://pubmed.ncbi.nlm.nih.gov/16953794.

24. Phebe Cramer, "Seven Pillars of Defense Mechanism Theory," *Social and Personality Psychology Compass* 2, no. 5 (2008): 1963–81, https://doi.org/10.1111/j.1751-9004.2008.00135.x.

25. Evgeny Morozov, *To Save Everything, Click Here* (New York: PublicAffairs, 2013).

26. On protests, see Lisa Mueller, "Crowd Cohesion and Protest Outcomes," *American Journal of Political Science* (forthcoming), https://doi.org/10.1111/ajps.12725. On lobbying, see Wiebke Marie Junk, "When Diversity Works: The Effects of Coalition Composition on the Success of Lobbying Coalitions," *American Journal of Political Science* 63, no. 3 (2019): 660–74, https://doi.org/10.1111/ajps.12437. On writing to lawmakers, see Christian R. Grose et al., "Explaining Explanations: How Legislators Explain Their Policy Positions and How Citizens React," *American Journal of Political Science* 59, no. 3 (2015): 724–43, https://doi.org/10.1111/ajps.12164.

27. Astra Taylor, "Against Activism," *The Baffler*, no. 30 (2016), https://thebaffler.com/salvos/against-activism.

28. Evgeny Morozov, *The Net Delusion: The Dark Side of Internet Freedom* (New York: PublicAffairs, 2012), 179–203.

29. Zachary C. Steinert-Threlkeld et al., "Online Social Networks and Offline Protest," *EPJ Data Science* 4, no. 19 (2015): https://doi.org/10.1140/epjds/s13688-015-0056-y.

30. Sebastián Valenzuela, "Unpacking the Use of Social Media for Protest Behavior: The Roles of Information, Opinion Expression, and Activism," *American Behavioral Scientist* 57, no. 7 (2013): 920–42, https://doi.org/10.1177/0002764213479375.

31. Yu-Hao Lee and Gary Hsieh, "Does Slacktivism Hurt Activism? The Effects of Moral Balancing and Consistency in Online Activism," Proceedings of the SIGCHI Conference on Human Factors in Computing Systems, April 27–May 2, 2013, Paris, pp. 811–20, https://doi.org/10.1145/2470654.2470770.

32. Henrik Serup Christensen, "Political Activities on the Internet: Slacktivism or Political Participation by Other Means?" *First Monday* 16, no. 2 (2011), https://firstmonday.org/article/view/3336/2767.

33. Kyle A. Thomas et al., "The Psychology of Coordination and Common Knowledge," *Journal of Personality and Social Psychology* 107, no. 4 (2014): 657–76, http://nrs.harvard.edu/urn-3:HUL.InstRepos:14330738.

34. Tadeg Quillien, "Is Virtue Signalling a Vice?" *Aeon*, April 4, 2022, https://aeon.co/essays/why-virtue-signalling-is-not-just-a-vice-but-an-evolved-tool.

35. Zachary C. Steinert-Threlkeld, "Spontaneous Collective Action: Peripheral Mobilization During the Arab Spring," *American Political Science Review* 111, no. 2 (2017): 379–403, https://doi.org/10.1017/S0003055416000769.

36. Dina Bishara, "The Generative Power of Protest: Time and Space in Contentious Politics," *Comparative Political Studies* 54, no. 10 (2021): 1722–56, https://doi.org/10.1177/0010414020970227.

37. Killian Clarke and Korhan Kocak, "Launching Revolution: Social Media and the Egyptian Uprising's First Movers," *British Journal of Political Science* 50, no. 3 (2020): 1025–45, https://doi.org/10.1017/S0007123418000194.

38. Brian Ross and Matthew Cole, "Egypt: The Face that Launched a Revolution," *ABC News*, January 25, 2011, https://abcnews.go.com/Blotter/egypt-face-launched-revolution/story?id=12841488&page=1.

39. Mary Joyce, "Five Reasons Not to Use the Word 'Slacktivism,'" *Open Society Foundation: Voices*, April 30, 2012, https://www.opensocietyfoundations.org/voices/five-reasons-not-use-word-slacktivism.

40. Zeynep Tufekci, "#Kony2012, Understanding Networked Symbolic Action & Why Slacktivism Is Conceptually Misleading," *Technosociology*, March 10, 2012, https://technosociology.org/?p=904.

41. Jan Matti Dollbaum and Graeme B. Robertson, "The Activist Personality: Extraversion, Agreeableness, and Opposition Activism in Authoritarian Regimes," *Comparative Political Studies* (2023), https://doi.org/10.1177/00104140231152772.

42. See, for example, https://www.truity.com/test/big-five-personality-test.

43. J. William Stoughton, Lori Foster Thompson, and Adam W. Meade, "Big Five Personality Traits Reflected in Job Applicants' Social Media Postings," *Cyberpsychology, Behavior, and Social Networking* 16, no. 11 (2013): 800–805, http://doi.org/10.1089/cyber.2012.0163.

44. Andreu Casas and Nora Webb Williams, "Images that Matter: Online Protests and the Mobilizing Role of Pictures," *Political Research Quarterly* 72, no. 2 (2019): 360–75.

45. Sarah Repucci and Amy Slipowitz, *Democracy Under Siege*, Freedom House, 2022, https://freedomhouse.org/report/freedom-world/2021/democracy-under-siege.

46. Adrian Shahbaz, Allie Funk, and Kian Vesteinsson, *Countering an Authoritarian Overhaul of the Internet*, Freedom House, 2022, https://freedomhouse.org/report/freedom-net/2022/countering-authoritarian-overhaul-internet #Shattering.

47. Adrian Shahbaz and Allie Funk, *The Crisis of Social Media*, Freedom House, 2019, https://freedomhouse.org/sites/default/files/2019-11/11042019_Report_FH_FOTN_2019_final_Public_Download.pdf.

48. William R. Hobbs and Margaret E. Roberts, "How Sudden Censorship Can Increase Access to Information," *American Political Science Review* 112, no. 3 (2018): 621–36, https://doi.org/10.1017/S0003055418000084.

49. Christopher M. Sullivan, "Political Repression and the Destruction of Dissident Organizations: Evidence from the Archives of the Guatemalan National Police," *World Politics* 68, no. 4 (2016): 645–76, https://doi.org/10.1017/S0043887116000125.

50. Mai Hassan, "Coordinated Dis-Coordination," *American Political Science Review* (forthcoming), https://doi.org/10.1017/S0003055423000291.

51. Neil Postman, *Amusing Ourselves to Death: Public Discourse in the Age of Show Business* (New York: Penguin, 1985), xix.

52. Anna Lembke, *Dopamine Nation: Finding Balance in the Age of Indulgence* (New York: Dutton, 2021).

53. A key exception is Johann Hari, *Stolen Focus: Why You Can't Pay Attention—and How to Think Deeply Again* (New York: Crown, 2022).

54. Zeynep Tufekci, "'Not This One': Social Movements, the Attention Economy, and Microcelebrity Networked Activism," *American Behavioral Scientist* 57, no. 7 (2013): 849, https://doi.org/10.1177/0002764213479369.

55. Lembke, *Dopamine Nation*.

56. Marietta Pohl et al., "The Association of Internet Addiction with Burnout, Depression, Insomnia, and Quality of Life among Hungarian High School Teachers," *International Journal of Environmental Research and Public Health* 19, no. 1 (2022): 438, https://doi.org/10.3390/ijerph19010438.

57. Gloria Mark, *Attention Span: A Groundbreaking Way to Restore Balance, Happiness and Productivity* (New York: Hanover Square Press, 2023).

58. Sophie Leroy, "Why Is It So Hard to Do My Work? The Challenge of Attention Residue When Switching Between Work Tasks," *Organizational Behavior and Human Decision Processes* 109 (2009) 168–81, https://doi.org/10.1016/j.obhdp.2009.04.002.

59. Cal Newport, *Deep Work: Rules for Focused Success in a Distracted World* (New York: Grand Central Publishing, 2016).

60. Edward O. Wilson, *Consilience: The Unity of Knowledge* (New York: Vintage Books, 1998), 238.

61. James McMaster, "In Defense of Virtue Signaling," *Journal of Dramatic Theory and Criticism* 35, no. 2 (2021): 125, https://muse.jhu.edu/article/801572/summary.

62. Adom Getachew, "A 'Common Spectacle' of the Race: Garveyism's Visual Politics of the Founding," *American Political Science Review* 115, no. 4 (2021): 1197, https://doi.org/10.1017/S0003055421000484.

63. Sue Tait, "Bearing Witness, Journalism and Moral Responsibility," *Media, Culture & Society* 33, no. 8 (2011): 1220–35, https://doi.org/10.1177/0163443711422460.

64. Anne Bogart, *A Director Prepares: Seven Essays on Art and Theatre* (New York: Routledge, 2001), 63.

65. Sylvia Boorstein, *Don't Just Do Something, Sit There* (San Francisco: HarperSanFrancisco, 1996).

66. Getachew, "A 'Common Spectacle' of the Race," 1201.

67. Getachew, "A 'Common Spectacle' of the Race," 1206.

68. Getachew, "A 'Common Spectacle' of the Race," 1202.

69. Getachew, "A 'Common Spectacle' of the Race," 1197.

70. Peggy Orenstein, "The Revolutionary Power of a Skein of Yarn," *New York Times*, January 27, 2023, https://www.nytimes.com/2023/01/27/opinion/sunday/knitting-fabric-michelle-obama.html.

71. El Teatro Campesino, "Our History," https://elteatrocampesino.com/our-history.

72. Scott James, "From Homelessness to Donald Trump, This Art Group Takes on All," *New York Times*, March 10, 2020, https://www.nytimes.com/2020/03/10/arts/indecline-street-art-2020-election.html.

CHAPTER 3: GIVE PEACE A CHANCE

1. Tom Bartlett, "The Protesting of a Protest Paper," *Chronicle of Higher Education*, July 7, 2020, https://www-chronicle-com.eu1.proxy.openathens.net/article/the-protesting-of-a-protest-paper.

2. Brad Oswald, "Yes, She's the Queen of All Media, but to Discovery, She's Life Itself," *The Free Press*, January 26, 2010, https://www.winnipegfreepress.com/arts-and-life/entertainment/tv/2010/01/26/yes-shes-queen-of-all-media-but-to-discovery-shes-life-itself.

3. Loully Saney, "From 'Sexiest Internet Executive' to Politics Professor: Omar Wasow," *Daily Princetonian*, September 26, 2013, https://www.dailyprincetonian.com/article/2013/09/from-sexiest-internet-executive-to-politics-professor-omar-wasow.

4. Omar Wasow, "Agenda Seeding: How 1960s Black Protests Moved Elites, Public Opinion and Voting," *American Political Science Review* 114, no. 3 (2020): 638–59.

5. Roudabeh Kishi and Sam Jones, "Demonstrations & Political Violence in America: New Data for Summer 2020," Armed Conflict Location & Event Data Project, September 2020, https://acleddata.com/2020/09/03/demonstrations-political-violence-in-america-new-data-for-summer-2020.

6. Liz Sawyer, "Brainerd Man Sentenced to 4 Years for Minneapolis Police Station Fire During Floyd Protests," *Minneapolis Star Tribune*, April 28, 2021,

https://www.startribune.com/brainerd-man-sentenced-to-four-years-in-federal-prison-for-role-in-burning-minneapolis-police-third/600051280.

7. Nathan J. Robinson, "Has the American Left Lost Its Mind?" *Current Affairs*, June 15, 2020, https://www.currentaffairs.org/2020/06/has-the-american-left-lost-its-mind.

8. Dylan Matthews, "How Today's Protests Compare to 1968, Explained by a Historian," *Vox*, June 2, 2020, https://www.vox.com/identities/2020/6/2/21277253/george-floyd-protest-1960s-civil-rights.

9. Bartlett, "The Protesting of a Protest Paper."

10. Carol Kaesuk Yoon, *Naming Nature: The Clash Between Instinct and Science* (New York: W. W. Norton, 2009).

11. *Collective effervescence* is a classic term popularized by the sociologist Émile Durkheim. It is when "the group comes together and communicates in the same thought and participates in the same action, which serves to unify a group of individuals." See "Émile Durkheim," *Internet Encyclopedia of Philosophy*, https://iep.utm.edu/emile-durkheim.

12. Yoon, *Naming Nature*.

13. Louise Connell, "What Have Labels Ever Done for Us? The Linguistic Shortcut in Conceptual Processing," *Language, Cognition and Neuroscience* 34, no. 10 (2019): 1308–18, https://doi.org/10.1080/23273798.2018.1471512.

14. Mark Engler and Paul Engler, *This Is an Uprising: How Nonviolent Revolt Is Shaping the Twenty-First Century* (New York: Nation Books, 2016), 10.

15. Malcolm X and Alex Haley, *The Autobiography of Malcolm X* (New York: Random House, 1964), 413.

16. Jari Tiihonen et al., "Genetic Background of Extreme Violent Behavior," *Molecular Psychiatry* 20, no. 6 (2014): 786–92.

17. Karen Rothenberg and Alice Wang, "The Scarlet Gene: Behavioral Genetics, Criminal Law, and Racial and Ethnic Stigma," *Law and Contemporary Problems* 69, nos. 1/2 (2006): 343–65, https://www.jstor.org/stable/27592131.

18. Robert Sapolsky, *Behave: The Biology of Humans at Our Best and Worst* (London: Vintage, 2017), 672.

19. Donatella Della Porta, "Repertoires of Contention," in *The Wiley-Blackwell Encyclopedia of Social and Political Movements*, ed. David A. Snow et al. (Oxford: Blackwell, 2013), https://doi:10.1002/9780470674871.wbespm178.

20. Emily Kalah Gade, "Social Isolation and Repertoires of Resistance," *American Political Science Review* 114, no. 2 (2020): 314, https://doi.org/10.1017/S0003055420000015.

21. Siddhartha Mukherjee, *The Gene: An Intimate History* (New York: Scribner, 2016).

22. Malcolm X, speech, location and date unknown, https://www.youtube.com/watch?v=kXo0lgcOHhg.

23. Tamara Fakhoury, "Violent Resistance as Radical Choice," *Feminist Philosophy Quarterly* (forthcoming), https://philarchive.org/rec/FAKVRA-2.

24. Martin Luther King Jr., "The Other America," speech delivered at Stanford University, April 14, 1967.

25. Dacher Keltner, *Awe: The New Science of Everyday Wonder and How It Can Transform Your Life* (New York: Penguin, 2023), 11.

26. Keltner, *Awe*.

27. Ernestine H. Gordijn et al., "Emotional Reactions to Harmful Intergroup Behavior," *European Journal of Social Psychology* 36, no. 1 (2006): 15–30.

28. Wasow, "Agenda Seeding."

29. Erin R. Pineda, *Seeing Like an Activist: Civil Disobedience and the Civil Rights Movement* (New York: Oxford University Press, 2021), 162–65.

30. Brian Purnell, *Fighting Jim Crow in the County of Kings: The Congress of Racial Equality in Brooklyn* (Lexington: University Press of Kentucky, 2013), 249.

31. Erica Chenoweth and Maria Stephan, *Why Civil Resistance Works: The Strategic Logic of Nonviolent Conflict* (New York: Columbia University Press, 2011).

32. Wasow, "Agenda Seeding."

33. Will Jennings and Clare Saunders, "Street Demonstrations and the Media Agenda: An Analysis of the Dynamics of Protest Agenda Setting," *Comparative Political Studies* 52, nos. 13–14 (2019): 2283–2313, https://doi.org/10.1177/0010414019830736.

34. Louis Menand, "When Americans Lost Faith in the News," *New Yorker*, January 30, 2023, https://www.newyorker.com/magazine/2023/02/06/when-americans-lost-faith-in-the-news.

35. Ryan D. Enos, Aaron R. Kaufman, and Melissa L. Sands, "Can Violent Protest Change Local Policy Support? Evidence from the Aftermath of the 1992 Los Angeles Riot," *American Political Science Review* 113, no. 4 (2019): 1012–28, https://doi.org/10.1017/S0003055419000340.

36. R. Richard Banks, Jennifer L. Eberhardt, and Lee Ross, "Discrimination and Implicit Bias in a Racially Unequal Society," *California Law Review* 94, no. 4 (2006): 1172–73.

37. Devorah Manekin and Tamar Mitts, "Effective for Whom? Ethnic Identity and Nonviolent Resistance," *American Political Science Review* 116, no. 1 (2022): 161–80, https://doi.org/10.1017/S0003055421000940.

38. Pearce Edwards and Daniel Arnon, "Violence on Many Sides: Framing Effects on Protest and Support for Repression," *British Journal of Political Science* 51, no. 2 (2021): 488–506, https://doi.org/10.1017/S0007123419000413.

39. Jane Rhodes, "Fanning the Flames of Racial Discord: The National Press and the Black Panther Party," *Harvard International Journal of Press/Politics* 4, no. 4 (1999): 95–118, https://doi.org/10.1177/1081180X9900400406.

40. Cornel West, "The New Cultural Politics of Difference," in *The Postmodern Turn: New Perspectives on Social Theory*, ed. Steven Seidman (New York: Cambridge University Press, 1994), 71.

41. Lisa Mueller, "Do Americans Really Support Black Athletes Who Kneel During the National Anthem? Estimating the True Prevalence and Strength of Sensitive Racial Attitudes in the Context of Sport," *Communication & Sport* 10, no. 6 (2022): 1070–91, https://doi.org/10.1177/21674795211 019670.

42. Adam N. Glynn, "What Can We Learn with Statistical Truth Serum? Design and Analysis of the List Experiment," *Public Opinion Quarterly* 77, no. S1 (2013): 159–72.

43. Hakeem Jefferson, "The Politics of Respectability and Black Americans' Punitive Attitudes," *American Political Science Review* (forthcoming), https://doi.org/10.1017/S0003055422001289.

44. Jacquie L'Etang, "Public Relations, Activism and Social Movements: Critical Perspectives," *Public Relations Inquiry* 5, no. 3 (2016): 207–11.

45. USC Annenberg School for Communication and Journalism, *2020 Global Communication Report*, April 2020, https://annenberg.usc.edu/research/center-public-relations/global-communication-report.

46. Raynee Sarah Gutting, "Contentious Activities, Disrespectful Protesters: Effect of Protest Context on Protest Support and Mobilization Across Ideology and Authoritarianism," *Political Behavior* 42 (2020): 865–90, https://doi.org/10.1007/s11109-018-09523-8.

47. Cátia P. Teixeira, Russell Spears, and Vincent Y. Yzerbyt, "Is Martin Luther King or Malcolm X the More Acceptable Face of Protest? High-Status Groups' Reactions to Low-Status Groups' Collective Action," *Journal of Personality and Social Psychology* 118, no. 5 (2020): 919–44, https://doi.org/10.1037/pspi0000195.

48. For more on this topic, see Fakhoury, "Violent Resistance as Radical Choice."

49. Teixeira, Spears, and Yzerbyt, "Martin Luther King or Malcolm X," 938.

50. Killian Clarke, "Revolutionary Violence and Counterrevolution," *American Political Science Review* (forthcoming), https://doi.org/10.1017/S000 3055422001174.

51. Paul Dosh, *Demanding the Land: Urban Popular Movements in Peru and Ecuador, 1990–2005* (University Park: Penn State University Press, 2010), 29.

52. Sean J. Westwood et al., "Current Research Overstates American Support for Political Violence," *Proceedings of the National Academy of Sciences of the United States of America* 118, no. 12 (2022): e2116870119, https://doi.org/10.1073/pnas.2116870119.

53. Pedro Rodriguez, Arthur Spirling, and Brandon M. Stewart, "Embedding Regression: Models for Context-Specific Description and Inference," *American Political Science Review* (forthcoming), https://doi.org/10.1017/S000 3055422001228.

54. Fakhoury, "Violent Resistance as Radical Choice."

CHAPTER 4: "THE PEOPLE UNITED WILL NEVER BE DEFEATED!"

1. Pew Research Center, "America's Abortion Quandary," May 6, 2022, https://www.pewresearch.org/religion/2022/05/06/americas-abortion-quandary.

2. Eric Groenendyk, Erik O. Kimbrough, and Mark Pickup, "How Norms Shape the Nature of Belief Systems in Mass Publics," *American Journal of Political Science* (forthcoming), https://doi.org/10.1111/ajps.12717.

3. See, for example, William Booth, "Doctor Killed During Abortion Protest," *Washington Post*, March 11, 1993, https://www.washingtonpost.com/wp-srv/national/longterm/abortviolence/stories/gunn.htm.

4. Michele Wilson and John Lynxwiler, "Abortion Clinic Violence as Terrorism," *Terrorism* 11, no. 4 (1988): 263–73.

5. Poppy Noor, "Pro-Choice Militants Are Targeting 'Pregnancy Crisis Centers' Across US," *The Guardian*, June 11, 2022, https://www.theguardian.com/world/2022/jun/11/pro-choice-militants-pregnancy-crisis-centers-attacks-us.

6. Alice Reid, "Group Claims Credit for Madison Anti-Abortion Office Attack, Warns of More," NBC 26, May 22, 2022, https://www.nbc26.com/news/state/report-group-claims-credit-for-madison-anti-abortion-office-attack-warns-of-more.

7. Karen Garcia and Madalyn Amato, "Feeling Anxious about the End of Roe vs. Wade? Experts Discuss Mental Health Implications," *Los Angeles Times*, June 30, 2022, https://www.latimes.com/california/story/2022-06-30/feeling-anxious-about-the-roe-vs-wade-overturn-experts-talk-about-the-mental-health-implications.

8. Concern Health, *Roe v. Wade: Coping with the Emotional Fallout*, https://myusf.usfca.edu/sites/default/files/documents/HR/benefits/Roe%20v.%20Wade%20Decision%20-%20Coping%20with%20the%20Emotional%20Fallout.pdf, accessed November 1, 2023.

9. Translated from Wolof into French, and then into English. Chadidjatu Faye, "Y'en a Marre! A Discourse Analysis of Music and Political Contestation in Senegal," bachelor's thesis, University of Leiden, https://hdl.handle.net/1887/3244170.

10. Lisa Mueller, *Political Protest in Contemporary Africa* (New York: Cambridge University Press, 2018), chapter 4.

11. World Bank Group, Poverty and Equity Briefs, *Senegal*, April 2020, https://databankfiles.worldbank.org/public/ddpext_download/poverty/33EF03BB-9722-4AE2-ABC7-AA2972D68AFE/Global_POVEQ_SEN.pdf.

12. UNESCO Institute for Statistics, World Bank Open Data, September 19, 2023, https://data.worldbank.org/indicator/SE.ADT.LITR.ZS?locations=SN.

13. Mueller, *Political Protest in Contemporary Africa*, 63.

14. Mueller, *Political Protest in Contemporary Africa*, 112.

15. Mueller, *Political Protest in Contemporary Africa*, 112.

16. Ernest Harsch, "An African Spring in the Making: Protest and Voice Across a Continent," *Whitehead Journal of Diplomacy & International Relations* 45 (2012): 45–62.

17. Barbara Hinkley, "Coalitions in Congress: Size and Ideological Distance," *Midwest Journal of Political Science* 16, no. 2 (1972): 197.

18. Nisrin Elamin and Zachariah Mampilly, "Recent Protests in Sudan Are Much More than Bread Riots," *Washington Post*, December 28, 2018, https://www.washingtonpost.com/news/monkey-cage/wp/2018/12/28/recent-protests-in-sudan-are-much-more-than-bread-riots.

19. German Lopez, "Teens Started March for Our Lives, but All Ages Participated," *Vox*, March 30, 2018, https://www.vox.com/policy-and-politics/2018/3/30/17177432/march-for-our-lives-gun-control-children-age.

20. Adam Gopnik, "What Happens When You Kill Your King," *New Yorker*, April 17, 2023, https://www.newyorker.com/magazine/2023/04/24/the-blazing-world-jonathan-healey-book-review.

21. Bryn Rosenfeld, "Reevaluating the Middle-Class Protest Paradigm: A Case-Control Study of Democratic Protest Coalitions in Russia," *American Political Science Review* 111, no. 4 (2017): 637–52, https://doi.org/10.1017/S000305541700034X.

22. Jeffrey M. Jones, "LGBT Identification in U.S. Ticks Up to 7.1%," Gallup, February 17, 2022, https://news.gallup.com/poll/389792/lgbt-identification-ticks-up.aspx.

23. The group now goes simply by "PFLAG" (PFLAG is no longer an acronym).

24. Kathryn Schulz, "How One Mother's Love for Her Gay Son Started a Revolution," *New Yorker*, April 10, 2023, https://www.newyorker.com/magazine/2023/04/17/how-one-mothers-love-for-her-gay-son-started-a-revolution.

25. Angie Y. Chung, "The Powers that Bind: A Case Study of the Collective Bases of Coalition Building in Post-Civil Unrest Los Angeles," *Urban Affairs Review* 37, no. 2 (2001): 205–26, https://doi.org/10.1177/10780870122185262.

26. Joyce Gelb and Colleen J. Shogan, "Community Activism in the USA: Catholic Hospital Mergers and Reproductive Access," *Social Movement Studies* 4, no. 3 (2005): 209–29, https://doi.org/10.1080/14742830500329879.

27. Myra Marx Ferree and Silke Roth, "Gender, Class, and the Interaction between Social Movements: A Strike of West Berlin Day Care Workers," *Gender and Society* 12, no. 6 (1998): 626–48, https://www.jstor.org/stable/190510.

28. Dana R. Fisher, Dawn M. Dow, and Rashawn Ray, "Intersectionality Takes It to the Streets: Mobilizing Across Diverse Interests for the Women's March," *Science Advances* 3, no. 9 (2017): eaao1390, https://www.science.org/doi/10.1126/sciadv.aao1390.

29. Matt Broomfield, "Women's March Against Donald Trump Is the Largest Day of Protests in U.S. History, Say Political Scientists," *Independent*, January 23, 2017, https://www.independent.co.uk/news/world/americas/womens-march-anti-donald-trump-womens-rights-largest-protest-demonstration-us-history-political-scientists-a7541081.html.

30. Amsa Khalid, "Women's March Divisions Offer Lessons for Democrats on Managing a Big Tent," NPR, January 17, 2019, https://www.npr.org/2019/01/17/685289036/womens-march-divisions-offer-lessons-for-democrats-on-managing-a-big-tent.

31. Farah Stockman, "Women's March Roiled by Accusations of Anti-Semitism," *New York Times*, December 23, 2018, https://www.nytimes.com/2018/12/23/us/womens-march-anti-semitism.html.

32. Ellen Barry, "How Russian Trolls Helped Keep the Women's March Out of Lock Step," *New York Times*, September 2022, https://www.nytimes.com/2022/09/18/us/womens-march-russia-trump.html.

33. Farah Stockman, "One Year After Women's March, More Activism but Less Unity," *New York Times*, January 15, 2018, https://www.nytimes.com/2018/01/15/us/womens-march-anniversary.html.

34. Benita Roth, "'Organizing One's Own' as Good Politics: Second Wage Feminists and the Meaning of Coalition," in *Strategic Alliances: Coalition Building and Social Movements*, ed. Nella Van Dyke and Holly J. McCammon (Minneapolis: University of Minnesota Press, 2010), 99–118.

35. Reuven Y. Hazan, "Does Cohesion Equal Discipline? Towards a Conceptual Delineation," *Journal of Legislative Studies* 9, no. 4 (2003): 1–11.

36. Sally J. Scholz, *Political Solidarity* (University Park: Penn State University Press, 2008).

37. D. Michael Lindsay, "Evangelicals in the Power Elite: Elite Cohesion Advancing a Movement," *American Sociological Review* 73, no. 1 (2008): 71, https://www.jstor.org/stable/25472514.

38. Thad Dunning and Lauren Harrison, "Cross-Cutting Cleavages and Ethnic Voting: An Experimental Study of Cousinage in Mali," *American Political Science Review* 104, no. 1 (2010): 21, https://doi.org/10.1017/S0003055409990311.

39. John McCauley, "The Political Mobilization of Ethnic and Religious Identities in Africa," *American Political Science Review* 108, no. 4 (2014): 801–16, https://doi.org/10.1017/S0003055414000410.

40. Émile Durkheim, *Suicide: A Study in Sociology* (New York: The Free Press, 1951), 159. First published as *Le suicide: Étude de sociologie* (Paris, 1897).

41. Emily Crockett, "Can You Be a 'Pro-Life Feminist'? The Women's March on Washington Offered Some Insights," *Vox*, January 22, 2017, https://www.vox.com/identities/2017/1/22/14335292/womens-march-washington-abortion-pro-life-feminists.

42. Johanna K. Kaakinen et al., "Influence of Text Cohesion on the Persuasive Power of Expository Test," *Scandinavian Journal of Psychology* 52, no. 3 (2011): 201–8, https://pubmed.ncbi.nlm.nih.gov/21265860.

43. Danielle S. McNamara and Joe P. Magliano, "Toward a Comprehensive Model of Comprehension," in *The Psychology of Learning and Motivation*, ed. Brian Ross (New York: Elsevier Science, 2009), 297–394.

44. Bruce K. Britton and Sami Gülgöz, "Using Kintsch's Computational Model to Improve Instructional Text: Effects of Repairing Inference Calls on Recall and Cognitive Structures," *Journal of Educational Psychology* 83 no. 3 (1991): 329–45, https://doi.org/10.1037/0022-0663.83.3.329.

45. Lisa Mueller, "Crowd Cohesion and Protest Outcomes," *American Journal of Political Science* (forthcoming), https://doi.org/10.1111/ajps.12725.

46. Mueller, "Crowd Cohesion and Protest Outcomes."

47. Ulrike Bergermann, "P/occupy Milieus: The Human Microphone and the Space between Protesters," in *Interventions in Digital Cultures: Technology, the Political, Methods*, ed. Howard Caygill et al. (Lüneburg: Meson Press, 2017), 87–103.

48. Sophia J. Wallace, Chris Zepeda-Millán, and Michael Jones-Correa, "Spatial and Temporal Proximity: Examining the Effects of Protests on Political Attitudes," *American Journal of Political Science* 58, no. 2 (2014): 433–48, https://doi.org/10.1111/ajps.12060.

49. Robert D. Putnam, *Bowling Alone: The Collapse and Revival of American Community* (New York: Simon & Schuster, 2000).

50. Robert M. Sapolsky, *Behave: The Biology of Humans at Our Best and Worst* (New York: Penguin, 2017), 409.

51. Greenpeace, "Toolkit: Everything You Need to Write, Edit and Place an Opinion Piece," https://www.greenpeace.org/usa/toolkits/everything-you-need-to-write-edit-and-place-an-opinion-piece, accessed November 1, 2023.

52. Ann-Marie Szymanski, *Pathways to Prohibition: Radicals, Moderates, and Social Movement Outcomes* (Durham, NC: Duke University Press, 2003), 45.

53. Christian Davenport, *How Social Movements Die: Repression and Demobilization of the Republic of New Africa* (New York: Cambridge University Press, 2014).

54. Craig Volden and Clifford J. Carrubba, "The Formation of Oversized Coalitions in Parliamentary Democracies," *American Journal of Political Science* 48, no. 3 (2004): 521–37, https://doi.org/10.1111/j.0092-5853.2004.00085.x.

55. Jonathan S. Coley, "Social Movements and Bridge Building: Religious and Sexual Identity Conflicts," *Intersectionality and Social Change* 37 (2014): 125–51, https://doi.org/10.1108/S0163-786X20140000037005.

56. Amin Ghaziani, "Post-Gay Collective Identity Construction," *Social Problems* 58, no. 1 (2011): 99–125, https://doi.org/10.1525/sp.2011.58.1.99.

57. Daniel B. Cornfield and Holly J. McCammon, "Approaching Merger: The Converging Public Policy Agendas of the AFL and CIO, 1938–1955," in *Strategic Alliances: Coalition Building and Social Movements*, ed. Nella Van Dyke and Holly J. McCammon (Minneapolis: University of Minnesota Press, 2010), 80.

58. Deirdre Walsh, "AFL-FIO Steps Up Get-Out-the-Vote Effort," CNN, October 25, 2010, https://edition.cnn.com/2010/POLITICS/10/25/union.vote.campaign.

59. Pennsylvania AFL-CIO, "Pennsylvania AFL-CIO Leading Massive GOTV Push for General Election," news release, October 30, 2014, https://www.prnewswire.com/news-releases/pennsylvania-afl-cio-leading-massive-gotv-push-for-general-election-280941432.html.

60. Sirianne Dahlum, "Joining Forces: Social Coalitions and Democratic Revolutions," *Journal of Peace Research* (forthcoming), https://doi.org/10.1177/00223433221138614.

61. Wibke Marie Junk, "When Diversity Works: The Effects of Coalition Composition on the Success of Lobbying Coalitions," *American Journal of Political Science* 63, no. 3 (2019): 660–74, https://doi.org/10.1111/ajps.12437.

62. Jeb Aram Middlebrook, "Organizing a Rainbow Coalition of Revolutionary Solidarity," *Journal of African American Studies* 23 (2019): 406, https://doi.org/10.1007/s12111-019-09454-6.

63. Brittney Cooper, "Intersectionality," in *The Oxford Handbook of Feminist Theory*, ed. Lisa Disch and Mary Hawkesworth (New York: Oxford University Press, 2016), 385–406.

64. Robert Mitchell, "The Police Raid That Killed Two Black Panthers, Shook Chicago and Changed the Nation," *Washington Post*, December 4, 2019, https://www.washingtonpost.com/history/2019/12/04/police-raid-that-left-two-black-panthers-dead-shook-chicago-changed-nation.

65. Tabitha Bonilla and Alvin B. Tillery Junior, "Which Identity Frames Boost Support for and Mobilization in the #BlackLivesMatter Movement? An Experimental Test," *American Political Science Review* 114, no. 4 (2020): 947–62, https://doi.org/10.1017/S0003055420000544.

66. Black Lives Matter, "About," https://blacklivesmatter.com/about, accessed November 1, 2023.

67. Peter Callaghan, "'Fired Up About Rondo:' Land-Bridge Concept for St. Paul Neighborhood Gets a Boost," *Minnesota Post*, March 29, 2018, https://www.minnpost.com/politics-policy/2018/03/fired-about-rondo-land-bridge-concept-st-paul-neighborhood-gets-boost.

68. Thor-André Skrefsrud, "Teachers as Intercultural Bridge-Builders: Rethinking the Metaphor of Bridge-Building," *Teaching Theology & Religion* 23, no. 3 (2020): 137–213, https://doi.org/10.1111/teth.12550.

69. Martin Hartmann, *The Feeling of Inequality: On Empathy, Empathy Gulfs, and the Political Psychology of Democracy* (New York: Oxford University Press, 2023).

70. Fred Rose, *Coalitions Across the Class Divide: Lessons from the Labor, Peace, and Environmental Movements* (Ithaca, NY: Cornell University Press, 2018), 166.

71. Rose, *Coalitions Across the Class Divide*, 167.

72. Hinkley, "Coalitions in Congress," 197.

73. Winnifred R. Louis et al., "Emerging Research on Intergroup Prosociality: Group Members' Charitable Giving, Positive Contact, Allyship, and Solidarity with Others," *Social and Personality Psychology Compass* 13, no. 3 (2019): e12436, https://doi.org/10.1111/spc3.12436.

74. Juilana Carlson et al., "What's in a Name? A Synthesis of 'Allyship' Elements from Academic and Activist Literature," *Journal of Family Violence* 35 (2020): 889–98.

75. Alicia Garza, *The Purpose of Power: How We Come Together When We Fall Apart* (New York: One World, 2020), 216.

76. Michael E. McCullough and Charlotte vanOyen Witvliet, "The Psychology of Forgiveness," in *Handbook of Positive Psychology*, ed. C. R. Snyder and Shane J. Lopez (New York: Oxford University Press, 2002), 446.

77. Ezra Klein, "Transcript: Ezra Klein Interviews Natalie Wynn and Will Wilkinson," *New York Times*, April 27, 2021, https://www.nytimes.com/2021/04/27/podcasts/ezra-klein-podcast-cancel-culture-transcript.html.

78. Karen Wyatt, *7 Lessons for Living from the Dying: How to Nurture What Really Matters* (London: Watkins, 2020).

79. McCullough and Witvliet, "The Psychology of Forgiveness," 447.

80. Danya Ruttenberg, *On Repentance and Repair: Making Amends in an Unapologetic World* (Boston: Beacon Press, 2022), 25.

81. M. E. McCullough et al., "Interpersonal Forgiving in Close Relationships: II. Theoretical Elaboration and Measurement," *Journal of Personality and Social Psychology* 75, no. 6 (1998): 1586–1603, https://psycnet.apa.org/record/1998-03003-013.

CHAPTER 5: MONEY TALKS

1. Michelle Watson, "Black Lives Matter Executive Accused of 'Syphoning' $10M from BLM Donors, Suit Says," CNN, September 5, 2022, https://www.cnn.com/2022/09/04/us/black-lives-matter-executive-lawsuit/index.html; Ryan Grim and Akela Lacy, "Under Attack Again, Women's March Releases Tax Documents and Justifies Spending," *The Intercept*, November 29, 2018, https://theintercept.com/2018/11/29/womens-march-financial-tax-form.

2. Grim and Lacy, "Under Attack Again, Women's March Releases Tax Documents and Justifies Spending."

3. Grim and Lacy, "Under Attack Again, Women's March Releases Tax Documents and Justifies Spending."

4. Leila Demarest, "Staging a 'Revolution': The 2011–12 Electoral Protests in Senegal," *African Studies Review* 59, no. 3 (2016): 70, https://doi.org/10.1017/asr.2016.78.

5. World Bank and OECD National Accounts data, https://data.worldbank.org/indicator/NY.GDP.PCAP.CD?locations=SN, https://data.worldbank.org/indicator/NY.GDP.PCAP.CD?locations=US.

6. Bob Edwards and John D. McCarthy, "Resources and Social Movement Mobilization," in *The Blackwell Companion to Social Movements*, ed. David A. Snow, Sarah A. Soule, and Hanspeter Kriesi (Malden, MA: Blackwell Publishing, 2004), 125.

7. Edwards and McCarthy, "Resources and Social Movement Mobilization," 128.

8. John D. McCarthy and Mayer N. Zald, "Resource Mobilization and Social Movements: A Partial Theory," *American Journal of Sociology* 82, no. 6 (1977): 1212–41, https://www.jstor.org/stable/2777934.

9. James Q. Wilson, *The Amateur Democrat: Club Politics in Three Cities* (Chicago: University of Chicago Press, 1962).

10. Tom Wolfe, "Radical Chic: That Party at Lenny's," *New York*, June 8, 1970, https://nymag.com/news/features/46170.

11. Charlotte Curtis, "The Bernsteins' Party for Black Panther Legal Defense Stirs Talk and More Parties," *New York Times*, January 24, 1970, https://www.nytimes.com/1970/01/24/archives/the-bernsteins-party-for-black-panther-legal-defense-stirs-talk-and.html.

12. Ira Silver, "Buying an Activist Identity: Reproducing Class Through Social Movement Philanthropy," *Sociological Perspectives* 41, no. 2 (1998): 303–21, https://doi.org/10.2307/1389479.

13. Hahrie Han, Elizabeth McKenna, and Michelle Oyakawa, *Prisms of the People: Power and Organizing in Twenty-First-Century America* (Chicago: University of Chicago Press, 2021), 20.

14. J. Craig Jenkins, "Social Movement Philanthropy and American Democracy," in *Philanthropic Giving: Studies in Varieties and Goals*, ed. Richard Magat (New York: Oxford University Press, 1989), 301.

15. Sheelah Kolhatkar, "The C.E.O. of Anti-Woke, Inc." *New Yorker*, December 12, 2022, https://www.newyorker.com/magazine/2022/12/19/the-ceo-of-anti-woke-inc.

16. The Claremont Institute Center for the American Way of Life, BLM Funding Database, https://dc.claremont.org/blm-funding-database, accessed November 1, 2023.

17. Herbert H. Haines, "Black Radicalization and the Funding of Civil Rights: 1957–1970," *Social Problems* 32, no. 1 (1984): 31–43, http://www.jstor.org/stable/800260.

18. J. Craig Jenkins and Craig M. Eckert, "Channeling Black Insurgency: Elite Patronage and Professional Social Movement Organizations in the Development of the Black Movement," *American Sociological Review* 51, no. 6 (1986): 821, https://www.jstor.org/stable/2095369.

19. J. Craig Jenkins and Abigail Halci, "Grassrooting the System? The Development and Impact of Social Movement Philanthropy, 1953–1990," in *Philanthropic Foundations: New Scholarship, New Possibilities*, ed. Ellen Condliffe Lagemann (Bloomington: Indiana University Press, 1999), 229–56.

20. Jenkins and Eckert, "Channeling Black Insurgency," 823.

21. Eleanor L. Brilliant, "Women's Gain: Fund-Raising and Fund Allocation as an Evolving Social Movement Strategy," *Nonprofit and Voluntary Sector Quarterly* 29, no. 4 (2000): 554–70, https://doi.org/10.1177/0899764000294005.

22. Women's Funding Network, "Our Story," https://www.womensfundingnetwork.org/who-we-are/our-story, accessed November 1, 2023.

23. Women's Funding Network, "Women's Economic Mobility Hubs," https://www.womensfundingnetwork.org/what-we-do/strategy-development/economic-mobility-hub, accessed November 1, 2023.

24. Brilliant, "Women's Gain," 565.

25. Bill & Melinda Gates Foundation, "Foundation Fact Sheet," https://www.gatesfoundation.org/about/foundation-fact-sheet, accessed November 1, 2023.

26. The Gates Foundation, in particular, has rigorous standards for impact evaluation.

27. Frederick M. Hess, "Philanthropy Gets in the Ring," American Enterprise Institute, April 24, 2012, https://www.aei.org/articles/philanthropy-gets-in-the-ring.

28. Doug McAdam and W. Richard Scott, "Organizations and Social Movements," in *Social Movements and Organization Theory*, ed. Gerald F. Davis et al. (New York: Cambridge University Press, 2005), 10.

29. Tim Bartley, "How Foundations Shape Social Movements: The Construction of an Organizational Field and the Rise of Forest Certification," *Social Problems* 54, no. 3 (2007): 229–55.

30. Catherine Corrigall-Brown, "Funding for Social Movements," *Sociology Compass* 10, no. 4 (2016): 333, https://doi.org/10.1111/soc4.12362.

31. Haymarket People's Fund, *2022 Haymarket Grantees Glossary*, https://www.haymarket.org/_files/ugd/625fa0_25e90405d1c04d41af55c7ec9c947fe6.pdf, accessed November 1, 2023.

32. Haymarket People's Fund, "About Haymarket," https://www.haymarket.org/about, accessed November 1, 2023.

33. Susan A. Ostrander, *Money for Change: Social Movement Philanthropy at Haymarket People's Fund* (Philadelphia: Temple University Press), 90.

34. Human Rights Campaign, "Human Rights Campaign Refuses Money from Disney Until Meaningful Action Is Taken to Combat Florida's 'Don't Say Gay or Trans' Bill," March 9, 2022, https://www.hrc.org/press-releases/human-rights-campaign-refuses-money-from-disney-until-meaningful-action-is-taken-to-combat-floridas-dont-say-gay-or-trans-bill.

35. Luis Cortes Romero, "Activism Leads, the Law Follows: DACA and Its Fate at the Supreme Court," *American Bar Association*, April 27, 2020, https://www.americanbar.org/groups/crsj/publications/human_rights_magazine_home/immigration/activism-leads-the-law-follows.

36. Spencer Buell, "Massachusetts Companies Donated $65,000 to Help DACA Applicants Pay Fees," *Boston*, September 26, 2017, https://www.bostonmagazine.com/news/2017/09/26/massachusetts-donated-65000-daca-fees.

37. Jenkins and Halci, "Grassrooting the System," 255.

38. Victoria Carty, *Wired and Mobilizing: Social Movements, New Technology, and Electoral Politics* (New York: Routledge, 2011), 124 and 133.

39. Charis Chang, "The Political Force that Terrifies the Liberal Party," News.com.au, May 4, 2019, https://www.news.com.au/national/federal-election/the-political-force-that-terrifies-the-liberal-party/news-story/5c2e2162139a4fa60eef27245a6c39ed.

40. John F. Kihlstrom, "The Cognitive Unconscious," *Science* 237 (1987): 1445–52, https://www.science.org/doi/abs/10.1126/science.3629249.

41. Saif Ullah and Yulin Zhou, "Gender, Anonymity and Team: What Determines Crowdfunding Success on Kickstarter," *Journal of Risk and Financial Management* 13, no. 4 (2020): 1–26, https://doi.org/10.3390/jrfm13040080.

42. Alessandro Cordova, Johanna Dolci, and Gianfranco Gianfrate, "The Determinants of Crowdfunding Success: Evidence from Technology Projects," *Procedia* 181, no. 11 (2015): 115–24, https://doi.org/10.1016/j.sbspro.2015.04.872; Jascha-Alexander Koch and Michael Siering, "Crowdfunding Success Factors: The Characteristics of Successfully Funded Projects on Crowdfunding Platforms," *Proceedings of the 23rd European Conference on Information Systems* (2015): 12, https://ssrn.com/abstract=2808424; Mi Zhou et al., "Project Description and Crowdfunding Success: An Exploratory Study," *Information Systems Frontiers* 20, no. 2 (2018): 259–74, https://pubmed.ncbi.nlm.nih.gov/29755287.

43. Ajay K. Agrawal, Christian Catalini, and Avi Goldfarb, "The Geography of Crowdfunding," NBER Working Paper Series no. 16820 (2011): 1–61, https://www.nber.org/papers/w16820.

44. Dennis M. Steininger, Mark Lorch, and Daniel Veit, "The Bandwagon Effect in Digital Environments: An Experimental Study on Kickstarter.com," *Multikonferenz Wirtschaftsinformatik* (2014): 546–56, https://www.researchgate.net/publication/260088116_The_Bandwagon_Effect_in_Digital_Environments_An_Experimental_Study_on_Kickstartercom.

45. Xin Tian et al., "Herding Behavior in Supplier Innovation Crowdfunding: Evidence from Kickstarter," *International Journal of Production Economics* 239 (2021): 108184, https://doi.org/10.1016/j.ijpe.2021.108184.

46. Zhou et al., "Project Description and Crowdfunding Success."

47. Koch and Siering, "Crowdfunding Success Factors," 11.

48. Koch and Siering, "Crowdfunding Success Factors," 11.

49. Lauren Rhue and Lionel P. Robert Jr., "Emotional Delivery in Pro-Social Crowdfunding Success," *Extended Abstracts of the 2018 CHI Conference on Human Factors in Computing Systems* (2018): 1–6, https://doi.org/10.1145/3170427.3188534.

50. Koch and Siering, "Crowdfunding Success Factors," 11; Ullah and Zhou, "Gender, Anonymity and Team," 13.

51. Ullah and Zhou, "Gender, Anonymity and Team," 13.

52. Jens Hainmueller, Daniel J. Hopkins, and Teppei Yamamoto, "Causal Inference in Conjoint Analysis: Understanding Multidimensional Choices via Stated Preference Experiments," *Political Analysis* 22, no. 1 (2014): 1–30, https://doi.org/10.1093/pan/mpt024.

53. Lisa Mueller, "United We Stand, Divided We Fall? How Signals of Activist Cohesion Affect Attraction to Advocacy Organizations," *Interest Groups & Advocacy* 10 (2021): 1–18, https://doi.org/10.1057/s41309-020-00108-7.

54. Sarah Mathey and Zoe Howard, "Q3 2019: On Track for a $1 Billion Year," ActBlue (blog), October 17, 2019, https://blog.actblue.com/2019/10/17/q3-2019-on-track-for-a-1-billion-year.

55. Rob Pope, *Becoming Forest: The Extraordinary True Story of One Man's Epic Run Across America* (New York: HarperNorth, 2023).

56. Christopher Y. Olivola and Eldar Shafir, "The Martyrdom Effect: When Pain and Effort Increase Prosocial Contributions," *Journal of Behavioral Decision Making* 26, no. 1 (2013): 91–105, https://doi.org/10.1002/bdm.767.

57. This quote is from Smiley's 2016 visit with the national team. Kevin Lilley, "Major Motivation: Wounded Warrior Scotty Smiley Speaks to Team USA Hoops," *Army Times*, July 28, 2016, https://www.armytimes.com/off-duty/military-sports/2016/07/28/major-motivation-wounded-warrior-scotty-smiley-speaks-to-team-usa-hoops.

58. Rebecca K. Ratner, Min Zhao, and Jennifer A. Clarke, "The Norm of Self-Interest: Implications for Charitable Giving," in *The Science of Giving: Experimental Approaches to the Study of Charity*, ed. Daniel M. Oppenheimer and Christopher Y. Olivola (New York: Psychology Press, 2011), 113–32.

59. Peter Singer, *The Life You Can Save: How to Do Your Part to End World Poverty* (New York: Random House, 2010), 3.

60. GiveWell, "Why Is It So Expensive to Save Lives?" https://www.givewell.org/cost-to-save-a-life, accessed November 1, 2023.

61. Geof Magga, "Mosquito Nets as Wedding Gowns and Fishing Nets in Uganda," *Africa Report*, February 10, 2012, https://www.theafricareport.com/7659/mosquito-nets-as-wedding-gowns-and-fishing-nets-in-uganda.

62. Nicolette Naylor and Nina Blackwell, "Freeing Ourselves from Colonial, White Savior Models of Philanthropy," *Nonprofit Quarterly*, June 16, 2022, https://nonprofitquarterly.org/freeing-ourselves-from-colonial-white-savior-models-of-philanthropy.

63. Cynthia Cryder and George Loewenstein, "The Critical Link Between Tangibility and Generosity," in Oppenheimer and Olivola, *The Science of Giving*, 237–52.

64. See Cryder and Loewenstein, "The Critical Link Between Tangibility and Generosity," for summaries and citations.

65. Samson Ntale et al., "At Least 45 People Killed During Ugandan Protests," CNN, November 24, 2020, https://www.cnn.com/2020/11/23/africa/ugandan-protest-death-toll-intl/index.html.

66. "France to Probe Paris Migrant Camp Dismantling After 'Shocking' Scuffle Images," France 24, November 24, 2020, https://www.france24.com/en/france/20201124-police-use-tear-gas-to-disperse-refugees-living-in-migrant-camp-in-central-paris.

67. Julian Go, "The Imperial Origins of American Policing: Militarization and Imperial Feedback in the Early 20th Century," *American Journal of Sociology* 125, no. 5 (2020): 1193–1254, https://doi.org/10.1086/708464.

68. Go, "The Imperial Origins of American Policing," 1194.

69. David Pion-Berlin and Igor Acácio, "Explaining Military Responses to Protests in Latin American Democracies," *Comparative Politics* 54, no. 2 (2022): 229–51, https://doi.org/10.5129/001041522X16195268352999.

70. Astead W. Herndon, "How a Pledge to Dismantle the Minneapolis Police Collapsed," *New York Times*, September 26, 2020, https://www.nytimes.com/2020/09/26/us/politics/minneapolis-defund-police.html.

71. Aurelien Breeden, "France Lawmakers Pass Contentious Bill Extending Police Powers," *New York Times*, April 15, 2021, https://www.nytimes.com/2021/04/15/world/europe/france-security-bill-passes.html.

72. Joseph Ax, "Defying 'Defund Police' Calls, Democrat Adams Leads NYC Mayor's Race," Reuters, June 22, 2021, https://www.reuters.com/world/us/defying-defund-police-calls-democrat-adams-leads-nyc-mayors-race-2021-06-23.

73. See details and citations in Kai M. Thaler, Lisa Mueller, and Eric Mosinger, "Framing Police Violence: Repression, Reform, and the Power of History in Chile," *Journal of Politics* (forthcoming), https://doi.org/10.1086/724967.

74. "High-dose" frames, which also included photographs of recent and historical violence, were especially powerful.

CONCLUSION

1. Kurt Weyland, *Making Waves: Democratic Contention in Europe and Latin America Since the Revolutions of 1848* (New York: Cambridge University Press, 2014).

2. Michael K. Miller, Michael Joseph, and Dorothy Ohl, "Are Coups Really Contagious? An Extreme Bounds Analysis of Political Diffusion," *Journal of Conflict Resolution* 62, no. 2 (2018): 410–41, https://doi.org/10.1177/0022002716649232.

3. Kurt Weyland, "Crafting Counterrevolution: How Reactionaries Learned to Combat Change in 1848," *American Political Science Review* 110, no. 2 (2016): 225, https://doi.org/10.1017/S0003055416000174.

4. Weyland, "Crafting Counterrevolution," 215.

5. Charles Taylor, *The Ethics of Authenticity* (Cambridge, MA: Harvard University Press, 1991), 26.

6. Rigoberta Menchú and Elisabeth Burgos-Debray, ed., *I, Rigoberta Menchú* (New York: Verso, 2009), 262.

7. Neil deGrasse Tyson, *Starry Messenger: Cosmic Perspectives on Civilization* (New York: Henry Holt, 2022), 176.

8. William MacAskill, *Doing Good Better: How Effective Altruism Can Help You Help Others, Do Work That Matters, and Make Smarter Choices About Giving Back* (New York: Avery, 2015).

9. MacAskill, *Doing Good Better*.

10. Larissa MacFarquhar, *Strangers Drowning: Impossible Idealism, Drastic Choices, and the Urge to Help* (New York: Penguin, 2015).

11. Michael Specter, "The Dangerous Philosopher," *New Yorker*, August 29, 1999, https://www.newyorker.com/magazine/1999/09/06/the-dangerous-philosopher.

INDEX

Page numbers for illustrations appear in italics.

abolitionists, 5
abortion access, 9, 24, 103–4, 113, 114, 115
Ace Metrix, 52
ActBlue, 159–60
activism: deep, 51, 70; defined, 3; "disciplining" of, 7; quiet, 3; science *vs.*, 14–18
activist personality, 64–65
The Advantage of Disadvantage (Gause), 33
advertising, 52, 152–56, *153*
Aegis surveillance system, 66
aesthetic practices, 71–75
affirmative action policies, 95
AFL-CIO, 124
"African Spring," 108
Against Malaria Foundation, 165, 176–77
agreeableness, 64–65
al-Bashir, Omar, 18–19
Algeria, 66
allies and allyship, 104, 109–10, 131–34
altruism, effective, 45–46, 175–77
Amalgamated Clothing and Textile Workers Union, 130

American Dream and Promise Act, 152
American Federation of Labor and Congress of Industrial Organizations (AFL-CIO), 124
American Revolution, 171
Amini, Masha, 29
Anoll, Allison, 41
anti-racist activism, 93
applied utilitarianism, 176–77
Arab Spring: effectiveness of, 1, 2; online coordination of, 59, 62; organizing hubs for, 31; protests modeled on, 4; and protest waves, 171, 172; and repression, 19; violence in, 95
Armistead, Lewis, 121
Arnon, Daniel, 90
Artful Activists, 74
artist-activists, 74–75
athlete-activists, 91–92, *92*
attention economy, 69
"attention residue," 70
autocrats, and online activists, 66–68
Autrey, Wesley, 52–53, 57
awe, 86–87

Bahrain, 32
Balogun, Jumoke, 50

"bandwagon effect," 155
Banerjee, Abhijit, 6
Barro, Fadel, 106, 107
Bay of Pigs invasion (1961), 96
bearing witness, 71–72
Beem, Angie, 112
beneficiaries, 164–66
Ben & Jerry's, 52
Benno Bokk Yaakaar, 111
Berlin Wall, 28
Bernstein, Leonard, 142–43
Berry, Mr. and Mrs. Lee, 142–43
Biden, Joe, 24, 151
Big Five, 64–65
Bill and Melinda Gates Foundation, 147
Bingham, Hiram, 121
Black Americans, social esteem of, 41
Black Lives Matter (BLM), 2; and advantage of disadvantage, 33–34; and coalitions, 131, 134; crowd size of, 27; effectiveness of, 172; fundraising for, 137, 144; as intersectional, 126–27; media coverage of, 93; and online recruiting, 65; police repression of, 166, 167; and slacktivism, 59–60; and violence, 78, 98
#BlackLivesMatter, 51, 57, 59–60, 61, 96, 122
Black Lives Matter Funding Database, 144
Black Lives Matter Global Network Foundation, 34
"black nationalist hate groups," 91
Black Panther Party, 4, 91, 125–26, 142–43
BLM. *See* Black Lives Matter (BLM)
Bloomberg, Michael, 53
"Blow Away the AfD," 40
board of directors, and fundraising, 148–49

Boko Haram, 49–50
Bonilla, Tabitha, 126–27, 128
Brady Campaign, 60
branding problems, 52
Brave New World (Huxley), 68
bridge builders, 104, 128–30, 135
Bridge Builders, 123
#BringBackOurGirls, 50, 51, 54, 57, 58
brown, adrienne maree, 8
Brulle, Robert J., 12
Butcher, Charles, 31–32

Canada, COVID-19 vaccine mandate by, 29
Capitol Hill riot, 23–24, 33–34, 98
Carmona, Rachel O'Leary, 138
the carrot and the stick, 38–43
Casas, Andreu, 65
cause(s): and effect, 5; prioritization of, 175–77
censorship, 19, 66–67, 68
Center for Artistic Activism, 74
Chambers, Gary, Jr., 46
Chapek, Bob, 149
Chavez, Cesar, 74
Chenoweth, Erica, 18–19, 29–30, 32, 88, 96
Chile, 28, 59, 66, 168–69
China, 2, 21–22, 28, 35–36, 66, 67
"Chinese solution," 32
CHIRLA, 152–54, *153*
Chung, Angie, 110
Civil Rights Movement. *See* US Civil Rights Movement
Civis Analytics, 79
cladistics, 81–82
Claremont Institute, 144
Clarke, Jennifer, 163
Clarke, Killian, 96–97, 99
Clinton, Hillary, 113, 128
coalition(s), 103–35; allyship in, 104, 109–10, 131–34; average citizens in, 107–8; bridge

builders in, 104, 128–30, 135; categories of protesters in, 110–11; cohesive demands in, 104, 113–14, 115–25, *118*; common ground in, 111, 121, 1114; cross-cutting cleavages in, 114, 121; defined, 104, 108; diversity in, 124–25; healing of, 131–34; heterogeneous interests in, 109–10, 112, 113; naming of, 123; opportunities for new, 123–24; "oversized" ("big tent"), 122–23; purity tests in, 122–23; "rainbow" (intersectional), 125–28; resources in, 110, 131–32; sequencing in, 127–28; success *vs.* failure of, 112–14; tactics for enhancing cohesion in, 120–22; targeting in, 127; teamwork in, 105–12
Coalition for Humane Immigrant Rights of Los Angeles (CHIRLA), 152–54, *153*
Coalitions Across the Class Divide (Rose), 130
Cobb, Charles E., Jr., 84–85, 86
coercion, 38, 41–43, 96
cognitive dissonance, 60
cohesion gaps, 115
cohesive demands, 104, 113–14, 115–25, *118*
Coley, Jonathan, 123
collective action: cooperation problems in, 37–43; coordination problems in, 35–37; individual activism *vs.*, 22–23, 44–47
collective effervescence, 82, 196n11
"color revolutions," 1
community-based knowledge, 7
"compound treatment" problem, 157–60, *159*
computer science, manipulation of, 18–19
Concern Health, 104

concessions, crowd size and, 31–32
Confederate monuments, 46
Congress of Racial Equality (CORE), 87–88, 93, 145
conjoint experiment, 157–60, *159*
"conscience adherents," 141–43
Consumer Financial Protection Bureau, 97
cooperation problems, 37–43
cooptation, fundraising and, 143–48
coordination problems, 35–37
CORE, 87–88, 93, 145
counterrevolutions, 96, 172–73
COVID-19 pandemic: and Canadian mandate of vaccine, 29; and distrust of science, 10–12; and protest participation, 26, 36; and slacktivism, 52, 61–62; talking points on, 122; and Women's Funding Network, 146–47
Crenshaw, Kimberlé, 125
Crime and Human Nature (Wilson and Herrnstein), 83
Croatia, 66
"cross-cutting cleavage," 114, 121
crowdfunding, 151–56, *153*
crowd size, 27–33
Crowds on Demand, 39
Cruz, Verónica, 24
Cryder, Cynthia, 166
"cult of the irrelevant," 7
Czech Republic, 116

DACA (2012), 150–51, 152–54, *153*
Dahlum, Sirianne, 124–25
Dakota Access Pipeline, 167
Dalai Lama, 87
data analytics, manipulation of, 18–19
Davenport, Christian, 122
Davis, Angela, 121
Deacons for Defense and Justice, 84

deep activism, 51, 70
Deferred Action for Childhood Arrivals (DACA, 2012), 150–51, 152–54, *153*
Delano Grape Strike, 74, 75
demands, cohesive, 104, 113–14, 115–25, *118*
Demarest, Leila, 138
disadvantage, advantage of, 33–35
disagreeableness, 64–65
discretionary purchases, 165
dissatisfaction: and protest participation, 25–27, 37
Dixon, Benjamin, 79
Dobbs v. Jackson Women's Health Organization (2022), 103–4, 114
Doing Good Better (MacAskill), 6, 45
Dollbaum, Jan Matti, 64–65
"Don't Do It" campaign, 52, 55–56, 57
"Don't Say Gay" Bill, 149–50
"doom scrolling," 72, 74
Dosh, Paul, 97
DREAM Act and Dreamers, 150–51
Dubner, Stephen, 6
Du Bois, W. E. B., 73
Duflo, Esther, 6
Durkheim, Émile, 114, 196n11

East Germany, 27–28, 32–33
Eckert, Craig, 145
Edwards, Bob, 139
Edwards, Pearce, 90
effective altruism, 45–46, 175–77
Egypt, 62–63, 171, 172
Elamin, Nisrin, 109
Electoral Reform Society, 119
elite universities, prestige of, 53–54, 56–57
El Salvador, 39
El Teatro Campesino, 74, 75
Emergency Strategy (brown), 8
empathy, 72

"empathy gulfs," 129
empirical science, 14
empirical social science, 6–7
"End of the Godfathers," 116
#EndSARS campaign, 166–67
Enos, Ryan, 89
esprits, 108
eugenics, 82
European Union, 28–29
Evidence Revolution, 6–10, 17
excludable goods, 38
expected value framework, 45–46
extroversion, 64–65

Facebook, 18–19, 41, 49, 50, 62
Fakhoury, Tamara, 85
fangzu, 22
Farrakhan, Louis, 112
Fauci, Anthony, 11
Fawcett Society, 119
#FeesMustFall, 117
feminism, 113, 127, 146
Ferris, William, 73
#Fightfor15, 51
Fisher, Dana, 109, 112, 113, 116
Five Factor Model, 64–65
Floyd, George: and BLM movement, 78; and bridge building, 128–29; and coalitions, 131; and crowd size, 27, 29; and hashtags, 52; and performative protesting, 72; and police reform, 167; and science *vs.* activism, 16; and social signaling, 56; and violent protests, 98
Fontaine, Danielle, 3
foot-binding, 21–22
Forest Stewardship Council, 147–48
forgiveness, 133–34, 135
France, 167
Freakonomics (Levitt and Dubner), 6
"freedom convoy," 29
Freedom House, 66

Freedom Summer Project, 78
free riding, 37–43; coercion for, 41–43; defined, 37; and "non-excludable goods," 37; selective incentives for, 38–41
free speech, 66–67, 68
French Revolution, 171, 172
Friedrich Wilhelm IV of Prussia, 173
fun, as incentive, 40
"Fundamental Problem of Causal Interference," 5
Fundly, 151
fundraising, 137–69; advertising and, 152–56, *153*; audience and timing of, 154–55; and board of directors, 148–49; by classical *vs.* professional SMOs, 141–43, 145; from "conscience adherents," 141–43; and cooptation, 143–48; via crowdfunding, 151–56, *153*; disdain for, 144; framed in historical events, 166–69; goals of, 154; history lessons on, 140–52; identifying clear "victim" in, 164–66; involving stakeholders in, 161–64; market research on, 156–60, *159*; and martyrdom effect, 160–61; and mission drift, 148–50; and organizational fields, 147–48; psychological strategies for, 160–69; and "radical flank effect," 145–47; and refusal of donations, 149–50; and resource mobilization theory, 141; scrutiny of, 137–39; tax constraints on, 144; and violence, 160
FundRazr, 151
Funk, Patricia, 42

Gade, Emily Kalah, 84
Gandhi, Mahatma, 87
Garvey, Marcus, 72–74
Garza, Alicia, 98, 131
gate-keeping, 63
gateway effect, 67, 76
Gause, LaGina, 33, 34–35
genetics, 83–84
Getachew, Adom, 71, 73, 74
GetUp!, 151, 152
Ghaziani, Amin, 123
GiveWell, 165, 175
GoFundMe, 151, 154, 156
Gopnik, Adam, 109
Greenpeace, 119, 122
Gridiron Club, 89
Guatemala, 67–68
guerrilla theater, 74–75
gun(s), 84–86
gun control, 60, 109
Gutting, Raynee Sarah, 94

Haines, Herbert, 145
Haitian Revolution, 95, 171
Halci, Abigail, 151
Hamilton (musical), 2
Hampton, Fred, 125–26
Han, Hahrie, 143
Hanson, Susan, 3
Harlem riots, 85–86
Harvard University, 53–54
hashtags, 50–52, 53, 58, 59, 74, 122, 190–91n6
Haymarket People's Fund, 148–49
"herding behavior," 155
heroes, 52–53
Herrnstein, Richard J., 83
Hess, Frederick, 147
historical frames, 166–69, 209n74
Hobbs, William, 67
Honecker, Erich, 27–28, 33
Hong Kong, 2, 28, 35–36, 38, 66
Hoover, J. Edgar, 91
Hsieh, Gary, 59–60
Human Rights Campaign, 149–50
Humphrey, Hubert, 8

Hussein, Saddam, 32
Huxley, Aldous, 68

identifiable "victim" effect, 165–66
immigration reform, 150–51, 152–54, *153*
incentives, 38–41
Indecline, 74–75
individual activism, 22–23, 44–47
"influencers," 45–46
"informational cascade," 27
Instagram, 67, 69
institutions, 97
International Organization of Good Templars, 122
internet, fundraising via, 151–56, *153*
internet activism. *See* slacktivism
intersectionality, 125–28
Iran, 28–29
Iraq, 32

Jane's Revenge, 103–4
January 6 US Capitol insurrection, 23–24, 33–34, 98
Jaunā Vienotība, 111
Jefferson, Hakeem, 93
Jenkins, J. Craig, 145, 151
#JeSuisCharlie, 51
Jonathan, Goodluck, 50
Jordan, David Starr, 81
Joyce, James, 72
Joyce, Mary, 63

Kaepernick, Colin, 91, 92
Kaufman, Aaron, 89
Kavanaugh, Brett, 38
Kefferpütz, Roderick, 19
Keltner, Dacher, 86–87, 88, 99
Keur Gui, 106
Kickstarter, 154
King, Martin Luther, Jr.: on allies, 132; on coordination of protests, 36–37; and violent *vs.*

nonviolent protests, 4, 7–8, 80, 82–83, 84–86, 87, 88–89
King, Rodney, 89
Kohl, Herbert, 23
Koreatown and West Adams Public Safety Association, 110
Kremer, Michael, 6
Krenz, Egon, 28, 32–33
Krzyzewski, Mike, 161–63, 164
Ku Klux Klan, 85

Las Libres, 24
Latinx Americans, social esteem of, 41
"The League," 54
Lee, Robert E., 46
Lee, Yu-Hao, 59–60
Le Mouvement 23 Juin, 107, 138
Lennon, John, 80
Lesbian and Bisexual Women's Task Force, 123
Les Misérables (musical), 2
Letting Feet Out Society, 22
Levitt, Steven, 6
Lewis, Michael, 6
LGBTQ+ rights, 40–41, 110, 112, 123, 127, 149–50
LinkedIn, 54
list experiment, 91–92, *92*
Loewenstein, George, 166
Lomax, Louis, 144
Lorde, Audre, 156–57

MacAskill, William, 5, 6, 45, 176
MacFarquhar, Larissa, 176
Malcolm X, 82, 84, 85
Mallory, Tamika, 112, 137–38
Mampilly, Zachariah, 109
Mandela, Nelson, 57
Manekin, Devorah, 90–91, 94, 99
Manford, Jeanne, 110
Mansour, Abdel Rahman, 62–63
March for Life, 9, 113–14, 115, 116, 120

March for Our Lives (2017), 109, 112–14
March for Science (2017), 11–12
March On, 113
March On the Polls, 113
marginalized people: protests by, 33–35; social esteem of, 41
Mark, Gloria, 69–70
marriage equality, 40–41
Martin, Deborah G., 3
martyrdom effect, 160–61
material incentives, 38–39
McCarthy, John, 139, 141
McClendon, Gwyneth, 40–41
McKenna, Elizabeth, 143
McMaster, James, 71
Menchú, Rigoberta, 174–75
Meta-Activism Project, 63
#MeToo, 51, 57, 95
Mexico, 24
Miller, Lulu, 81–82
Minneapolis-Saint Paul, 128–29, 167
"Miracle of Leipzig," 33
mission drift, 148–50
Mitts, Tamar, 90–91, 94, 99
mobilization, of masses, 107–9
Monday demonstrations, in East Germany, 27–28, 32–33
Moneyball: The Art of Winning an Unfair Game (Lewis), 6
Moneyball for Government (Nussle and Orszag), 6
Money for Change (Ostrander), 149
Mongolia, 32, 66
mono-tasking, 69–70
Montgomery Bus Boycott, 23
moral balancing, 59
moral beauty, 87
morality, 174–75
moral responsibility, 176
Morozov, Evgeny, 58–59, 71
Mosinger, Eric, 167
movement(s): size of, 23–24; starting, 35–43

MoveOn.org, 151, 152
Mulford Act (1967), 91
Muslim countries, protests in, 31–32, 33

NAACP, 84, 146
National Black United Fund, 146
National Committee Against Discrimination in Housing, 145
National Committee for Responsive Philanthropy, 146
National Highway Traffic Safety Administration, 97
National Press Club, 89
National Rifle Association, 60, 91
Nation of Islam, 83, 112
Native Americans, water rights of, 167
Natural Resources Defense Council, 143
natural selection, 55, 56–57
neglectedness, 176
The Net Delusion (Morozov), 58, 71
New Economics Foundation, 119
Newport, Cal, 70
Newton, Huey, 91
Nicaragua revolt (2018), 2
Nigeria, 49–50, 166–67
Nike, 52, 55–56, 57, 144
1984 (Orwell), 68
Nixon, Richard, 8, 79, 89, 126
non-excludable goods, 37
non-material incentives, 39–41
"nonnormative" protests, 94–95
nonviolent protest. *See* violent *vs.* nonviolent protest
"normative" protests, 94–95
normative questions, 14
Nussle, Jim, 6

Obama, Barack, 60, 106, 110, 150
Obama, Michelle, 50
Occupy London, 118–19, 172
Occupy Nigeria, 172

Occupy Wall Street, 2, 95, 119, 172
O'Keefe, Benjamin, 131
Old Hippies, 24, 26
Olivola, Christopher, 161
online activism. *See* slacktivism
Operation Black Vote, 119
Orenstein, Peggy, 74
Oreskes, Naomi, 4, 11
organizational fields, 147–48
Orszag, Peter, 6
Ortega, Daniel, 2
Orwell, George, 68
Ostrander, Susan, 149
Oxfam, 166
Oyakawa, Michelle, 143

pacifism, 80, 82–83. *See also* violent *vs.* nonviolent protest
pageantry, 73
paid protesting, 38–39
Palestinian resistance, 84
Parada, Claudia, 104
parades, 73
Parents and Friends of Lesbians and Gays (PFLAG), 109, 200n23
Parks, Rosa, 23
"Peace Pop" campaign, 52
peer-reviewed publications, 17
"people's microphone," 120–21
"performative" protesting, 70–75
personal fit, 176
Peru, 97
Peters, Cynthia, 9
PFLAG, 109, 200n23
philanthropy. *See* fundraising
Pinckney, Jonathan, 31–32
Pineda, Erin, 87–88
Pinochet, Augusto, 168–69
police reform, 166–69
Pope, Rob, 160–61
posters, 120
Postman, Neil, 68–69
PR, 93–94

President's Emergency Plan for AIDS Relief, 97
Pride Alliance, 123
pride rally, 40–41
Procter and Gamble, 166
Prohibition Party, 122
pro-life movement, 9
propaganda, 68
protest(s): caveats on predicting effects of, 173–74; dissatisfaction and, 25–27; emotional and spontaneous, 12–14; history of, 1–2; normative questions about, 14; percentage participation in, 24–26, *25,* 37; repression of, 28–29, 32–33; size of, 23–24, 27–33; success or failure of, 2, 3–6, 172–73; in twenty-first century, 2–3; wave-like, 171–72
protesters, violent, 81–86
protesting: costs of, 33–35; paid, 38–39; "performative," 70–75
Prussia, 172, 173
"publicly engaged academic work," 17
public relations (PR), 93–94
The Purpose of Power (Garza), 131
pussyhats, 74
Putnam, Robert, 121

Qiu Jin, 22

"race riots," 78–79, 89
racial inequality, 95
racialized punitive policies, 93
racist double standards, 33–34
"radical chic," 142–43
"radical flank effect," 145–47
Radical Reconstruction period, 83
Rainbow Coalition, 125–28
Rainforest Action Network, 147–48
Ramaswamy, Vivek, 144
randomized controlled trial, 117–18, *118*

Ratner, Rebecca, 163
Reagan, Ronald, 91
recruitment, slacktivism and, 62, 64–65
"Redeem Team," 162–63
religious organizations, 114
"repertoires of contention," 84
repression, of protests, 28–29, 32–33
research, 17, 18
resource mobilization theory, 141
"respectability politics," 93
Response, Recovery, and Resilience Collaborative Fund, 146
revenge cycles, 132–33
revolutions, 95–96
#RhodesMustFall, 51, 117
Rhue, Lauren, 156
riot, as language of the unheard, 85–86
Robert, Lionel, Jr., 156
Roberts, Margaret, 67
Robertson, Graeme, 64–65
Roe v. Wade (1973), 9, 24, 103, 113, 115
Rondo (Minnesota), 129
Rose, Fred, 130
Roselle, Mike, 147
Rosenfeld, Bryn, 109
Roth, Benita, 113
Russell, Bertrand, 175
Russia, 66
Russian opposition supporters, 65
Ruttenberg, Danya, 133

Sagan, Carl, 18
Said, Khaled, 62–63
Sall, Macky, 106
same-sex marriage, 40–41
sanctions, 28–29; social, 42–43
Sandinista Revolution (1979), 2
Sands, Melissa, 89
Sapolsky, Robert, 83, 121
SARS (Special Anti-Robbery Squad), 166–67

Sarsour, Linda, 137–38
Saudi Arabia, 28
scale, 176
scholar-activists, 7
science, trusting, 10–14
The Science of Giving (Ratner, Zhao, and Clarke), 163
scientific evidence, 18
"security trap," 97
selective incentives, 38–41
self-defense, 84–86
self-licensing effect, 59
Semptian, 66
Senegal, 105–8, 138
sequencing, 127–28, 135
Shafir, Eldar, 161
shaming, 42–43
Shor, David, 78–80, 99–100
signaling theory, 55–56
Silver, Ira, 143
Singer, Peter, 164–65, 176–77
Skrefsrud, Thor-André, 129
slacktivism, 49–76; attention economy and, 69–70; autocrats and, 66–68; aversion to, 51–57; defense of, 70–75; defined, 49; examples of, 49; key action items for, 75–76; motivation to engage in, 50–51; overview of, 49–51; and real-world activism, 58–64; and recruitment, 62, 64–65; use of term, 63–64
slam poetry, 74
slave revolts, 84
Smiley, Scotty, 162, 163
SMOs, 141–42, 143–46, 147–49; classical *vs.* professional, 141–43, 145
social disapproval, 41–43
social esteem, 40–41
social media: convergence of attitudes on, 61; coordination on, 35–37; and deep activism, 70; and slacktivism, 50–51, 58–59

social movement organizations
  (SMOs), 141–42, 143–46,
  147–49; classical *vs.* professional, 141–43, 145
social movement theory, 9
social pressure, 42–43
social sanctions, 42–43
social science, 6–7, 8–9, 14–18
social signaling, 55–56
Sontag, Susan, 70
South African experiment, 117–18, *118*
Southern Christian Leadership Conference, 82
Spears, Russell, 94–95, 99
Special Anti-Robbery Squad (SARS), 166–67
spectacle, 71–75
Springtime of the Peoples, 171
stakeholders, 161–64
"stall-in," 87–88
Stephan, Maria, 29, 88, 96
structural inequality, 93
Student Nonviolent Coordinating Committee, 84
Students for a Democratic Society, 125
success, 19–20
Sudanese "bread riots," 108–9
Sullivan, Christopher M., 67
sumud, 84
surveillance, 19, 66, 68

"tactical identities," 5
Take Back Parliament, 118–19, 120
talking points, 121–22
targeting, 127, 135
taxonomy, 81–82
Taylor, Astra, 58
Taylor, Charles, 174
Tea Party rallies, 30, 37
Teixeira, Cátia, 94–95, 99
Thaler, Kai, 167

This Nonviolent Stuff'll Get You Killed (Cobb), 84, 86
"3.5 percent rule," 29, 32
Thunberg, Greta, 98, 171
Tiananmen Square demonstrations, 32
TikTok, 69
Tillery, Alvin, Jr., 126–27, 128
tokenizing, 164
toolkits, 122
tractability, 176
tribe, 43, 190n60
Trump, Donald: and DACA, 150, 152; and Environmental Protection Agency, 97; and January 6 riot, 23–24; and March for Our Lives, 109; and paid protesters, 38; performative protests of, 74–75; and Women's March on Washington, 9, 128, 137
t'shuvah, 133
Tufekci, Zeynep, 63–64, 69
Tunisia revolution, 171, 172
Twitter: and slacktivism, 50, 59, 62, 65; and violent *vs.* nonviolent protests, 79, 88, 89–90, 98–99
"tyranny of experts," 7
"tyranny of metrics," 7
Tyson, Neil deGrasse, 18, 175
Tyson, Prince Jordan, 39

Uganda, 28, 43, 167
Ukraine war, 26
Ullah, Saif, 154, 155
UNIA, 72–74
UNICEF, 26
United Farm Workers, 74
"Unite the Right" rally (Charlottesville, VA, 2017), 38
"Universal Negro," 74
Universal Negro Improvement Association (UNIA), 72–74
Unraveling (Orenstein), 74

US Citizenship Act of 2021, 152
US Civil Rights Movement, 1, 4–5; guns and, 84–86; and "radical flank effect," 145–46
utilitarianism, applied, 176–77

victims, 164–66
Vietnam War resistance, 125
violence: and fundraising, 160; genetics and, 83–84
violent *vs.* nonviolent protest, 77–101; activists *vs.* scientists on, 78–80, 98–99; advice on, 97–100; biases in judging, 90–93, *92*; effectiveness of, 86–97, *92*; effects on election outcomes of, 78–80, 88–89; emotional responses to, 87–88; geographic proximity of, 89; inherent nature of, 81–86; long-term effects of, 95–97; media coverage of, 89–90, 91, 93; and morality, 174–75; and "radical flank effect," 145; and revolution, 96; support for, 98; threat to community from, 94
virtual private networks (VPNs), 67
virtue signaling, 56, 71
Voter Education Project, 144, 145
voting by mail, 42
Voting Rights Act (1965), 2
voyeurism, 72
VPNs, 67

Wade, Abdoulaye, 105–6, 107, 138
Walt Disney Company, 149–50
Wasow, Omar, 7–8, 77–80, 88, 89–90, 92, 98, 99–100, 174
Watts riots, 85–86
weather, and protest participation, 30–31
West, Cornel, 91
We the People (website), 60

Weyland, Kurt, 171–72
WFN, 146–47
"What Works Movement," 6–10
Why Fish Don't Exist (Miller), 81
Williams, Bernard, 177
Williams, Nora Webb, 65
Wilson, Edward O., 8
Wilson, James Q., 83
Wine, Bobi, 167
Winfrey, Oprah, 77
Woke, Inc. (Ramaswamy), 144
Wolfe, Tom, 142
Women's Christian Temperance Union, 122
Women's Economic Mobility Hubs, 146
Women's Funding Network (WFN), 146–47
Women's March(es), 2
Women's March on Washington (2017): as coalition, 112–14; fundraising for, 137–38; lack of cohesive demands in, 9, 112–14, 115, 116, 120; and paid protesters, 38; and performative protesting, 74; and sequencing, 128
women's movement, 113
Wood, Elisabeth, 39
Worthy, William, 84–85
Wyatt, Karen, 133
Wynn, Natalie, 132

Y'en a Marre, 105–8, 110
Young Lords, 125
Young Patriots, 125
Yousafzai, Malala, 50, 57
YouTube, 69
Yzerbyt, Vincent, 94–95, 99

Zald, Mayer, 141
Zhao, Min, 163
Zhou, Yulin, 154, 155
Zuckerberg, Mark, 49